# *Programmer Productivity*

Achieving an Urgent Priority

# *Programmer Productivity*

## Achieving an Urgent Priority

Girish Parikh

Reston Publishing Company
*A Prentice-Hall Company*
Reston, Virginia

*Library of Congress Cataloging in Publication Data*

Parikh, Girish,
Programmer productivity.

Bibliography: p.
Includes index.
1. Electronic digital computers—Programming—Labor productivity. I. Title.
QA76.6.P366 1984 001.64'2'0683 83-16081
ISBN 0-8359-5650-4



Other books by Girish Parikh

*How to Measure Programmer Productivity*, 1981
*Techniques of Program and System Maintenance*, 1982
*Tutorial on Software Maintenance* (with Nicholas Zvegintzov), 1983
*The Guide to Software Maintenance* (forthcoming)

Published by
Reston Publishing Company, Inc.
11480 Sunset Hills Road
Reston, Virginia 22090



10 9 8 7 6 5 4 3 2

PRINTED IN THE UNITED STATES OF AMERICA

*To My Parents*

# *Contents*

# *Foreword*

When Girish Parikh asked me to write a Foreword to his latest book, I immediately said 'Yes' and then wondered how he had approached the topic. I was confident that, as always, there would be arguments over syntax as well as style, and theory as well as pragmatism. We would discuss our plans and ambitions over tables of mixed Vietnamese and Indian dishes lovingly prepared by our wives. We would also marvel at the intertwining of our lives (working together in three organizations), and those of the friends and colleagues who tie into our various networks.

Subsequent discussions and review of the manuscript confirmed these expectations. Topics like productivity measurement, the relative merits of different methodologies, the transportability of experience across national and linguistic boundaries, and the merits of various research approaches remain wide open. They still merit review, research, and reasoned response.

As I read this manuscript, several points emerge:

- Productivity improvement must start with an internal commitment; such commitment may stem from the Christian notion of stewardship, vedantic philosophy, or Smith's "enlighted self-interest". It cannot be mandated.
- Data processing is on the verge of a professional standing, on its long march from magic, through art, to science (see my Guide-55 paper, "The Model, The Romance, and The Marriage Broker").
- Humanism, in this late 20th century, requires us to recognize the virtues and vices of computers. They are not merely inferior inorganic beings, but rather partners of the thinking mind in exactly the same way that machines are partners to the exercised body.

Were I writing this book, I would have undoubtedly selected different threads, yet the fabric has been woven and cut into garments that are both sturdy and suggestive. The intent to raise productivity is always clear; the possibilities are varied and tantalizing. Nonetheless, any mixture of philosophy and technology carries risks of boredom and discontinuity. Girish impresses me most because he willingly takes those risks. He challenges each of his friends and his beloved readers to find the flaws and, better yet, to resolve them. The "not-invented-here" rule has no place in his unusually successful efforts to contain his ego, while he bursts the shackles of "acceptable" topics for data processing research. Consider his pioneering efforts on software maintenance, programmer productivity measurement, and improving programmer productivity.

Those of you who read this book will pay Girish the profoundest compliment by subjecting his recommendations to the most careful scrutiny, applying them to personal circumstances, and then *reporting the findings*.

One of the tragedies of research is the popular view that only professional researchers should do it, coupled with the view that much of what is researched is on esoteric subjects. Simple research projects conducted with due concern for constraints on time, money, and skill do produce significant results. Indeed, I assert that productivity improvements become statistically significant only when adopted by the common citizen, not the sometime hero.

Finally, Girish's discussion of being ego-less does not mean to give up one's pride, but rather to achieve the grace to share work, play, and by no means least, *success*. My recommendation is to take courage, seek out the camaraderie of your peers, and move ahead. Productivity improvements are there for the taking; the other side of the coin is that corporate survival and personal careers depend on taking the first step.

Jon Cris Miller, Principal
*The Catalyst Group*
*Peat, Marwick, Mitchell & Co.*
Brookfield, Illinois

# *Acknowledgements*

Swami Bhashyananda of Vivekananda Vedanta Society, Chicago, provided a view of the Vedanta system, an ancient philosophy of India, which was considered by Albert Einstein to include some of the most scientific thinking in religion. Vedanta helped to broaden my view. Ultimately, all logic and sciences merge into Vedantic truth. Vedanta means end of Vedas, or knowledge, the ultimate, the one without second, the absolute. I am also grateful to Swami Bhashyananda for reviewing the chapter "How to be Egoless."

I thank my wife Hasu, without whose encouragement and patience I could not have written this book.

I acknowledge with profound gratitude the influence of my teachers, who include former supervisors, authors of professional books and articles, and colleagues.

I am especially grateful to my programming guru, Gerald M. Weinberg, for his encouragement and guidance which began even before we corresponded and met. The period immediately following my data processing training was most frustrating, as without experience, I was unable to get a programming job. One employment agent in Chicago even gave me enticing advice: "You are a civil engineer with several years of field experience. We can get you a job in that field with a good salary. Why are you banging your head against a stone wall by trying to get a job as a programmer?"

Fortunately, I discovered and studied an early book coauthored by Weinberg: *Computer Programming Fundamentals* (second edition, McGraw-Hill Book Company, 1966). I loved that book. I thanked God I was in the right field. Much later, I benefitted from Weinberg's counsel and encouragement in writing *Techniques of Program and System Maintenance* and *The Guide to Software Maintenance.*

I thank Jon Cris Miller for his inspiration and editorial help in developing the "Programmer Productivity Reports" now included in this book, and for writing the Foreword. I also learned many things from my discussions with him.

I thank Jean Dominique Warnier for reviewing the chapter "Logical Retrofit for Enhancing Maintenance Programming Productivity." Dr. Helmut Epp, Chairman of the Computer Science Department, DePaul University, Chicago, gave me an opportunity to teach graduate courses on software methodologies, information systems analysis and design, and software maintenance; where I used some of the material from the book.

I thank Charles F. Durang, computer science editor, Reston Publishing Company, for accepting this project. I thank all the publishers and authors who gave me permission to reprint material from their works. Also, Siva P. Raparla gave invaluable help in preparing the manuscript, in checking the proofs and in compiling the index.

I thank Janet Walsh, the production editor, Shelley Gelbert, and Annie Guerard, the former production editors, and other staff at Reston Publishing Company for producing an excellent book. I thank the freelance copy editor, Barbara Zieders, of Service to Publishers for the excellent editing of the manuscript.

I cannot repay the debt to my late parents Haribhai J. Parikh, and Kankuben, to whom this book is dedicated. I was influenced by my father, who was a high school teacher and an author. He encouraged me to write.

# *Programmer Productivity*

Achieving an Urgent Priority

# *Introduction*

Programmer productivity is one of the key issues of the data processing industry in the 1980s. For instance, James Martin, at one of his famous five-day lectures, warned: "Most of the U.S. work force will be needed as programmers by the end of this decade if programmer productivity is not increased." It is becoming more critical as hardware costs are plummeting and software (especially programming) costs are skyrocketing! The main purpose of this book is to reduce costs and increase efficiency in the crucial areas of software development and maintenance by increasing programmer productivity.

Let me briefly describe the genesis of this book and, indeed, the diverse forces which led me to it.

I worked for seven years in India, mostly as a civil engineer. In the late 1960s I decided to come to the United States. Soon there came the turning point for me—away from civil engineering and toward computer programming. I took a FORTRAN course at the Milwaukee School of Engineering. The professor was inspiring. (This is yet another example of what a good teacher can do.) Also during that period I read an article in *Fortune* magazine entitled "Help Wanted: 50,000 programmers." These two events changed my mind. I decided to become a computer programmer.

While scribbling flowcharts and writing short FORTRAN programs, I knew I had found my life's work. I did not know the term "software"; but I had found my field.

I started as a tab operator in night shifts at a large corporation and kept looking for a programming job during the day. After six months I got a job that involved programming and computer operations. Then I changed jobs and became a full-time programmer, and kept accumulating experience in the field. Like a typical programmer, I kept changing jobs every one and a half years; however, most of the time I was searching for better ways of programming.

By the mid-1970s, my programming work consisted substantially of maintenance, much of it painful. Had I anticipated the painful maintenance, I might have had second thoughts about entering data processing! While working on some of the most depressing maintenance assignments of my career at a large midwest retailer, I started thinking about better ways of doing maintenance work. I thought: "There has to be a better way." I discussed the problem with my supervisor. To my good fortune, he sent me to a presentation on structured programming (then called "Improved Programming Technologies") given by an IBM systems engineer.

One of the attendees in that presentation was Jon Cris Miller, whom I had known personally and professionally since he had hired me as a programmer some years previously. Indeed, he had recommended me for the current job. He shared my concern over the kind of maintenance problems I was facing. Miller and I were impressed by the presentation and its claims of improvements in programmer productivity, particularly in maintenance, measured in multiples, not fractions, for systems developed with those techniques.

Independently we both started to think about using structured techniques to improve maintenance environment. Miller researched for about a month and developed a company report "Improved Programming Technologies Retrofit (A study of the Application of Improved Programming Technologies to Systems Developed Without Improved Programming Technologies)." I was intrigued by the report, summarized its content, and presented it to my management. I believed that some of the concepts of the structured techniques could be applied to increase maintenance programming productivity. I applied some of the ideas on my own, and kept studying the subject.

Meanwhile, I started researching the subject of maintenance and decided to write a book. The material from Miller's report was to form one part of it. After about a year's part-time study of Miller's work and other material, I prepared the report "Improved Maintenance Techniques." My company, Shetal Enterprises, published the report in May 1977. This activity gave me a greater understanding of the time it would take to put together an original manuscript on maintenance. Believing that the topic required something sooner, I edited articles gathered in my research, and *Techniques of Program and System Maintenance* became the first American book on software maintenance.

"Improved Maintenance Techniques" became the first report in the series "Programmer Productivity Reports." Later I published four more reports: "How to Document Program Changes and Enhancements Internally,"

"How to Increase COBOL Programming Productivity Using a Preprocessor," "How to Make the Most of HIPO," and "A Powerful Structured Tool: The Warnier/Orr Diagram."

I approached each report in the series by focusing on a specific topic distilling thorough research, experience, and/or interviews with professionals in a few pages. I packed them with practical tips, techniques, and guidelines, as well as selected case studies and annotated references. I designed the reports to serve as an introduction to specific topics, readable by data processing managers as well as professionals.

Reports addressed computer professionals, primarily data processing managers and programmers; business, industry, government, and educational organizations using computers; data processing trainers and educators; and researchers.

I learned the lesson the hard way to "write about what you know best." As soon as I started writing about computer programming I began to be published. (In case you missed it, there is a moral here: Doing what you know best will make you productive.) However, in the beginning it was not easy. I published five reports before my first book, *Techniques of Program and System Maintenance* was published by Ethnotech (Lincoln, Nebraska) founded by Gerald M. Weinberg. The second edition of the book is now published by Little, Brown and Company.

The book in your hand is based on experience, studies, and interviews with professionals. For each major report, the introduction gives the context and background under which it was written. When my thinking has changed, the introduction includes my present thinking.

The central theme of the book is programmer productivity; its achievement is an urgent priority. I had been a programmer for most of my data processing career, and have drawn from the variety of my experience. My work in programming included positions with user organizations in different industries, consulting firms, and service bureau environments as well as a stint as a free-lance programmer. Since May 1, 1980, I have been on my own, dividing my time among teaching part-time, writing books and articles, and consulting assignments.

The book includes an annotated bibliography that includes important works related to programmer productivity. It also includes a comprehensive index.

Here are some suggestions on how to make the most of this book:

First take a pen or transparent marker in hand and go through the entire book, including the Preface and Introduction. This first reading is to put things in context. Mark the lines and the passages that appeal or apply to you. After this first pass, reread the passages marked for details and subtle relationships to other sections.

Discuss the material from the book with your colleagues, and your supervisor. Look for ways to apply the appropriate techniques in your work, and then apply them! Make notes of your experience using the techniques. Share your experiences. I, for one, actively solicit feedback, as do other students of the field.

Improving productivity is an ongoing process. The book gets you started. Continue a professional approach to professional development; look for original sources cited in the bibliography and watch for additional treatment in trade and technical publications. In fact, learning should never stop. The more you learn, think about, and apply appropriate techniques, the more productive you become. Good luck!

# *Improved Maintenance Techniques: How To Use Structured Techniques In Maintenance*

# 1

The pioneering work of Jon Cris Miller was a major influence in writing this chapter. In 1975–1976, Miller and I were working for a large midwestern retailer. Miller was in quality assurance and I was a senior programmer in applications, where less than 20% of the work was in new development. The undocumented, unstructured BAL and COBOL programs were almost impossible to maintain. The work was terribly depressing.

Miller was concerned not only about the maintainability of the system, but also took a personal interest in the maintenance problems I faced, partly because he had recommended me for that job. (I had previously worked for Miller in a consulting company, and our personal and professional relationship had continued.)

Miller, who had angrily denounced the *Datamation* (December, 1973) articles on structured programming, began to reexamine the underlying premises, rather than the mere style recommended by structured programming advocates.

In the fall of 1975, Miller and I attended an in-house presentation on improved programming technologies (structured programming, top-down development, development support libraries, HIPO, chief programmer teams, and structured walkthroughs) by an IBM systems engineer. The unforgettable message was: "Many companies report that improved programming technologies improve programmer effectiveness by up to 400% and maintenance programmers achieve improvements of up to 1600% when operating on such code!"

The IBM systems engineer's presentation was the catalyst. Miller saw the tremendous opportunity in maintenance, provided that some

---

Most of the introduction to this chapter is based on material from *Tutorial on Software Maintenance* by Girish Parikh and Nicholas Zvegintzov (see the Bibliography). 

means could be found to introduce structured techniques to existing systems. I, who had been losing sleep over maintenance assignments, saw a ray of hope—after all, there *was* a better way! The challenge was: how to apply improved programming technologies to systems developed without using those techniques.

Management was weighing the alternatives: to rewrite the whole system or redo the worst parts. Miller spent a month researching and interviewing in-house staff and in January 1976 issued the report "Improved Programming Technologies Retrofit: A Study of the Application of Improved Programming Technologies to Systems Developed Without Improved Programming Technologies." Its premise was how to defer major rewritings of the system and extend its life. (Incidentally, management did decide to rewrite the system!)

Meanwhile I had began a research study on maintenance. Literature on the subject was rare, and there was not a single book available! I started work on an original book. Miller's work was to become a part in it. I spent countless hours interpreting Miller's findings, and inspired by Miller and his research, published the report "Improved Maintenance Techniques" in May 1977.

In the Introduction to my earlier book, *Techniques of Program and System Maintenance* (Parikh, 1982a), I gave the following brief background:

> In 1976, while working on some of the most depressing maintenance assignments of my career, I started work on an original book on software maintenance. I did some research, put together some of my experience, talked with some professionals and outlined the book.
>
> After about a year's part-time effort, I condensed and published a section of it in the form of a report "Improved Maintenance Techniques." It attempted to answer the question: "How can the Improved Programming Technologies be used to maintain existing systems?"
>
> That report became the first in the series "Programmer Productivity Reports."

This chapter outlines some ideas for applying improved programming technologies in a maintenance environment; however, other structured technologies can also be applied in maintenance work.

"Improved Programming Technologies Retrofit" (now called "Structured Retrofit") pioneered by Miller, and introduced in this chapter, was a step forward in solving some of the problems of maintaining existing unstructured programs. However, I have recently conceived the concepts of "Logical Retrofit," (outlined in the chapter "Logical Retrofit for Enhancing Maintenance Programming Productivity") primarily based on "data" structured concepts pioneered by Jean-Dominique Warnier.

## Acknowledgments

I thank Jon Cris Miller, then project manager, Applied Information Development (now president, The Catalyst Corporation, Brookfield, Illinois), for encouraging me to write this report. His pioneering work in improved programming technologies retrofit provided some material. He also reviewed the manuscript critically and offered some excellent suggestions. William Hersh, Advisory Systems Engineer, IBM, helped me in the research and reviewed the manuscript. Gordon W. Terrill, then senior education specialist, Montgomery Ward Corporate Systems Division (now with Sysorex International, Cupertino, California), and Sharon L. Miro, project manager, Montgomery Ward Corporate Systems Division, also reviewed the manuscript. In preparing the manuscript, my daughter Sharmila (now Mrs. Sharmila P. Houck) gave invaluable help.

---

"As long as I live so long do I learn."
*Ramakrishna Paramahamsa*

This chapter describes the use of improved programming technologies to maintain and enhance existing systems and programs developed without using those techniques. The two approaches described for using these techniques are: "direct" maintenance (for immediate problems), and/or "retrofit" (for long-term benefits). In the "direct" maintenance approach, a librarian, (un)structured walkthroughs, chief programmer teams, HIPO, top-down program development, and structured programming are used. The "retrofit" method includes extensions to development support libraries (standard media definitions, and library management systems), HIPO, program classification by functions, reformatting and restructuring programs, team operations to develop functional documentation and HIPO, and a librarian (as a "programmer technician").

"He that will not apply new remedies must expect new evils."
**Bacon**

Here are some results reported by the users of improved programming technolgies:

*Infotech International*, a British training organization, has found an 80% reduction in program maintenance and 50% cuts in project times in its study of 1000 users of structured programming techniques.

*Yale University* estimates that new functions can be added to existing programs between 200 and 1000% faster, depending on complexity.

*Marathon Oil* found that with structured design and programming, together with HIPOs, people think in terms of functions, and their thinking becomes easier to follow and to implement.

At *Hartford Insurance*, the finished product was of excellent quality and concluded ahead of schedule, using fewer resources than projected.

I understand that the reports cited above relate to new developments using improved programming technologies. Many other organizations using improved programming technologies for new developments report similar results.

## What This Chapter Can Do For You

"How can I use improved programming technologies to maintain existing systems (developed without using those techniques)?" is the commonly asked question by those exploring or using improved programming technologies. This chapter explores the possibilities of using improved programming technologies to maintain systems developed without using those techniques. I report on experience with a librarian, a "mini" walkthrough (explained later), and an "informal" chief programmer team; the concepts have proved extremely successful in such maintainence.

The improved maintenance techniques (IMTs) presented in this chapter use improved programming technologies to maintain and enhance the existing systems more effectively and economically. Naturally, this is not a panacea for all maintenance problems. However, using improved programming technologies to maintain the existing systems will provide many benefits, such as:

1. More understanding will be obtained and the documentation developed will be valuable in maintenance (and for future redesign).
2. Problems come into sharper focus.
3. Some parts can be salvaged from "rewrite" candidates.
4. Job satisfaction can be provided to maintenance personnel.

On the whole, proper and continued use of these techniques, depending on the situation, will provide a disciplined approach and make the lives of those responsible for maintenance a little easier.

## THE MANAGEMENT COMMITMENT IS MANDATORY

Without management understanding and commitment, attempts by programmers, individually or in groups, to use IMT may result in frustration or failure through misdirected management pressure, unrealistic expectations, or organizational constraints. With management involvemnt, a plan of action can be addressed. If you are a new user of improved programming technologies, I suggest the plan described below. If you are already using the technologies in new developments, but not in maintenance, start from step 3. (If you have innovated to use improved programming technologies in maintenance, this report will give you more ideas.)

### A Suggested Plan of Action

1. Education in improved programming technologies.
2. Use the technologies in new developments to build up a thorough understanding of the techniques. (Implement *slowly*, preferably one technique at a time. Study the article by Edward Yourdon, "Making the Move to Structured Programming," listed in the Bibliography.)
3. Start using improved programming technologies to maintain the existing systems. Make a step-by-step plan for your environment, using the ideas given in this report. All "improved programming technologies retrofit" guidelines described in this report need not be done on a system or program(s). It can stop any time, with whatever work done benefiting the installation. The guidelines chosen to be used should be subject to management review.

Of course, education must be a continuous process; especially as these technologies are still evolving. As the current technologies are refined and/or new techniques are developed, they can be incorporated in the plan, if applicable.

## WHAT ARE IMPROVED PROGRAMMING TECHNOLOGIES?

Improved programming technologies, loosely called structured (programming) techniques, comprise the following six techniques:

1. HIPO (hierarchy plus input-process-output).
2. Top-down program development.
3. Chief programmer teams.
4. Development support libraries.
5. Structured programming.
6. Structured walkthroughs.

### Capsule Description of Improved Programming Technologies[1]

**HIPO** (pronounced "high po"). A design aid and documentation technique consisting of a visual table of contents and a set of operational diagrams which graphically describe *functions* from the general to the detail level. It shows what a system or program does and what data it uses and creates. HIPO supports top-down development.

***Top-Down Program Development.*** A method of development in which programming originates at the highest level of control logic within the system and proceeds downward through the lower level modules. The development of top functions is usually done by inserting stubs for the lower-level functions, which are replaced with actual coding (which may again have stubs) as development progresses.

***Chief Programmer Teams*** (also called "team operations"). A highly structured team of programming specialists working under strict operational discipline. A typical team consists of a chief programmer, backup programmer and librarian, plus additional programmers, analysts, and technicians as re-

[1]The material in this subsection is based on "Glossary/Index" in "Structured Programming" Independent Study Program Workbook (SR20–7150), IBM Corporation.

quired. The chief programmer teams could be nested, forming a hierarchy of teams, depending on the size and nature of a development project.

***Development Support Libraries*** (DSL). A set of office and computer procedures designed for use in a program development environment to provide constantly up-to-date representations of the programs and test data in both computer- and human-readable form. The design of the procedures permits the clerical and record-keeping operations to be handled by a librarian.

***Structured Programming***. The design, writing, and testing of a program made up of interdependent parts in a definite pattern of organization. A method of programming according to a set of rules that enhances a program's readability and maintainability. The three basic structures used in structured programming are Sequence, IF THEN ELSE, and DO WHILE. DO UNTIL and CASE are two additional structures.

***Structured Walkthroughs***. In team operation, a generic name given to a series of reviews, each with different objectives and each occurring at different times in the development cycle. the reviewee subjects his or her work product to review by other team members, with emphasis on design- and coding-error detection, thus contributing to increased team and project productivity.

## HOW TO USE IMPROVED PROGRAMMING TECHNOLOGIES TO MAINTAIN EXISTING SYSTEMS

### The Two Approaches

Any one, or both of the following two approaches could be taken, depending upon the time and resources available.

1. Improved programming technologies in "direct" maintenance.
2. Improved programming technologies retrofit for long-term benefits.

A pilot project, using these two approaches in stages depending on your needs, will help you to evaluate and adapt those powerful techniques in your environment.

Let us take a closer look at each approach.

## Improved Programming Technologies In Direct Maintenance

What is direct maintenance? Modifying or enhancing the program(s) and/or system in the affected part(s) only, without disturbing the rest of the program(s) and/or system, is defined as direct maintenance for the purpose of this chapter. Direct maintenance solves the problem, sometimes on an emergency basis, either by patching or, if possible, by devising a better, permanent solution. Normally, a better, permanent solution comes later, if at all.

Some, if not all, concepts of improved programming technologies can be used in direct maintenance, depending on the situations. The concepts may even need modification. Let us examine how the concepts of improved programming technologies can be used in direct maintenance.

### *The Human Librarian*

The librarian, both human and computerized, can be very useful in direct maintenance. There will be more about the computerized librarian (library management systems) later, but here, the human librarian would be directly useful.

A service bureau where I worked at one time experimented with sharing a librarian among five programmers. The experiment was extremely successful. It released the programmers to concentrate on the technical tasks. Following are some of the tasks a librarian can do:

1. Maintain source, compile, and linkage-edit listings.
2. Help create and maintain the test data and job control language (JCL) decks.
3. Maintain the test listings, dumps, etc.
4. Handle the program moves to production.
5. Maintain the documentation of changes.
6. Maintain the centralized library of programming and system manuals and other pertinent information.
7. Help in the testing of jobs, submit jobs, and provide light technical help (particularly JCL) in testing the job streams.
8. Do light keypunching and typing.
9. Act as the centralized information source for project status information.

***How Do You Justify a Librarian?*** If you are a manager, how do you justify a librarian in your department? Ask your programmers to keep an accurate record of the time they spend doing clerical and routine tasks (these should be defined; the list above will provide a guideline), preferably by each task, for a few weeks. If the average weekly hours spent on such tasks for the department total 40 or more, a full-time librarian is justified; otherwise a part-time librarian will be appropriate. (If you decide to add a librarian, the data, classified by tasks, will help you define the librarian's job in your environment, as well as indicating what training to give him or her if needed.

By the suggestion above, I do not mean to imply that a librarian's function is limited to clerical and routine tasks, although in a maintenance environment, those tasks may be his or her primary responsibility. We shall see later that he or she can act as a "programmer technician" in retrofit activities.

I strongly recommend assigning a librarian in most programming areas. If a librarian is used properly, better organized documentation and improved overall production should result.

## *(Un)structured Walkthroughs*

Two or more minds focusing in harmony on the same problem have more chances to come up with a correct or a better solution to a problem. Walkthroughs need not be formal. The informal "mini" walkthrough is also a powerful method, often giving deep insight into the program and the problem(s). The purpose of the mini walkthrough is to identify and isolate problem(s) and consider solution(s) with the help of another programmer.

Before coding a complex segment for the existing program, a mini walkthrough (with analyst and/or programmer) can ensure the logic, possibly through pseudocode or a flowchart. The approach(es) for interfacing of the new routine with the existing program may also be reviewed in a walkthrough. Problem definition should be clear in order to conduct an effective walkthrough. If possible, write it down.

The other member in a walkthrough provides the objectivity to the problem solution; the error(s) not spotted by the programmer may be located by the walkthrough member. The walkthrough can be used effectively in the testing stage to solve a problem. If the walkthrough procedure is formally used, the other member may act as the backup programmer. A "dry-run" walkthrough, in which one member acts as the computer while the other helps evaluate the processing of the input data record(s), is also a valuable method.

I sometimes "self"-walkthrough a program with the data to identify a problem. Self-walkthroughs can be done easily as often as needed and can eliminate the logical errors, saving time. When a problem cannot be solved in a reasonable time, request help from another member. Exchanging walk-through help, without ego involvement, will go a long way toward forming a strong team, proud of its accomplishments.

## Chief Programmer Team

The chief programmer team can be implemented as follows.One person having the responsibility for an assignment may act as a chief programmer. The backup programmer, who is also knowledgeable in the system, may assist him. The analyst can be consulted as needed. If the size or complexity of the assignment and/or the target date justify, one or more programmers may be added as needed.

Here is how an unsuccessful team operation expanded to a successful one. I was responsible for a major enhancement assignment involving several programs (most of them BAL, one of about 6000 statements) in a system with very little documentation. For several weeks I struggled but made no progress. The backup programmer was also baffled. Both of us agreed that it was hopeless in the time allotted. But management wanted it and we had no way to go but ahead.

In a meeting with the project manager, I suggested that she assign another BAL programmer to help make crucial changes in the front-end program. She agreed but warned, "If the other programmer can't, you'll have to do it!" With her help we made a breakthrough. Encouraged, we worked harder, consulted with the analyst and another programmer who was not in the team (both of whom knew the system better than any of us, especially since the originators of those programs were long gone), and finished the assignment.

Part of the problem had been understaffing. The benefits of adding limited staff, however, were more than proportional. I must add that throughout the assignment the backup programmer kept my spirits high with his cheerful nature. The team operation can work very well on large to medium-size maintenance assignments. A team working in harmony, by some mental chemistry, can produce results unattainable by any single member. The team operation can also take the form of a task force, with a responsible senior programmer acting as the chief, in a maintenance environment.

## HIPOs

HIPOs can be used to write the specifications for a maintenance or an enhancement assignment.

### *Top-Down Program Development*

This technique can also be used for adding new routines and enhancing the existing system.

### *Structured Programming*

This method can also be used for enhancements and new features, and can be called "structured maintenance" or "structured enhancements." Before coding the proposed additions, design them using the program design techniques described in the literature on structured programming. Pseudocode can be used to establish the logic. The structured flowcharts are optional, but my experience, and that of many others, indicates that "informal" flowcharting (i.e., sketching flowcharts) prior to coding saves time in the long run. (Macro packages for structuring BAL programs are available from some vendors. Refer to a good software product directory.)

## Improved Programming Technologies Retrofit for Long-Term Benefits

Improved programming technologies retrofit involves restructuring and reformatting of programs, mechanically and/or manually, to improve their maintainability. It includes standardization of media definitions.

### *Development Support Libraries*

A broad view of the development support library is taken here, in the sense that the contents of the libraries, especially the record format definitions, and library management systems are considered.

***Standard Media Definitions.*** The systematic assignment of program and module names, the standard data names within a record, the standard record and file names, etc., are defined as standard media definitions. If each program has hard-coded data names within a record, when the format is changed, the programs that use these formats may need hard changes (changes in program to be done manually by a programmer). Because of different data names or labels used for definitions, it is difficult to determine which programs are affected. Even in recompiling programs, there are chances of coding errors. Misunderstanding may also arise. By changing the format represented by the member in the library, all the programs that use this format will automatically get this changed format when they are recompiled. By issuing a copy of the listing of the new format to all concerned, effective communication will be established. Also the names will be standardized, providing effective documentation: for example, in COBOL, M-LAST-NAME, M-FIRST-NAME, where the prefix "M" is for Master.

*How to Implement Standard Media Definitions.* Use of library management systems can help in standardizing media definitions. Substituting hard-coded data definitions with the library-maintained source books and replacing the references manually or mechanically is a major step in changing documentation from the program to the system level. On time-sharing systems, this replacement can be done quickly. Once done, the programs become easier to maintain. The standard media definitions should be as comprehensive as possible so that they meet the needs of all the programs that use them. This applies particularly to repetitive fields, hierarchical groups, and fields with both alphabetic and numeric possibilities. As external documentation, a description of each field should be written and kept undated.

*Library Management System.* A library management system is an automated library system that can manage (add, change, delete, replace, change status to production, etc.) source programs, object and load modules, JCL, test data, etc. Some library management systems are so versatile they may well be called computerized librarians. A library management system helps the human librarian in many ways, but it does not replace him or her.

*Source Program Management.* The importance of well-organized source program management cannot be overemphasized. The external (human-readable) source program and related listings and documentation should be available to authorized persons whenever they need them.

Source program management should include:

1. Current and previous listings.
2. Program security. Production source program should always be backed up, preferably not on cards but on a reliable library system.
3. An audit trail of program modifications.
4. The facility to copy a production program to create a test version for modifications.

Refer to a good software product directory for information on source program management systems.

## *HIPO*

A hierarchy chart (or the visual table of contents) can be created for the entire system. Detailed (hierarchy) charts for the parts of the system that need a great deal of maintenance can be created if time permits. If resources and time are available, overall and detailed HIPOs may be constructed for the existing systems. HIPO or functional documentation developed for the existing system will be useful in rewriting the system. Partial HIPO packages may be useful and sufficient for "ordinary" maintenance. It may not be feasible to develop HIPOs for programs that are extremely unstructured, in either the traditional hierarchical sense or in the current structured programming sense. Instead of making formal IPO (input-process-output) diagrams, functional documentation can be developed by a team. This point will be developed later.

## *Program Classification by Functions*

How do you create a program classification by functions?

1. Make an inventory of all the programs and utilities (sort, merge, etc.) in the system.
2. Classify the inventory of programs and utilities by functions and subfunctions relative to the hierarchy chart. Some programs and/or utilities may be repeated in the classified list.

Such a classified list shows the group of programs to accomplish the various functions in the system. The classified list together with the hierarchy chart give a good overall picture of the system. It tells "what" is being accomplished through "which" programs, and briefly tells "how" through one-line descriptions of the programs and the utilities. The system hierarchy chart usually does not change much, but with modifications in the system, the program classification may change. It should be updated whenever it is changed. A program could be written to produce an updated list.

## *Top-Down Program Development*

The hierarchy chart (or the visual table of contents) should give a top-down picture of the system. Programs may be converted to top-down structure by using ideas outlined later. After retrofitting, automated flowcharts may show the top-down structure and may be more useful.

### Reformatting Programs

Some COBOL preprocessors with capabilities to reformat existing COBOL programs are available (refer to a good software product directory). No preprocessing system can correct fundamental logic flaws. It can make programs more "readable," so that logic flaws and other errors are readily apparent. In COBOL, by enforcing details such as alignment, paragraph numbering, level numbering, common names, etc., through an automatic tool, program maintenance productivity can be improved.

### Restructuring Programs

Restructuring of programs goes beyond reformatting, so that programs conform to the structured programming standards.

***Manual Restructuring of Programs.*** The unstructured flowchart of the existing program or its part(s) can be converted to a structured flowchart and then coded to comply with structured programming. [Assignment 3 in IBM's "Structured Programming," Independent Study Program (see the Bibliography) gives some techniques for structuring unstructured programs.] The Ashcroft-manna state-variable technique can be used to convert an unstructured flowchart to an equivalent structured flowchart. Another technique is to duplicate coding to eliminate branching into "common code."

Manual (or automated) routines (their discussion is beyond the scope of this chapter) can be developed to do the following in COBOL programs:

- ALTER removal.
- GO TO/PERFORM substitution.
- Closing subroutines.
- Highlighting the control structures.

Before undertaking manual restructuring, carefully evaluate the potential gain versus the effort and costs involved.

***Automated Restructuring of Programs.*** Guy de Balbine (1975) describes results achieved by restructuring existing FORTRAN programs into a "structured" FORTRAN superset called S-FORTRAN. Examples of restructured programs are easier to understand. Processors exist to translate most FORTRAN programs to S-FORTRAN, and vice versa.

### Structuring Engine

The "structuring engine" is a package that automatically transforms unstructured program into a structured program. [Jon Cris Miller, the pioneer of improved programming technologies retrofit concepts (now further refined and called "structured retrofit"), has developed the first commercial COBOL structuring engine. Automated restructuring and retrofitting services are available from the Catalyst Corporation, 9408 W. 47th Street, Brookfield, IL 60513.]

## *Structured Walkthroughs*

Structured walkthroughs are helpful in making decisions about retrofit projects. Walkthroughs of improved, modified programs with better structure can familiarize the team with the system more rapidly. It is helpful in the evaluation and maintenance of restructured programs.

## *Team Operation*

***A Retrofit Team.*** A retrofit team can be assembled to carry out retofit activities in an installation. It is a formal team for retrofit activity. A pilot project could be done and then the team made permanent if desired. The retrofit team establishes the priorities of action. They do testing prior to and after retrofitting and evaluate the retrofit project or assignments. The team becomes specialized in improved programming technologies retrofitting.

***Team Operation to Develop Functional Documentation and HIPO.*** Team operation could be extremely important in developing effective functional documentation and HIPO for the existing system. It could work as follows. If available documentation is not enough, constructing IPO diagrams may involve studying the entire program—even reading and interpreting the detail code and segments of code. To accomplish this, the chief programmer and backup programmer can divide up the code along major functional breaks, if possible, or by programs for reading. Each concentrates on his or her assigned part, and scans or reviews the other person's part. The segments are then reviewed in walkthrough sessions and notes made from the programming standpoint. The systems analyst then interprets the findings of the programmers from the systems viewpoint. Thus the entire program can be covered if necessary.

When the whole program or its necessary parts are thus covered, a meeting between the analyst and programmers (and possibly the users) is needed to complete the function chart and then the HIPO for the program. This method is slow, and some programs may be so unstructured and disorganized that they may not lead to a formal structure chart, but the overall HIPO and functional documentation can be developed. The narration of the program should be written down (preferably in pseudocode) while interpreting the programs.

The functional documentation and HIPO can be built in stages as you come across new maintenance activities.

*The Human Librarian.* The librarian may act as a "programmer technician" in an improved programming technologies retrofit environment. The librarian should keep definitions of media (records, reports, source document) current. It should be automated, but the librarian should make sure that it is done. Although a librarian is not expected to define a source library, he or she can contribute to the source library walkthroughs.

### Control Fuctions of the Librarian

The librarian makes the library work efficient for programming, systems and operating staff. He or she monitors program number and file name assignments, file and record composition, and general documentation. In the improved programming technologies retrofit environment, the librarian function becomes more ambitious on three counts:

1. Assembling and maintaining human-readable file of mechanically maintained source documentation.
2. Quantifying system status, identifying missing elements, such as documentation, source programs, status of test facilities, and data sets.
3. Building a priority of missing library elements with the chief programmer.

As the retrofit team begins operation, the librarian focuses first on the superficial aspects of retrofit, such as making existing programs more readable through reformatting packages and helping develop draft source books to displace hard coding.

As the effort continues, the librarian shifts to a monitoring scheduling role in recertification of the improved programming technologies retrofitted system from the technical and documentation standpoints. The project notebook provides the raw data for scheduling parallel runs and subsequent data set comparison runs. As technical certification continues, the librarian can round out narrative documentation with mechanical supplements, such as machine-generated flowcharts.

## CONCLUSION

To my knowledge, there are no available figures from cost/benefit studies regarding improved maintenance techniques and retrofitting activities. The following records kept by the librarian can help in the evaluation. The record of actual hours spent in retrofitting can be kept. After retrofitting—partial or complete—the hours spent to do the comparative maintenance assignments can be recorded. Although exact measurements may not be possible, the technically oriented manager may be able to evaluate the retrofit project fairly.

Once again, I should remind you that all IMT and retrofit activities need not be used and that a formal improved programming technologies retrofit team need not be assembled. The activity can stop any time, with whatever work done benefitting the installation. The IMT and retrofit activities could be flexible and the resources could, if needed, be diverted to other, more important work.

Thus, the concepts of improved programming technologies can contribute substantially to improving maintenance productivity for the existing systems and programs. The management should review the situations and use the techniques described in this chapter.

# *How To Make The Most Of HIPO*

# 2

When I sent out a news release announcing the HIPO report to editors of several computer periodicals in August 1978, I got the following letter from Richard Canning, the publisher of *EDP Analyzer*.

> **Dear Mr. Parikh:**
>
> **Most of the user experience with HIPO that we have come across has been negative. It looks to me as though HIPO has some basic flaws in its make-up.**
> **Since you have done this report on it, it would appear that you don't feel that way about it.**
> **Have you found the majority of HIPO users, that you have talked to, to be happy with it?**
> **Based on what we came across, I have backed off from writing on HIPO in a way that would encourage readers to consider using it. So I am just checking to see if you have found user experiences to be different from what we found.**
>
> **Sincerely,**
> **Richard G. Canning**

I replied to Mr. Canning as follows:

> **Dear Mr. Canning:**
>
> **Let me try to answer your question on HIPO:**
> **HIPO has certainly become controversial. Almost all the programmers I've talked to dislike HIPO.**
> **Personally, I do not like the basic HIPO form, though I do like the "hierarchy chart" of the HIPO method. During the last three years I had to work with HIPO on several projects. That ex-**

**perience, plus my study, prompted me to write the repoort ["How to Make the Most of HIPO"].**

**Several programming managers I've talked to like HIPO. Companies using Improved Programming Technologies promoted by IBM mostly use HIPO with other techniques.**

**I think those who are disappointed with HIPO have either carried it too far, or expected too much from it. When HIPO is kept functional, I've seen it working well.**

**However, HIPO does have some basic flaws. Eventually, HIPO will be replaced by a better (and hopefully, universal) design and documentation method (or possibly a combination of method(s), but (in my view) a single method has not yet emerged.**

**While HIPO remains in use, I hope my report will serve its users.**

**Sincerely,**
**Girish Parikh**

HIPO is certainly a milestone in the arena of structured technologies. Before the advent of HIPO, data processors used to think in terms of flow of events primarily using system and program flowcharts. They often viewed the trees instead of the forest, and got entangled in the details. HIPO was the graphic tool that had "function" (i.e., *what* was to be done, *not* how) as its basis. It required data processors to change their way of thinking from details of logic to the overview functional aspects of a system and programs. However, there were no standards for HIPO documentation. Some designers included logic in their processing charts, especially in detailed IPO (input-process-output) charts. This often defeated the main purpose of HIPO.

HIPO also has other weakness. For example, it produces too much paper and is hard to update. Thus it may become a maintenance nightmare. Transition from design done by HIPO to programming may also need additional work, as the detailed IPO charts usually do not contain logic. The programming logic may be developed using other tools, such as structured flowchart or pseudocode.

From my experience and study, I have found better tools than HIPO. After my flirtation with HIPO, I stumbled on the Warnier/Orr diagram. I found it to be a very powerful and versatile structuring tool. I have devoted an entire chapter (Chapter 3) to this powerful structured tool. However, if you are stuck with HIPO, the present chapter will give you many ideas to make the most of it.

### Acknowledgments

I thank Cris Miller, then project manager, Applied Information Development (now president, The Catalyst Corporation, Brookfield, Illinois); William Hersh, Advisory Systems Engineer, IBM; and Gordon W. Terrill, then senior education specialist, Montgomery Ward Corporate Systems Division (now with Sysorex International, Cupertino, California) for reviewing the manuscript critically. For helping me in the research, I thank Donald Leavitt, then associate editor, *Computerworld* (now technical editor, *Software News*); and Susan M. Lee, Marketing Representative, IBM. Technical discussions with my friend Lem Ejiogu [now Director of Lemcomm Softech, Chicago, and author of *Effective Structured Programming* (see the Bibliography)] provided insights. In preparing the manuscript, my daughter Sharmila (now Mrs. Sharmila P. Houck) gave invaluable help.


This chapter gives tips, trends, ideas, and sources to help you make the most of HIPO in new developments as well as in maintenance. You should be familiar with the HIPO method to make the most of this chapter. If you are not yet familiar with HIPO, the section "What HIPO Is" provides a capsule description. However, study the IBM publications "HIPO: Design Aid and Documentation Technique,"and "HIPO: Design Aid and Documentation Tool" (audio course) and Katzan (1976) (all listed in the Bibliography), for a deeper understanding of HIPO.

Except for a few tips, the chapter does not cover HIPO graphics and conventions. For these, the references mentioned in the preceding paragraph are excellent sources.

## AN OVERVIEW OF SYSTEM/ PROGRAM DESIGN AND DOCUMENTATION TOOLS

Figure 2-1 is an overview of system/program design and documentation tools: (The tools are not listed in order of importance.)Note that the classification is somewhat arbitrary. For instance, decision tables can also be used with

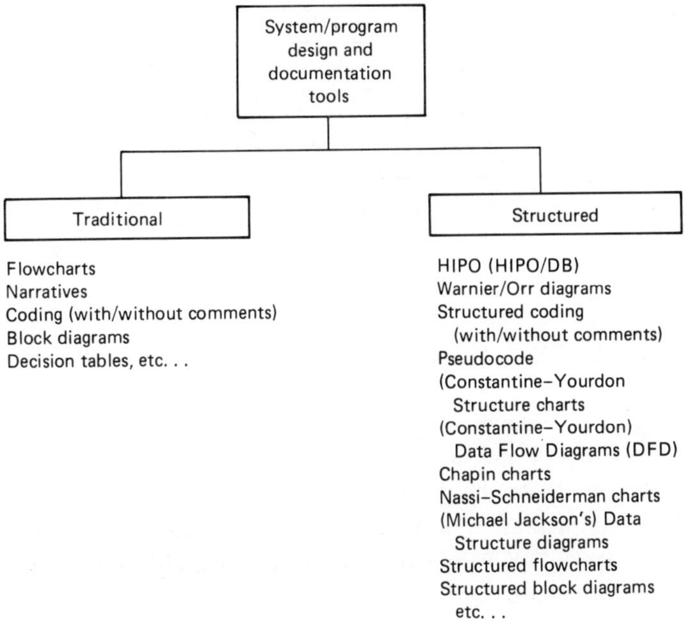


FIGURE 2.1 An overview of system/program design and documentation tools

structured methodologies. Some "structured" tools may also be used with traditional systems/programs; HIPO is one that we shall explore later.

Figure 2-1 also illustrates that HIPO is not the only tool available to help design, develop, and document systems/programs. Many tools of structured documentation have been developed over the last decade. These tools are still evolving and a great deal of experimentation is going on.

## WHAT HIPO IS

HIPO (hierarchy plus input-process-output; pronounced "high po") is a design aid and documentation technique originally developed by IBM. HIPO describes functions of a system from the general to the detailed level. It is one of the techniques in the improved programming technologies [also called structured (programming) techniques]; other techniques are: top-down program development, chief programmer teams, development support libraries, structured programming, and structured walkthroughs (see Chapter 1 for capsule description of improved programming technologies), and is the logical

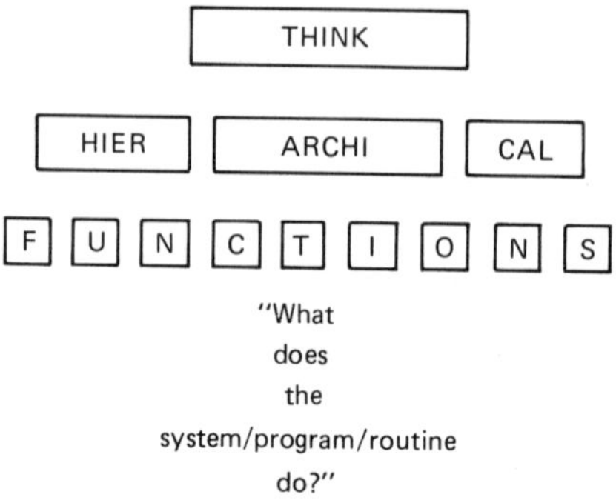


FIGURE 2.2 Hierarchical/functional nature of HIPO

extension of the top-down design and development effort. It shows graphically what a system or program does and what data it uses and creates. Figure 2-2 represents the hierarchical/functional nature of HIPO.

HIPO documentation usually contains three kinds of diagrams: a visual table of contents (VTOC) and overview and detailed HIPO diagrams. Figure 2-3 is a hierarchy chart showing the components of HIPO.

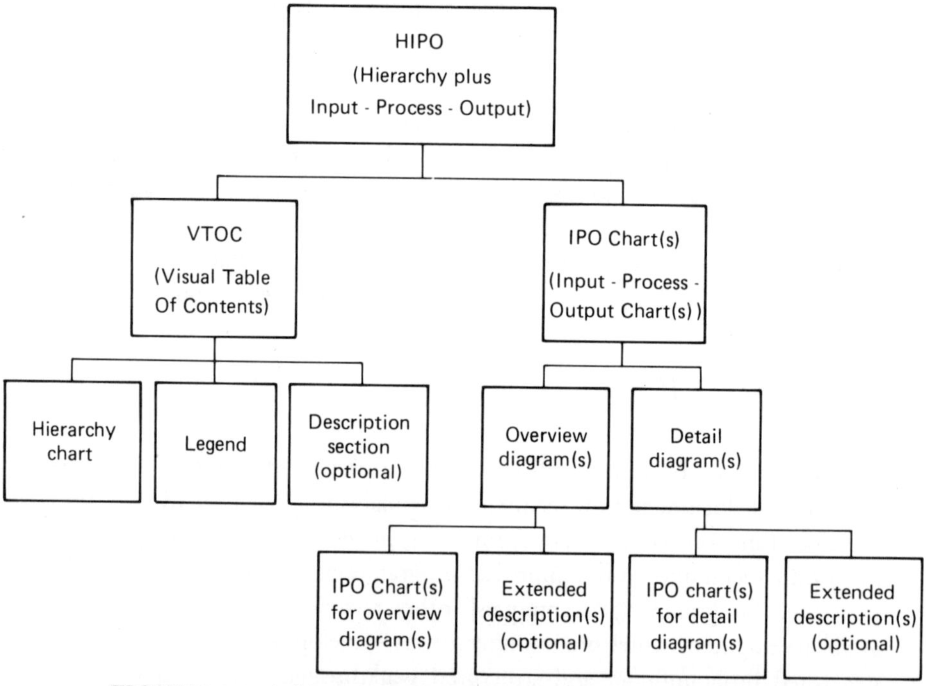


FIGURE 2.3 A hierarchy chart showing components of HIPO

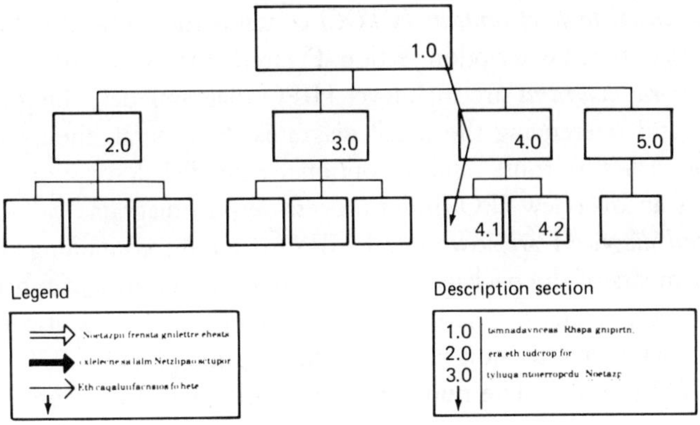


FIGURE 2.4 Visual Table of Contents (VTOC)

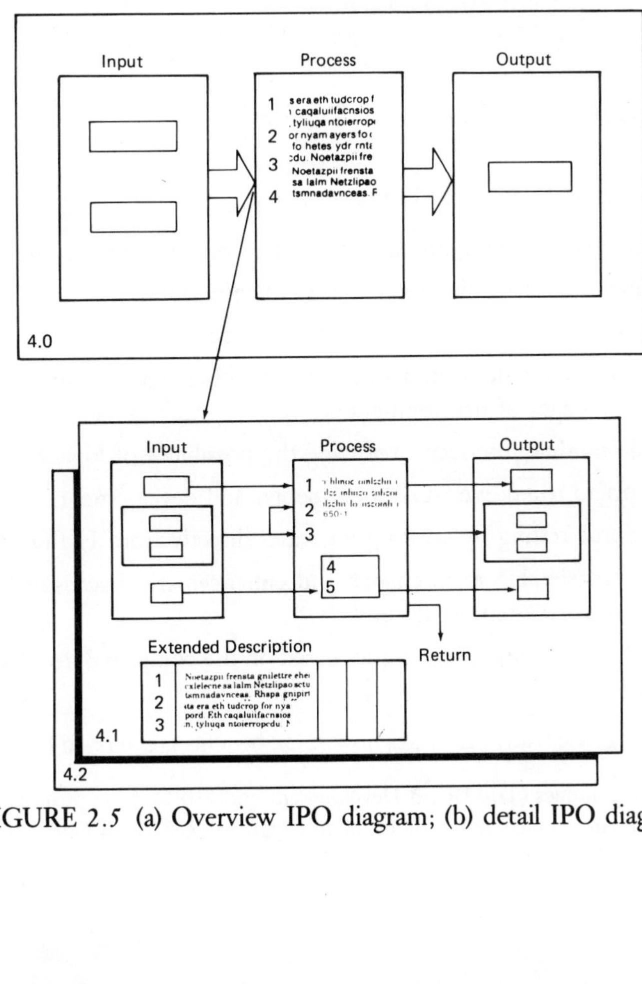


FIGURE 2.5 (a) Overview IPO diagram; (b) detail IPO diagram

The *visual table of contents (VTOC)* contains the hierarchy chart, a legend, and an optional description section. Figure 2-4 is a schematic of a VTOC.

*Overview diagrams* are high-level HIPO diagrams describing the major functions and referencing the detail diagrams. In general, they provide the inputs, processes, outputs, and an optional extended description. Figure 2-5(a) shows an overview IPO (input-process-output) diagram.

*Detail diagrams* are lower-level HIPO diagrams containing the fundamental elements of the package. They describe the specifics of functions and input and output items. The extended description section is also more specific, and may refer to non-HIPO documentation. Figure 2-5(b) shows a detailed IPO diagram. The number of levels of detailed diagram usually depends on the complexity and/or amount of information to be documented.

The two major kinds of HIPO packages are the initial design package and the detail design package. The maintenance package, the third kind, is optional. Each package contains all three types of HIPO diagrams: VTOC, overview, and detailed HIPO diagrams.

## SOME BENEFITS AND USES OF HIPO

Some benefits and uses of HIPO are:

- Easier user understanding and agreement on functional content.
- Highlighting of missing or inconsistent information.
- Easy documentation and modification of functions.
- Documentation done in a single effort rather than multiple efforts at different stages of development.
- Simple module interfaces, reducing the possibility of logic errors.
- Support to top-down, functional design and development.
- Functional testing by creating test cases directly from HIPO diagrams.
- More transferable maintenance and enhancement, because of the visibility of the system at all levels.
- Improved estimation techniques based on the completed detailed design phase.

The following case study illustrates how some benefits are derived from HIPO.

> Two techniques (Top-Down Development and HIPO) have proven invaluable in the chargeout environment of Crown Zellerbach Corp. (San

Francisco, California). Using Top-Down Development, a new application is defined at four consecutive levels: Feasibility, general design, detail design and implementation. At each level, HIPO charts are written and used to refine the problem with users and make "go/no go" decisions. At the end of the third level of development, the application has been desgined and documented down to modules of 50 source statements, and the user has accepted and understands that design. Yet, the total cost of that design at that point is only 15% to 20% of the total development cost, and the remaining programming effort has become fully predictable as to cost and time.[1]

## SOME DEFICIENCIES OF HIPO AND TIPS TO OVERCOME THEM

Here are some of the negative features of HIPO and suggestions (in brackets) to overcome them:

1. To draw and maintain formal HIPOs manually using a template is time consuming. [Drawing a freehand, informal HIPO (discussed later), when possible, may save time. Using a (human) librarian to finish formal HIPO, and/or an automated package may help. The time-saving simplified versions of IPO diagrams, discussed later, can also be used.]
2. Complete HIPO generates a lot of paperwork. [If possible, stop at the necessary level and/or draw IPOs for selected functions only. In some cases, hierarchy chart(s) may suffice.]
3. From a system design standpoint, HIPO lacks any notion of a data base as an integral part of the systems overview. [HIPO/DB (HIPO/Data Base), described later, helps overcome this deficiency.]
4. HIPO does not normally show the control structure. For example, if function A has subfunctions B and C, does function A require both B and C, or does it require either B or C to execute? [This deficiency can be corrected to some extent by using the pseudocode concept in the IPO charts to indicate (overall) control structures.]
5. HIPO is one of the most difficult techniques to learn for the developer. [Proper training and education are necessary to learn to develop HIPO. The IBM publications "HIPO: A Design Aid and

[1]From the IBM publication, *Advanced Systems Programs Productivity*, SM-75-012, June 25, 1975.

Documentation Technique," and "HIPO: Design Aid and Documentation Tool (audio course) and Katzan (1976) (all listed in the Bibliography) provide material for education.]

## WHAT IT TAKES TO CREATE GOOD HIPO

You cannot create good HIPO documentation merely by using HIPO form. To create good HIPO documentation requires discipline, hard thinking, criticism, creativity, and perserverance. Be prepared to redraw several times (called iteration, described later) until the best possible design is developed within time and budget constraints.

## HIERARCHY CHART AND HOW TO DEVELOP IT

The hierarchy chart is the heart of top-down functional design and development. The upper boxes in a hierarchy chart represent "controls" and the lower boxes indicate "actions." The top box in a hierarchy chart describes the entire system or program in terms of a single function. It names the system or program in a single sentence.

Use the technique called "functional decomposition" to develop a hierarchy chart. Each function is exploded into increasingly lower levels of detail until all subfunctions have been defined. Determining the main function, decomposing it into a hierarchy of subfunctions, and naming all functions requires insight, creativity, and experience on the part of the designer. Each designer may define the subcomponents of a function slightly differently.

When developing a hierarchy chart, first emphasis should be on the functional organization. Consideration of packaging the system into programs should come later.

### Iterative Process of Functional Design

As the process of design goes to the lower levels of hierarchy, some changes in the upper levels may be necessary. This is typical of the system/program development process and is called the "iterative process" of refinement. As the iteration progresses to further detail levels, the impact on top-level design should be minimal.

## Graphics for Hierarchy Charts: Varying Sizes of Boxes

Judicious varying of sizes of boxes allows more information in fewer pages. A one-page chart, if not too cluttered, may be easier to grasp than a two-page chart. Include in the legend:

> Note: The sizes of the boxes are varied for convenience only. They do not reflect the relative weight of any function.

## Numbering of Boxes in a Hierarchy Chart

Number each box in a hierarchy chart to reference the related IPO diagram. The particular function in a program should also be identified with the same number, if possible, as a prefix to the paragraph name(s) or with a comment statement preceding the block of code for that function. There are several methods of numbering boxes in use. Select the one most suitable to your environment, and follow it consistently.

## The Legend is Important

Sometimes there is a tendency to drop the legend from a VTOC. (The author has been a victim of this tendency.) It is important to include the legend. The graphic symbols and their meanings change, and it is a good practice to define them in the legend the way they are used in the HIPO package. If an installation has standards about graphic symbols, the standards also are subject to change. A comprehensive legend documents prior standards and eliminates the need to revise the HIPO documentation according to changed standards. It also helps those who are uninitiated in HIPO to understand the package.

## The Optional Description Section in a VTOC

The optional description section in VTOC provides a brief description of each function in the hierarchy chart. The boxes in the hierarchy chart contain only the title of the function. In some cases, the optional description section may eliminate the need to turn pages to the related overview and detail diagrams to get a further description of the functions.

## Checklist for Review and Analysis of a VTOC

Paul Noll gives the following checklist for review and analysis of a VTOC:

1. Are all the modules functional? (Can each one be described by one simple imperative statement?)
2. Is the VTOC complete? (Does each module have all of its subfunctions represented by subordinate modules?)
3. Are the verbs consistent? (Do the same verbs always imply the same subfunctions?)
4. Are the modules independent? (Are control codes only passed to the calling module?)
5. Is proper subordination shown? (Do the subordinates actually represent the subfunctions of the calling module?)
6. Are the control spans reasonable? (General guideline: From two to nine subordinate modules make for a reasonable control span.)
7. Are the modules too large? (General guideline: fifty lines or less of source code per module.)[2]

# IPO DIAGRAMS ARE NOT ALWAYS NECESSARY TO DEVELOP STRUCTURED PROGRAMS

The author has successfully completed several structured programs without IPO diagrams. The top-down development started with hierarchy charts, and then used structured flowcharts or pseudocode to develop an overall program structure and internal logic.

When IPO diagrams are not used, some functions may need additional documentation in the form of pseudocode, decision tables, or even structured

---

[2]Paul Noll, *The Structured Programming Cookbook*, p. 16. Copyright 1978 by Mike Murach & Associates, Inc., Fresno, CA 93705.

flowcharts. Using alternative documentation technique(s) when application allows may save significant paperwork and time.

Also, by eliminating IPO diagrams, development starts earlier. [However, after designing hierarchy chart(s), a strategy for implementing a program/function(s), using appropriate tool(s), should be developed before the actual coding begins.]

When you must use IPO diagrams, make the most of them, as discussed in the topics below.

## List Outputs First When Developing IPO Diagrams

> The first step in creating an input-process-output diagram is to list the outputs of the function. Listing of the outputs prior to developing the steps of the process and the inputs is preferred to concurrent development because the needed outputs of a function are generally known beforehand. If the topmost overview diagram of a system is being developed, then the outputs can be taken from the system requirements.
>
> Some analysts prefer to develop the process block first or to develop the three blocks concurrently; however, this a doubtful strategy. The effectiveness of a system, program, or function is determined by its outputs—otherwise, why have the system, program, or function in the first place? Thus, it would seem prudent to list the outputs first.[3]

## Should There Be an IPO Diagram for Every box in the Hierarchy Chart?

Theoretically, every box in the hierarchy chart should have an IPO diagram. However, the rule "draw IPO diagrams for every box in the hierarchy chart" may prompt the developer to manipulate the hierarchy chart to reduce the number of boxes, cutting down on the number of IPO diagrams he or she has to draw.

In practical applications, by eliminating IPO diagrams for trivial functions or drawing IPO diagrams for selected functions only, time-consuming paperwork can be reduced. (Boxes in the hierarchy chart for which IPO dia-

[3]From *Systems Design and Documentation: An Introduction to the HIPO Method* by Harry Katzan, Jr., © 1976 by Litton Educational Publishing, Inc.

grams are not drawn should be shown by a diagramming convention, such as dashed-line box, and so indicated in the legend.)

The next topic presents another idea that should help to reduce the number of IPO diagrams.

## How Many Levels of Functions an IPO Diagram Should Show

An IPO diagram should normally show the function (say at level L) being drawn and refer to its immediately lower-level functions (at level L+1). It should not refer to subfunctions at level L+2 or subsequent levels, except when a single IPO diagram is allowed to contain more levels (the number of levels should be limited) to minimize the number of IPO diagrams to be drawn, reducing effort and paperwork.

## How to Use the Process Box of an IPO Diagram Effectively

To develop a brief statement of function, begin the statement with an imperative statement, such as CREATE, READ, TEST, etc. On page 63 of the IBM manual "*HIPO—A Design Aid and Documentation Technique*" (GC20-1851-1) is a list of 94 verbs. Select the verbs commonly used in your installation. Write down their precise meanings, give examples, and develop standards for your staff.

## Using Pseudocode in the Process Box of an IPO Diagram

Pseudocode is "how", not "what." The lower-level IPO diagrams tend to go from "what" to "how." Several professionals advocate pseudocode in the process box or in the extended section of the lower-level IPO diagrams.

A question may arise: Instead of using pseudocode in IPO diagrams, why not use it independently? The answer seems to be: The IPO diagram puts pseudocode for a particular function in proper perspective. The function (whose pseudocode is in a particular IPO diagram) is organized hierarchically to make the structure of a system or program visible. The inputs used and outputs created by the function can be seen instantly. I call this method

"HIPO- Pseudocode" as opposed to "HIPO-Functional," described in the next section.

## KEEPING HIPO FUNCTIONAL

I feel that HIPO should be function-oriented as much as possible. (Use the pseudocode concept in the process box to indicate the overall structure only.) HIPO is a major breakthrough from its predecessors in emphasizing "what" rather than "how."

While developing a program, pseudocode or other appropriate, commonly used tool(s) can be used independently to develop the control structure (of a program) and the "how" of the function(s). All or part of the material thus generated (providing a *means* to the end result of a well-organized, maintainable, structured program) may later be included with the documentation package to complement the functional HIPOs.

When desiging a system or program, focusing on the functions and how they fit together saves considerable time. By mixing "how" while thinking "what," the view of the forest may be lost for the trees. Providing functions instead of pseudocode in the process box of the IPO diagram also makes maintenance easier, since such IPO diagrams can be studied easily and affected functions located faster. Also, functions do not change that often, requiring less redrawing of IPO diagrams.

In most cases, structured code, if well done and properly "commented," may be the best (and most up-to-date) documentation. However, the complicated functions should have additional documentation.

I call this method "HIPO-Functional" as opposed to "HIPO-Pseudocode" described in the preceding section. Try both methods, "HIPO-Functional" and "HIPO-Pseudocode"; then decide which is better for your environment.

### Be Consistent When Writing in a Process Box

When writing in a process box, be consistent in your indentation. Establish standards and follow them consistently. This becomes more important if you write psuedocode in the process box.

## Be Consistent in Applying Diagramming Conventions and Symbols

To produce effective and clear HIPO documentation, be consistent. In most cases, consistent use of diagramming conventions and symbols is more important then the conventions themselves.

If your installation has no standards for symbols, use symbols on the HIPO and flowcharting template jackets consistently. (It may be a good idea to review the jackets of these two templates periodically.)

## When to Show Specific Device Types in IPO Drawings

Specific device types are usually not necessary to the development of a logical design. The decision about device types may be deferred until the implementation stage is reached.

# SOME VARIATIONS OF IPO DIAGRAMS

## HIPO/DB (HIPO/Data Base)

According to Ken Orr, HIPO has had two main shortcomings: a lack of the concept of a logical systems data base in which various data are stored for future use; and that a considerable amount of work remained in developing a well-structured program from HIPO documentation. He developed HIPO/DB to correct these problems.

HIPO/DB has an additional "data base" box above the process box, and the function(s) in the process box are stated in a structured pseudolanguage that Orr called structured systems design language (SDL). Figure 2-6 is a simple illustration of HIPO/DB. Orr's modifications of the basic HIPO approach have been very successful. For more information on HIPO/DB, refer to the references by Orr (1977a; 1977b).

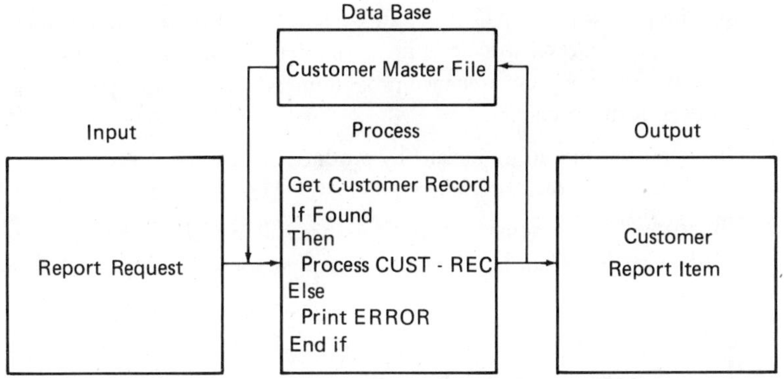


FIGURE 2.6 A simple illustration of HIPO/DB*

## "Son of HIPO" or "HIPO Jr."

Joseph T. Rigo introduces a new variation of HIPO:

> Consider a simplified approach. Call it Son of HIPO, or HIPO Jr.
>
> For illustration, assume a standard master file update program. On the left side of the page, put a list of inputs: the master file, a transaction file and perhaps a table of codes used in processing.
>
> On the right, put a list of outputs: the updated master file, a couple of reports and a parameter to be passed.
>
> Put a great big box in the middle. It is for a list of processing functions performed (or to be performed) by the module.
>
> A simple arrow connects each input item with the first processing function that uses it. Another arrow connects a processing function with the output it creates.
>
> There is still plenty of room on the page for miscellaneous text. The text includes identification of called and calling modules, job and procedure names and references to file and record layout forms as necessary.
>
> The result is a programmer's version of the flowchart that is customarily produced for the data center operations staff. The main difference is it emphasizes processing functions.

*(From Ken Orr, "Structured Systems Design: Blueprinting the Future," *Infosystems,* February 1977, p. 74. Copyright, Hitchcock Publishing Company)

The chart is easy to update. It can be maintained on a standard text editor. For best results, include it as comments in the program listing. If it is in the listing, maintenance programmers are more likely to use it and keep it up to date.

This approach has an important by-product. It introduces everyone to the fundamentals of HIPO charts.

The arrows, boxes, squares, and circles are still available. They can be added as needed when a more complex design application comes along. In the meantime, people may start using HIPO. It really does work.[4]

## Another Form of IPO Chart

Figure 2-7 illustrates an example of another form of an IPO chart.

It should be noted that the major processing tasks specified in the Processing section of the IPO Chart do not specify the manner in which any of the processing is to be accomplished nor are they necessarily listed in the sequence in which the processing is to take place within the program. Instead, the IPO Chart is used to merely specify the major processing tasks which must occur within the program. Thus, the IPO Chart is used to specify WHAT must take place within the program, not WHEN and HOW.[5]

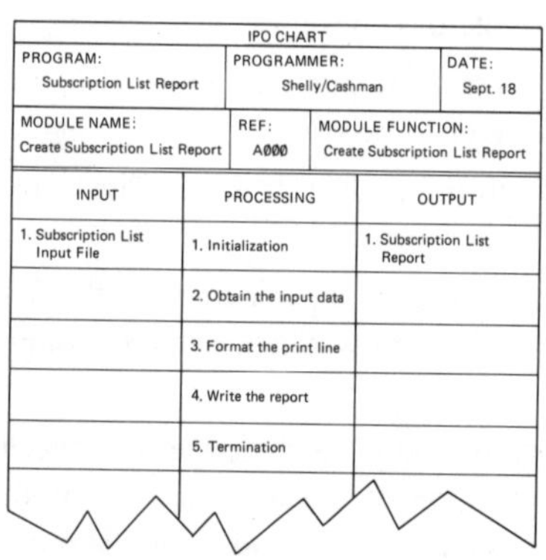

IPO CHART

| PROGRAM: | PROGRAMMER: | DATE: |
|---|---|---|
| Subscription List Report | Shelly/Cashman | Sept. 18 |

| MODULE NAME: | REF: | MODULE FUNCTION: |
|---|---|---|
| Create Subscription List Report | AØØØ | Create Subscription List Report |

| INPUT | PROCESSING | OUTPUT |
|---|---|---|
| 1. Subscription List Input File | 1. Initialization | 1. Subscription List Report |
| | 2. Obtain the input data | |
| | 3. Format the print line | |
| | 4. Write the report | |
| | 5. Termination | |

FIGURE 2.7 An example of another form of IPO chart*

[4]Joseph T. Rigo, "'Son of HIPO' Proposed as Easier Charting Vehicle", *Computerworld*, August 9, 1976, p. 21. Copyright 1976 by Computerworld, Inc., Newton, MA. 02160.

[5]Gary B. Shelly and Thomas J. Cashman, "Introduction to Structured Design and Structured Programming," *The Compiler*, Fall 1977, p. 6.

*(From Gary B. Shelly and Thomas J. Cashman, "Introduction to Structured Design and Structured Programming," *The Compiler*, Fall 1977, p. 6)

### Paul Noll's Simplified Version of HIPO

The main characteristics of Paul Noll's simplified version of HIPO are:

1. It does not connect input(s) to process step(s), or process step(s) to output(s). There are no arrows. The input(s) and output(s) are shown (in input and output boxes) against the step(s) that use or create them.
2. Pseudocode is used in the process box.
3. In the space between the process and output boxes, the number of called modules are written to the right of the steps that call them.
4. The calling module(s) are written above the upper left-hand corner of the process box.

For further information, see Noll (1977, 1978).

## DEVELOPING HIPO IN A SERIES OF MEETINGS

HIPO specifications for a new development can be developed in a series of meetings between the system designers/programmers and users. An early meeting may deal with generalities and produce a list of probable functions. Later meetings may concentrate on those functions one at a time, elaborating in more detail. After each meeting, the chief programmer documents the discussions together with HIPOs evolved during the meeting. As more functions evolve, relationships between them appear and can be arranged into a hierarchy. When the hierarchy is completed, the systems requirements will be defined and design will also be completed. Refer to Jones, (1976) for a case study of how HIPO was used for developing specifications in a series of meetings.

## INFORMAL, FREEHAND HIPO

During the process of system or program design, informal, freehand HIPOs are usually drawn quickly to record thoughts. If such HIPOs are legible, they can be used in walkthroughs. When the design is finalized, diagrams should be drawn with a template following standard graphic conventions. [A (human) librarian can prepare finished HIPOs from legible sketches.]

## HOW TO KNOW THAT A HIPO PACKAGE COMMUNICATES EFFECTIVELY

Apply this test to find out whether a HIPO package (or any documentation) communicates effectively. Can a reader (who knows how to read HIPO) understand it with minimal explanation? If not, there is something wrong. Either the HIPO method is not used properly or the method itself is inappropriate or insufficient for a particular application.

## GUIDELINES TO IMPROVE THE QUALITY OF HIPO DOCUMENTATION

Here is a partial list of guidelines to improve the quality of HIPO documentation.

1. A good hierarchy chart helps top-down design and development and improves the quality of the entire HIPO package.
2. A program librarian can help in drawing and updating HIPOs from the legible sketches drawn by programmers.
3. Guidelines and standards with actual examples of HIPOs, when followed, ensure consistent HIPO documentation.
4. If HIPOs are used widely in your company, a position of full- or part-time HIPO editor may be justified; otherwise, editing may be done by the project leader or lead analyst. Following are the suggestions for the HIPO editor:

    - Edit objectively.
    - Make constructive comments and suggestions for improvements.
    - Attend walkthroughs on HIPO.
    - Help to develop and update HIPO guidelines and standards.
    - Keep in touch with new developments in related areas.

Editing is also known as auditing, reviewing, and walkthrough. It applies to every phase of the development cycle. Editing done early in the cycle is by far the most significant in terms of effect on the final package.

Study Part III of "HIPO: Design Aid and Documentation Tool" (audio course) for more about HIPO editing.

## GUIDELINES VERSUS STANDARDS

When implementing a new technique such as HIPO, create guidelines for use. These may later become standards. (A standard specifies that you *will* do it this way, whereas guidelines specify that this is a suggestion. Generally, a guideline will help acceptance of a new technique, whereas standards may turn people away! Guidelines, with the consensus of HIPO developers and users, may later become standards.)

## HIPO ALONE MAY NOT BE ENOUGH

HIPO may not be enough in some situations. You may need other tools, such as decision tables, pseudocode, or even structured flowcharts to supplement or complement (since HIPO has limitations) HIPO documentation. Extended description entry(ies) can point to the non-HIPO documentation. System flowcharts can supplement HIPOs by indicating the flow (sequence) of events.

## THERE IS NO ABSOLUTELY RIGHT OR WRONG WAY TO USE HIPO

It must be remembered that there is no absolutely right or wrong way to use HIPO, just as there is no totally right or wrong way in writing or verbal communications. HIPO may be clear and complete, or ambiguous, just as written or verbal communications can be clear and concise or vague and confusing. Also, there may be many variations of HIPO, even within the conceptual framework established to use HIPO. HIPO may be right or wrong in degrees relative to that framework.

The HIPO conventions and symbols can be thought of as the grammar in communications. The conventions can help produce better HIPOs, but to create good-quality, HIPOs need something more than merely following conventions, and several revisions may be necessary before coming to a satisfactory version of HIPO.

## HIGHLIGHTING CHANGES TO HIPO SPECIFICATIONS UNDERGOING IMPLEMENTATION

The author, while working as a contract programmer, directly coded several programs from HIPO specifications. The designer, working nights, penciled changes to HIPO specifications without dating or initialing them. As a result, some changes were missed in the coding.

The designer accepted my suggestion to make changes with a red pencil or circle the changes with a red pencil, and to include date(s) of change. Incidentally, I was also able to justify the extra time spent in making the changes.

## WHAT TO DO WHEN HIPO IS THE INSTALLATION STANDARD AND YOU DON'T LIKE IT

If your installation requires HIPO and if you don't like it, you can proceed this way. With the consent of your boss, or perhaps privately, use the tool or technique you think appropriate (or feel comfortable with) to design and develop a system or program, and then translate to HIPO (within the time allotted) to conform to the standards.

Why do double work? It may not be that bad. Once design is done using any appropriate structured documentation tool, the hard part of the work is done. Translating to HIPO (or to any other structured documentation technique) should be relatively easy after that, provided that you know HIPO. It may also provide an additional check of the design. In fact, with the consent of my boss, in one system design assignment I used Warnier/Orr diagrams [described in Orr (1977a, 1977b)] to design the system and then translated them to HIPO.

## ESTIMATING TIME REQUIRED TO DRAW HIPO DIAGRAMS

Include thinking time in your estimate when preparing IPO diagrams. The typical IPO diagram requires about half an hour to draw after that.

### *A Rule-of-Thumb Method of Measuring Productivity of a System/Program Designer*

The number of completed function boxes per day in a hierarchy chart may be a rule-of-thumb measure of a system/programmer designer's productivity. However, remember that many factors are involved in the design, such as the complexity of the system/program, support of the users, and quality and completeness of specifications. The measurement and comparison of productivity of design personnel in different situations may not be accurate. Use this method with great caution.

Such a unit of measure may encourage creating more boxes, so some standard (e.g., equating each box to an averge of 50 lines of structured code) might be established. Experimentation with this unit of measure in a particular environment may lead to some useful results.

## HIPO IN MAINTENANCE

Chapter 1 provides guidelines for using HIPO in maintenance and for creating HIPO documentation for existing systems.

## HOW HIPO WAS USED TO DOCUMENT EXISTING SYSTEMS AT THE UNIVERSITY OF ILLINOIS

Here is how HIPO was used to document existing systems at the University of Illinois.[6] At the request of Mr. Henard (manager of the financial data systems group at the Urbana campus), staff members of the three data centers documented their existing systems. For this they used traditional flowcharting techniques, mainly because the university had not had time to train all of its

[6]The material on this topic is based on a case study in *Business Systems Planning and HIPO at the University of Illinois* [Installation Management, GK20-0967-0(4/76)], IBM Corporation.

personnel in HIPO. Mr. Henard and two of his associates grouped the flowcharts for the procurement and disbursement systems into functional packages. A third member took each package and fitted it into the visual table of contents. The team then expanded the original structure from the 14 functions to include 62 subfunctions listed on procedural flowcharts—a technique they adopted for this, their first major use of the HIPO technique.

The team analyzed each function and prepared HIPO overview diagrams for the functions that could benefit from these charts. The determining factors in the choice were the extent of the information available and the role of the function within the total system. In all, 23 overview diagrams were drawn.

Since the team's task was to identify functions rather than to design a system, the development of detailed HIPO diagrams was left for the people assigned to the next phase of the study.

Sandy Dennhardt, senior management methods analyst, describes the way she and her group used HIPO in phase 3, starting with the new material developed in the previous phase. First, they refined the visual table of contents during a thorough review of the system. This review produced a more elaborate structure than was possible during the initial study. The team then reviewed the overview diagrams and developed detailed HIPO diagrams to support each overview.

As the analysts worked on these diagrams, gaps appeared where the interviews had not provided the needed data. The analysts then filled in the material from their general knowledge of the business and marked the item for special review by the user.

Usually, as the analysts embarked on each new level of detail, they saw areas in the level they had just finished that needed further definition. At this point they were able to fill in the necessary information. Miss Dennhardt's experience is that two iterations after the first generally are sufficient to bring any level of diagram to satisfactory completion.

The analysts work in pencil so that they can easily insert modifications. Each page is numbered in a hierarchical fashion to allow rearrangement of the design simply by renumbering and physically reordering pages in the binder rather than redrawing diagrams.

## AUTOMATING HIPO

> There have been some attempts to automate the process. Clint Jurgens and Dick Olson of Sperry Univac in St. Paul described one effort at the ACM '75 (Fall) conference. . . .

> They modified a software package that normally produces electronic circuit diagrams. Their HIPO charts look like wiring diagrams for your television set, but they do thc job, and they are easy to update.[7]

Two software packages, HIPODRAW, and PANEL, from IBM automate HIPO. Check with your IBM representative for details and availability. For both packages a trial period is allowed. Try before deciding to buy. To make the most of the trial, read the material thoroughly and coordinate with your data processing organization before beginning the trial.

Here are some considerations while acquiring such a package:

1. How much front-end work is involved? Is the package good in developing new HIPOs as well as in maintaining existing HIPOs?
2. Does it need a dedicated staff member? How much training is needed?
3. After making an announcement of the trial period, how many persons come forth to try the package?
4. What are the education requirements of personnel?

## FUTURE OF HIPO

Some authors (see the specific references in the Bibliography) have assessed HIPO as follows:

Paul Noll feels that HIPO is the most effective form of documentation that is currently available and it is the one most likely to be around 10 years from now. Noll has developed a simplified version of HIPO, as we saw earlier.

Ed Yourdon, however, does not recommend detail HIPO diagrams. He considered HIPO "better than nothing." He emphasizes (Constantine-Yourdon) structure charts.

Ken Orr, in general, dislikes the basic HIPO forms. However, he considers HIPO "a clear step forward from no consistent method of design and documentation at all." He prefers Warnier/Orr diagrams, which he calls "the flowchart of the future."

Joseph T. Rigo, in a recent article, feels that HIPO charts (which he calls "a transition phenomenon") may belong to the past.

HIPO does not seem to have been universally accepted. For example, the otherwise excellent reference work, the *Encyclopedia of Computer Science*,

---

[7]Joseph T. Rigo, "'Son of HIPO' Proposed As Easier Charting Vehicle",*Computerworld*, August 9, 1976, p. 21. Copyright 1976 by Computerworld Inc., Newton, MA. 02160.

(Princeton, N.J.: Petrocelli/Charter, 1976, first ed.), called by its editor Anthony Ralston a "snapshot" of computer science, does not even mention HIPO; neither does Martin H. Weik's *Standard Dictionary of Computers and Information Processing* (Rochelle Parte, N.J.: Hayden Book Company, Inc., 1977, rev. 2nd ed.).

The important thing for the industry is that HIPO is a form for structured documentation.

## CONCLUSION

It should be remembered that HIPO is only a design and documentation tool. Drawing thousands of HIPOs will not guarantee a good design. Ed Yourdon, referring to the IBM manual "HIPO—A Design Aid and Documentation Technique" says: "The title of IBM's manual says it all: HIPO is a design *aid* and a *documentation technique*—it's not design, in and of itself."[8]

By following the applicable tips, trends, and ideas outlined in this chapter, and by studying the required sources for further study you will be able to make the most of HIPO.

---

[8]Ed Yourdon, "Users Want too Much from HIPO", *Computerworld,* May 31, 1976, p. 24. Copyright 1976 by Computerworld, Inc., Newton, MA. 02160.

# *A Powerful Structured Tool: The Warnier/Orr Diagram*

# 3

After first using the Warnier/Orr diagram to develop a system, I continued using it privately, since the installation standard was HIPO. The diagram proved equally effective for designing major modifications, and was a precise and effective tool for enhancements as well. The modified programs worked on a second or third effective test.

Excited about this powerful tool, I studied almost everything about the Warnier/Orr diagram that I could lay my hands on during this period (mid-1978 through 1980). I condensed the research, experience, and interviews into a report on the Warnier/Orr diagram. The manuscript of the report was reviewed by Jean-Dominique Warnier, the inventor of the diagram, and Ken Orr, who enhanced the diagram and made it popular in North America.

[Incidentally, I found the Warnier/Orr diagram, even in the functional design, clearly superior to HIPO. However, I do not understand why many data processing professionals, some veterans of many years, have not even heard about this diagram, let alone used it. To me, not knowing Warnier is like working in physics and not knowing Newton!]

The Warnier/Orr diagram is a graphic design and documentation tool that has been called a "little giant" of the structured revolution. The Bibliography includes references on the Warnier/Orr diagram, the Warnier/Orr methodology (also called DSSD—a trademark of Ken Orr and Associates), and Jean-Dominique Warnier's methods Logical Construction of Programs/Logical Construction of Systems (LCP/LCS). *Structured Requirements Definition* by Ken Orr includes an appendix on Warnier/Orr diagrams which describes the diagrams as a powerful graphic specification language. It also gives additional conventions and use of the Warnier/Orr diagram, such as concurrency, recursion, arithmetic operators, concatenated names, assembly-line diagrams, and in-out diagrams. *Logical Construction of Programs* by Jean-Dominique Warnier, *Structured Systems Development* by Ken Orr, and *Program Design and*

*Construction* by David Higgins are also key sources on Warnier and Warnier/Orr diagrams. The *Tutorial on Software Maintenance* by Parikh and Zvegintzov includes three papers (with introductions) on the Warnier/Orr methodology.

Warnier/Orr diagrams can also be used effectively in noncomputer applications. See the section "Warnier/Orr Diagrams Adapt to Noncomputer Use," later in this chapter.

## Acknowledgments

I am grateful to Jean-Dominque Warnier (then with Cii Honeywell Bull, France, now retired); and Ken Orr (Ken Orr and Associates, Topeka, Kansas) for helping me in the research and for reviewing the manuscript of this chapter. I thank Cris Miller (The Catalyst Corporation, Brookfield, Illinois) for reviewing the manuscript. For helping me in the research I thank Rick Fuette (Byte Publications, Inc.) and Edrey Maranger. In preparing the manuscript, my daughter Sharmila (now Mrs. Sharmila P. Houck) gave invaluable help.

---

If a man can write a better book, preach a better sermon, or make a better mousetrap, than his neighbor, though he builds his house in the woods, the world will make a beaten path to his door.

*Ralph Waldo Emerson*

Warnier-Orr diagrams are a giant leap in the right direction for structured programming. They represent an attitude which, for the first time since people have been playing with computers, can lead to consistently reliable software that is very easy to maintain. Currently, most data processing departments spend over 80% of their time and effort repairing old code that has suddenly gone bad. Warnier-Orr diagrams also provide the means to produce software of a quality that has never before been possible.[1]

*David A. Higgins*

[1]From "Structured Program Design" by David A. Higgins in the October, 1977 issue of Byte magazine. 

Not so long ago, I started to design the batch part of a claims system for an insurance company. The requirements, written in narrative English, were voluminous and ambiguous. The required inputs and the necessary processes were not clear. Not knowing where and how to begin, I was terribly depressed and about to give up.

Then one Friday I took home the book *Structured Systems Development* (Orr, 1977b). Once I started reading, I couldn't put it down, and read almost the entire night. During the weekend I almost finished it.

On Monday, I returned to work confident, and knowing exactly where to start. Fortunately, the systems requirements included the detailed descriptions of outputs. I started working from the outputs using the Warnier/Orr diagram. Following the guidelines given in the book, I completed the initial design in a few days.

Later, I converted the design documentation to HIPO, the installation standard. The conversion was easy, and in addition, provided an additional check on the design. The system has been in production for several months and is working well.

Many other users, such as the Office of the Administration for the Courts for the State of Washington (see McNurlin, 1979), report dramatic results using the Warnier/Orr diagram and related techniques.

## WHAT THIS CHAPTER CAN DO FOR YOU

This chapter introduces a powerful structured tool, the Warnier/Orr diagram. If you are already using the Warnier/Orr diagram, the chapter will help you introduce it to new users in your organization. A list of annotated references for further study is given in the Bibliography.

## AN OVERVIEW OF SYSTEM/ PROGRAM DESIGN AND DOCUMENTATION TOOLS

Each structured tool has advantages and disadvantages. The Warnier/Orr diagram maximizes advantages and minimizes disadvantages.

Figure 3–1 illustrates an overview of system/program design and documentation tools. Note that the classification into traditional and structured

- System/program design and documentation tools
  - Traditional
    - Flowcharts
    - Narratives
    - Coding (with/without comments)
    - Block diagrams
    - Decision tables
    - .
    - .
    - .
  - Structured
    - Warnier/Orr diagrams
    - HIPO (HIPO/DB)
    - Structured coding (with/without comments)
    - Pseudocode
    - (Constantine–Yourdon) structure charts
    - (Constantine–Yourdon) data flow diagrams (DFD)
    - Nassi–Shneiderman charts
    - Chapin charts
    - (Michael Jackson's) data structure diagrams
    - Structured flowcharts
    - Structured block diagrams
    - .
    - .
    - .

FIGURE 3.1 An assembly line Warnier-Orr diagram showing an overview of system/program design and documentation tools

is somewhat arbitrary. For instance, decision tables can also be used with structured methodologies. Some of the structured tools may also be used with traditional systems/programs.

Many tools of structured documentation have been developed in the past decade. These tools are still evolving, and a great deal of experimentation is going on.

## The Need for Proper Logical Tools

Imagine how slow the advances in mathematics would have been if Roman numerals (I, II, III, ...) had remained the standard. The logical tool of Arabic numerals (1, 2, 3, ...) has been one of the keys to advances in mathematics.

For instance, multiply two simple numbers using both tools, e.g., 23 × 15, and XXIII and XV).

In the same way, efficient and easy "logical" tools are essential for advances in software technologies: structured software design, development, and maintenance. The Warnier/Orr diagram is one such tool.

## A Tool Invented in France, Enhanced in America

The Warnier (pronounced Warn-yay),/Orr diagram, named after the French systems scientist Jean-Dominique Warnier, and Kenneth Orr, an American systems scientist, has an interesting history. During the early 1960s, while teaching Boolean algebra to explain hardware to engineers of CII Honeywell Bull, France, Warnier asked: "Why not use Boolean algebra to design systems and programs?" Supported by his company, he formed a group and started work. His people were enthusiastic, but others ridiculed his ideas.

In 1969, he completed the methodology called Logical Construction of Programs [LCP, described in Warnier (1974)], which noted the top-down design for all data (output, input, and programs) with a hierarchical diagram (known as a Warnier diagram), representing each level of subdivision with a bracket.

Ken Orr, then with Langston, Kitch and Associates, Topeka, Kansas, stumbled on Warnier's book [*Logical Construction of Programs*, Warnier (1974)] in the early 1970s. To eliminate some of the drawbacks of HIPO, he had already developed HIPO/DB (Orr 1977a, 1977b), which combined pseudocode and an additional data base box on top of the process box in the IPO (input-process-output) chart. Unfortunately, it produced too much paper.

He experimented with the Warnier diagram as a design and analysis aid. Users liked this new diagram. He then eliminated the hierarchy chart of VTOC (visual table of contents) of HIPO in favor of the Warnier diagram, providing logical structures and eliminating boxes. People related better to this new diagram. Further experience produced an enhanced version of the Warnier diagram, now known as the Warnier/Orr diagram.

The Warnier diagram is the primary tool of Warnier's LCP/LCS (Logical Construction of Programs/Logical Construction of Systems), and the Warnier/Orr diagram is the heart of Warnier/Orr methodology. However, I believe this versatile tool can also be used with most other structured methodologies. It can even be used to document and modify existing systems/programs, as we shall see later.

## THE WARNIER/ORR DIAGRAM

While the Warnier/Orr diagram has foundations in set theory and Boolean algebra, knowledge of those subjects is not necessary to use it. In fact, the Warnier/Orr diagram is surprisingly easy to read and use (after some practice).

The Warnier/Orr diagram provides a formal method of hierarchical decomposition of entries. The entries may consist of activities, functions, or data elements. For a particular decomposition, all the entries must be of the same type (Rudkin and Shere, 1979).

The Warnier/Orr diagram also includes a sequence of events or flow of control, and the basic structures of structured programming, (i.e., sequence, alternation, and repetition).

### How to Read a Warnier/Orr Diagram

The conventional hierarchy chart does not show the relationship between various functions. The Warnier/Orr diagram shows the hierarchical structure as well as the process flow [where and when (and how many times) an event occurs]. How does it show all this?

The events occur in sequence from left to right and top to bottom for each column (beginning from the left). The symbols in parentheses below the names of each item in the diagram show the number of times that item occurs. The brackets enclose logically related operations. The hierarchy is also from left to right, which can be observed by turning a Warnier/Orr diagram 90° clockwise.

Study the following simple symbols and conventions. Then follow the examples of a Warnier/Orr diagram shown in Figure 3-4.

> (N) The function is executed N times, where "N" is a variable. Usually, a meaningful variable is chosen. For example,
>
> PRINT POLICIES
> (P)
>
> means execute the PRINT POLICIES function P times for P number of policies.

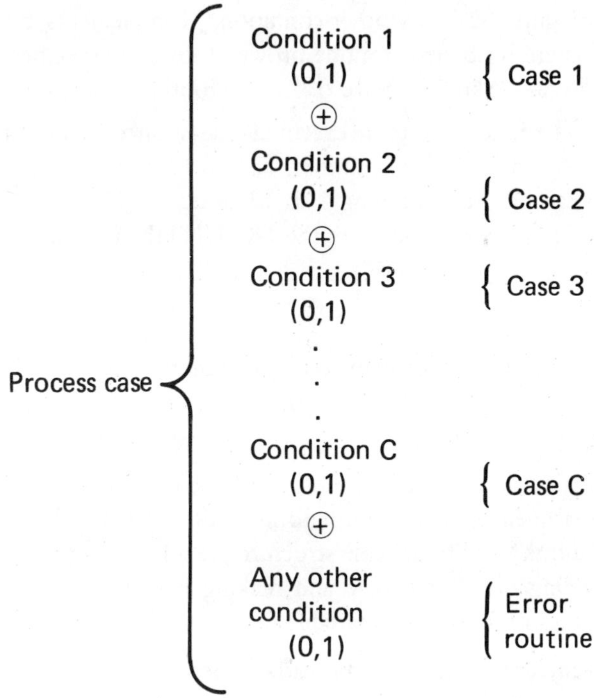


FIGURE 3.2 The case structure

Note that "N" could be zero. This notation provides a DO WHILE structure.[2]

When "N" is not a variable but a fixed number, such as 12 months in a year, it can be expressed as "(12)" if iteration is to be done 12 times; otherwise; the notation would be "(0,12)." If a function is executed only 1 time, the "(1)" is usually omitted.

(0,1) The function is executed 0 or 1 times, depending on whether the function has not or has been selected at this point.

This notation provides the alternation (or selection) structure (in conjunction with the exclusive OR symbol "⊕" explained later). The case structure is a "generalized"alternation with more than two cases to consider, as shown in Figure 3-2. The last case in

---

[2]For a DO WHILE structure, Warnier provides a better structure in his book, *Logical Construction of Programs* (Warnier 1974, pp. 52–53), making future modifications easier:

> . . . If a set of data is present A times in a set D and if A can be 0, the hierarchical organization of the data is described as follows:

Figure 3-2 "Any other condition," complements the structure. If there is no error routine provided for a nonspecified case, simply write "Skip" in place of "Error routine."

(1,t) The function is to be executed at least once, and possibly (t) times. When it is a fixed number, such as 12 months in a year, "(1,12)" can be used, meaning 1 to 12 times.
This notation provides the DO UNTIL structure.

The following symbol appears between the names of two (or more) functions:

⊕ Exclusive choice between two or more functions. [This is used in conjunction with "(0,1)" notation, and means one or the other, but not both.]

With the notations above, the three basic constructs of structured programming—sequence, alternation, and iteration (both DO WHILE and DO UNTIL)—and the additional case structure are added to the hierarchical diagram, providing order and logic and making it comprehensive. In case of iterations, it also tells (using a variable or a constant) how many iterations.

\+ Inclusive OR, i.e., one or the other or both. (This symbol is also used for concurrency.)

Note that in most applications, exclusive OR and sequential operations are used.

The remaining symbols are:

—— Appears above the name of a function *when* applicable): means *not*. For example, $\overline{\text{EQUAL}}$ means *not* equal.

?n This symbol, where n is an integer, is used to make footnotes to describe physical tests for the logical "number of times" in a Warnier/Orr diagram, when necessary for documentation purposes. See, for example, Figure 3-3. The symbol "?1" appearing with the logical notation for "number of times" (1,p) points to a note providing the physical implementation detail (end of policies = true).

The following symbol is not in the Warnier/Orr methodology; however, I believe it can be useful.

---

D { Group A (0 or 1 times) { Batch of data A times)

(from *Logical Construction of Programs* by Jean-Dominique Warnier, p. 52; published by Van Nostrand Reinhold Company).

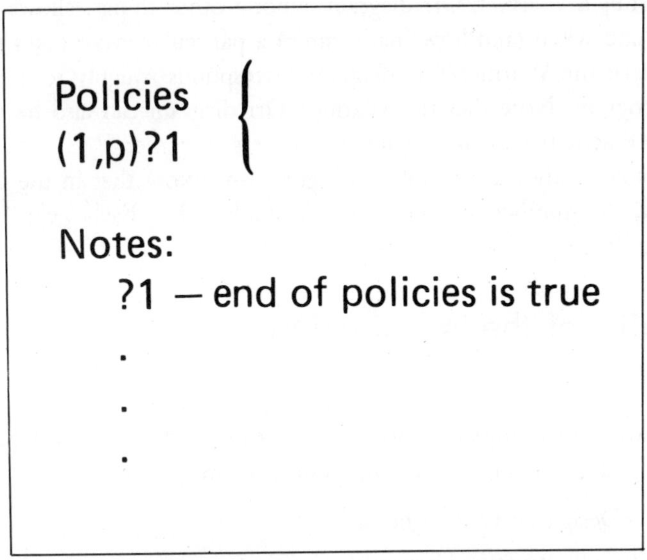


FIGURE 3.3 Physical constraint

Wiggly bracket used to draw WIGGLE Warnier/Orr diagram, when the design is not yet exact. (See Weinberg, 1979, for a description of WIGGLE.)

[A Warnier/Orr template including all of the above (except the Wiggly diagram) and a few additional symbols, with their explanations on the jacket, is available from Ken Orr and Associates, 1725 Gage Blvd. Topeka, Kansas 66604. Worksheets for documenting manual versions of Warnier/Orr diagram are also available from the same vendor.]

The following are conventions:

Each function comprises the subfunctions "Begin" (initialize, open files, etc.), "Process," and "End" (close files, print totals, etc.). The subsequent functions are decomposed in a similar fashion ("Begin," "Process," "End").

This structure of functions is based on the fact that logically, certain events can happen at the beginning of the functions, while others take place in the processing, and the remaining occur at the end. (This structure also makes future maintenance or modification of the program easy.)

Thus a Warnier/Orr diagram, among other things, allows you to see where and when (and how many times) a particular event takes place. Each bracket of the Warnier/Orr diagram corresponds roughly to a subfunction in a program. Note that the Warnier/Orr diagram can also be used to decompose activities or data elements, as we saw earlier.

Now study the examples in Figure 3-4. [Note that in the diagram on the left, the number of times, e.g., (Y) under "For Each Year," is omitted to simplify it.]

## Benefits of the Warnier/Orr Diagram

This and the following subsections describe some of the benefits of the Warnier/Orr diagram. The benefits for programmers are:

1. Design faster than before.
2. Code structured programs directly from Warnier/Orr diagrams with minimum effort.
3. Programs run correctly, usually on the first effective test.
4. Works for designing programs of any size.
5. Stresses design over coding. Once the problem is designed, it can be programmed in any language.
6. Is easy to learn and use. (Although the tool looks deceptively simple to use, it needs some practice.)
7. Indicates where and when (and how many times) a particular event takes place.
8. Organizes a program hierarchically, where each function has begin (initialize, etc.), the process, and the end (print final totals, etc.).
9. Helps develop a program that is logically correct, easy to read, already documented, and easy to maintain.

### *The Warnier/Orr Diagram Is a Versatile Tool*

The Warnier/Orr diagram is an excellent tool to combine and summarize the available related information from various sources into a logical and hierarchical organization, in a compact, pictorial format. Thus it becomes easy to reference, understand, communicate, check (verify), and work with.

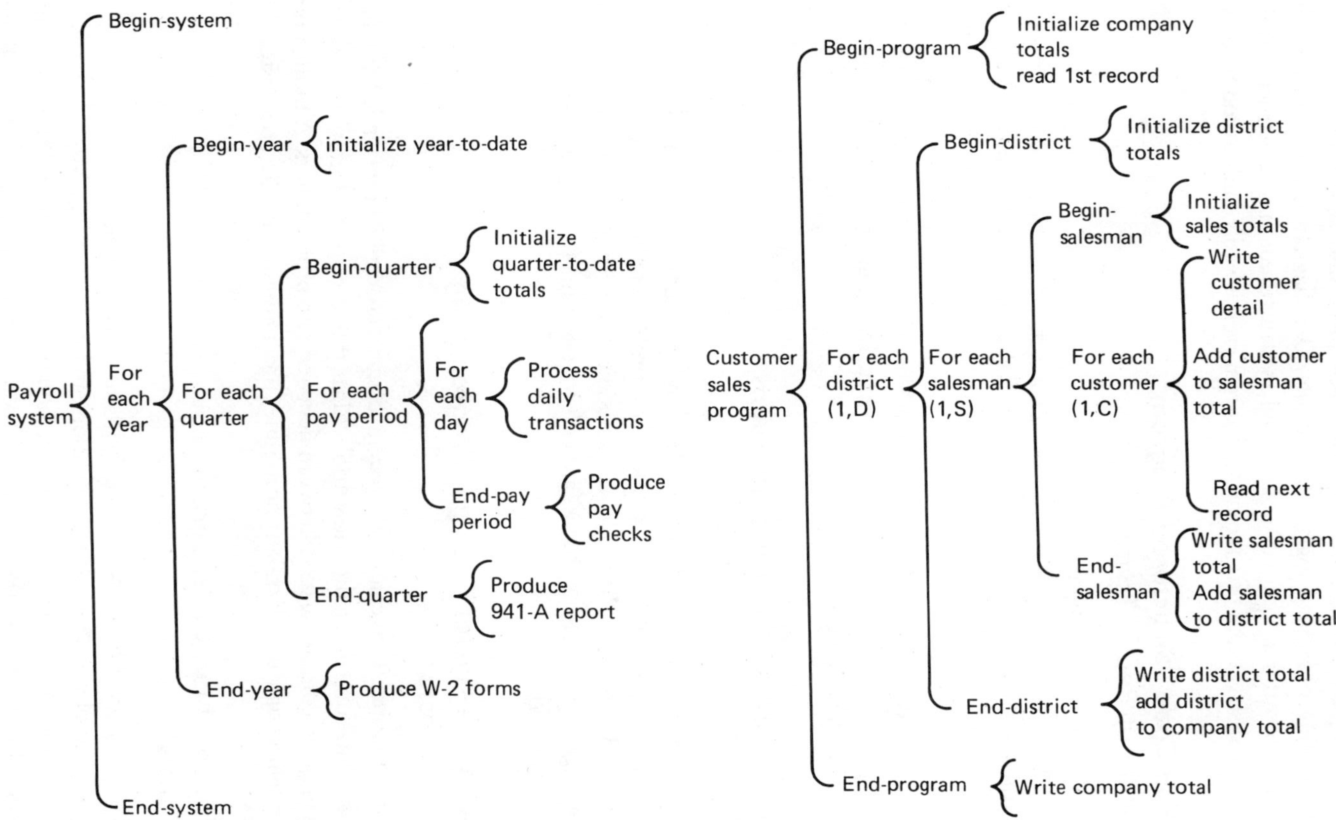


FIGURE 3.4 Examples of Warnier/Orr diagram*

*(From Ken Orr, "Structured Systems Design: Blueprinting the Future," *Infosystems*, February 1977. Copyright, Hitchcock Publishing Company)

By hierarchically decomposing each piece into simple pieces, and by combining order and logic, the Warnier/Orr diagram becomes one of the most powerful structured tools, useful in structured analysis, structured design, and structured programming. Moreover, it is easily understood by users.

## You Code "Structured Program" Without Really Trying

If Warnier/Orr diagrams are carried to sufficient detail, coding from them can be done rapidly. No extra design effort, or intermediate step (such as writing pseudocode), is necessary. Also, if Warnier/Orr diagrams are properly developed, you cannot code anything but a structured program from them. In other words, you code structured programs without really trying.

Perhaps the best way to eliminate (or reduce) the use of GOTOs in a structured program is to design them out. Designing with the Warnier/Orr diagram helps to do that.

## The Warnier/Orr Diagram Helps Develop Logical Design

The Warnier/Orr diagram helps develop logical design; thus the designer can concentrate on the logical solution of a problem before adding the physical details. Users also find the logical solution easier to understand. (For details on logical design using the Warnier/Orr diagram, see Higgins (1979), and Orr (1977b).)

## After the System Design, Programming Goes Faster

The Warnier/Orr charts for system design can easily be extended for implementation, using the same tool. Also, this precise tool ensures effective and quick communication between designers and programmers. Although the system design usually takes more time, programming usually goes faster.

## The Warnier/Orr Diagram Provides Consistency

The Warnier/Orr diagram is perhaps the only technique that uses a single graphic tool for design, data definition, and programming. Most other techniques use more than one documentation tool. For instance, HIPO uses the hierarchy chart and IPO charts; Jackson's method uses structure diagrams and schematic logic. Also, the Warnier/Orr diagram can be used throughout the system's life cycle, including maintenance.

## The Periodic Nature of an Activity or Output Is Shown

The periodic nature of an output or activity is often eliminated from a design unless it is specifically mentioned in the name of a function (e.g., PRODUCE WEEKLY PAYCHECKS) with other design tools. With the Warnier/Orr diagram, the periodic nature is shown explicitly in a hierarchical manner. If any report is missing, or shown with wrong period, the analyst or user can spot it quickly. Also, with the periodic nature of the system shown, it becomes a continuous operation, easier to visualize.

## Acceptance and Teachability

After selecting a structured tool, getting it accepted by designers and programmers is sometimes a problem for management. Management can force the tool by making it a standard, but this rarely works. Unless the tool has intrinsic value, it would not appeal to the practitioner for long. Although the shortcomings of a tool may not be apparent in the beginning, with disciplined and proper use the subtleties of a tool are revealed. When the weaknesses of a tool are found, even if the practitioner may not express it eloquently, the inherent frustration is there. The tool slowly goes into disuse or is not used as intended.

The remedy for these problems is to select a tool that has maximum advantages and minimum disadvantages. The Warnier/Orr diagram is such a tool. Also, the tool is teachable. The essence of this tool and related techniques can be imparted to a number of people. The Warnier/Orr diagram is perhaps the easiest tool to teach.

## The Warnier/Orr Diagram Can Be Used for Mini-Specs of Structured Analysis

Tom DeMarco in his book *Structured Analysis and System Specification* (DeMarco, 1978), describes the use of structured English to develop mini-specs. In my opinion, the Warnier/Orr diagram is a better tool, since the mini-specs developed using it need not be diluted to ensure the understanding of the user, thus saving time and effort.

The symbolic Warnier/Orr diagram is like a blueprint of the system. Take the analogy of an architect. He sketches a house using standard conventions. He does not write down "the bathroom is *X* feet long and *Y* feet wide" and so on, because his client does not know how to read a blueprint. He would explain the sketches verbally, but I doubt if he would go beyond that.

Users can easily be taught how to read a Warnier/Orr diagram, the tool used to develop the blueprint of the system.

## THE WARNIER/ORR DIAGRAM AND MAINTENANCE

The documentation developed with the Warnier/Orr diagram is like a schematic diagram of a system or program. It saves time and effort on the part of the maintenance programmer by providing reliable (when kept undated), compact documentation, which *is* consulted before going to the program listing. For continued usefulness, the diagrams must be kept updated. An automated diagramming package (such as Structure(s) of Ken Orr and Associates), makes it easier to update the diagrams.

The Warnier/Orr diagram can also be used for designing program/system modifications. Not long ago, I designed and coded major modifications to two structured programs (originally designed with other tools) using the Warnier/Orr diagram. The modified programs worked on the second effective test!

## USE OF THE WARNIER/ORR DIAGRAM TO DOCUMENT AN EXISTING SYSTEM

The Warnier/Orr diagram has been used successfully to document existing systems. The "in-out" or "assembly-line" version of the diagram is used.

Systems are often easier to document at the top. It is simpler to document at the procedure and program level than it is at levels below. Make the first cut at process documentation. This might be to develop Warnier/Orr diagrams of the major data files or data bases within the system. Diagrams should be made strictly from a logical standpoint. By documenting the data files, you can come up with a dictionary/directory describing what data exists and where they are used.

Redesign existing systems, starting with a systematic structuring of the existing outputs. Next, go through logical, physical systems design. Then a long-range plan for replacing the existing system can be developed.

## MAINTAINING WARNIER/ORR DIAGRAMS

While designing and/or developing a new system/program, keeping the documentation updated may become a major problem. Perhaps the most easily changed graphic technique to use is the Warnier/Orr diagram, and it becomes even easier with an automated diagramming package. The Warnier/Orr diagrams of the existing system/programs (after completing the necessary steps) can also be maintained with an automated package.

## SOME ADVANCED CONCEPTS OF THE WARNIER/ORR DIAGRAM

Concurrent and recursive operations can be shown with the Warnier/Orr diagram. The Warnier/Orr diagram is also a powerful tool to design teleprocessing, distributed data processing (DDP), process control, and communications systems. Real-time and on-line systems can also be efficiently designed using the Warnier/Orr diagram.

The assembly-line diagram is an offshoot of the Warnier/Orr diagram which is helpful in designing a system. In fact, I started the design of the claims system mentioned earlier with assembly-line diagrams.

Higgins (1979) includes two chapters on advanced concepts of the Warnier/Orr diagram.

## OTHER TOOLS ARE ALSO NEEDED

The Warnier/Orr diagram generally does the best job as a universal design and documentation tool. However, other structured tools are also needed for handling certain problems and for communicating with certain audiences. You can check if design/documentation done using other tools is structured by quickly translating it into a Warnier/Orr diagram.

A structured solution can be expressed using almost any structured tool. I think it is necessary to learn how to use more than one tool; a good craftsperson has several tools in his or her kit. If we know other tools, then when a need arises, we can quickly use the ones required.

## HOW TO INTRODUCE THE WARNIER/ORR DIAGRAM

Management commitment is mandatory for introducing the Warnier/Orr diagram in an organization. Initial training may consist of live classes (Orr's company offers courses on structured systems development which concentrate on use of the Warnier/Orr diagram) or an in-depth study of Higgins (1979) and Orr (1977b). On the first project, a qualified consultant may help ensure that you are on the right track. As you go along, study other appropriate references listed in the Bibliography. The managers and users should also be trained, especially in the procedural areas. Yourdon (1979) provides guidelines for selling the new techniques and setting up a pilot project.

## THE FUTURE OF THE WARNIER/ ORR DIAGRAM

Ken Orr thinks that the use of the Warnier/Orr diagram will extend outside of data processing in the future. The diagram will be used to plan procedures and lay out problems, manual procedures, and systems. (Interestingly, I used the Warnier/Orr diagram in the assembly line format while outlining this chapter.)

In his book *Structured Systems Development* (Orr, 1977b), Orr calls the Warnier/Orr diagram "the flowchart of the future." The ease of communication and the clean and transparent structure presented in a natural way by the Warnier/Orr diagram make it a powerful structured tool. The Warnier/Orr diagram has the potential to become the future universal structuring tool.

### Warnier/Orr Diagrams Adapt to Noncomputer Use

The versatile Warnier/Orr diagram can also be used by both programmers and managers for developing noncomputer procedures. The following guidelines include my experience. Although writers and publishers are used to illustrate the concepts, I believe the diagram can be of help in the development of almost all noncomputer procedures.

The Warnier/Orr diagram, a tool developed for designing computer systems and programs, can be used for planning purposes by writers and publishers. The diagram is surprisingly easy to read and use (after some practice) by laymen.

Orr predicted in a telephone interview that, in the future, the Warnier/Orr diagram will be used more for noncomputer procedures. I believe it can be used for planning writing and publishing activities, such as research, writing, scheduling, and marketing.

For noncomputer procedures, the diagram comprises a series of brackets, reading left to right, top to bottom, grouping activities or functions in a hierarchical, logical manner. It may include a sequence of events or flow of control. Perhaps the most commonly used form of Warnier/Orr diagram in noncomputer procedures is its assembly line version.

While the Warnier/Orr diagram has foundations in set theory and Boolean algerbra, knowledge of those subjects is not necessary in order to use it.

Figure 3-5 is a simple Warnier/Orr diagram showing how a writer (or reporter) can classify the research data into who, what, when, etc., and make sure that these key points are covered. Read the diagram from left to right, top to bottom.

Figure 3-6 is a completed Warnier/Orr diagram for the remaining activities I did at certain times for my book *Techniques of Program and System Maintenance*, while preparing the manuscript.

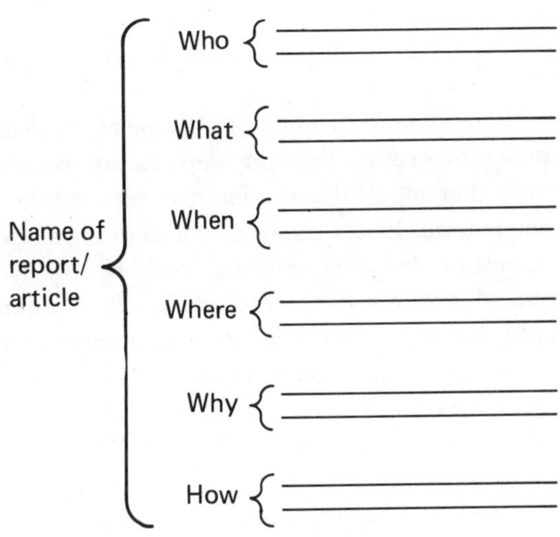


FIGURE 3.5

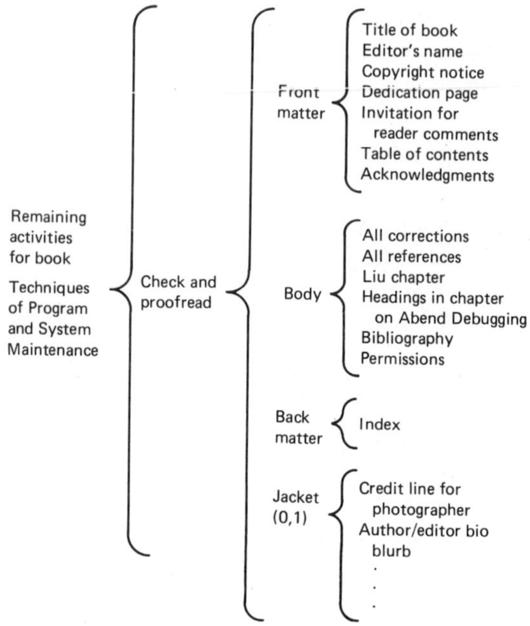


FIGURE 3.6 *Note:* (0,1) below *Jacket* means the jacket may or may not be there. The vertical ellipses mean there are other items not included here.

The activities or items are classified into related groups and subgroups, providing a logical organization and making it hard to forget any item(s). I kept this Warnier/Orr chart with me and checked off the activities as they were completed.

Of course, there is more to using the Warnier/Orr diagram in developing noncomputing procedures than this short section reveals; however, it may stimulate your thinking. If the idea interests you, use the Warnier/Orr diagram in its simple form. Its use can be extended (using a few, simple symbols and conventions) for designing strategies, including sequences (e.g., select a subject, write an ad, test, research, write), choices (e.g., commercially publish or self-publish), and repetitions (e.g., revise and rewrite until satisfied).

Concurrent operations (two or more activities to be done at the same time, e.g., when writers collaborate) and inclusive operations (one or the other or both) can also be shown with a Warnier/Orr diagram. Thus the possibilities seem to be limitless!

References in the Bibliography include technical material on the Warnier/Orr diagram.

## CONCLUSION

The best way to appreciate the power of the Warnier/Orr diagram is to use it. Try it on an application (development, maintenance, or even a noncomputer procedure) that you are working on. Study the appropriate references (especially Higgins, 1979, and Orr, 1977b) listed in the Bibliography.

The Warnier/Orr diagram is a little giant of the structured revolution. It can work wonders for you! Give it a chance.

# *How To Increase COBOL Programming Productivity Using a Preprocessor*

# 4

This chapter was originally published as a report in the series "Programmer Productivity Reports" in 1978. As COBOL is the most widely used commercial programming language, I expected the report to be the best seller in the series; however, it was the worst seller! (Incidentally, the Warnier/Orr report included in this book as Chapter 3 was the best seller.)

The chapter describes the COBOL preprocessor software tool used to boost the productivity of COBOL programmers. It can help increase productivity in almost every COBOL environment.

The original report included capsule descriptions of several COBOL preprocessors then available. I did extensive research on preprocessors and other COBOL aids for the report. While revising the report, I contacted the same vendors for updated information on their packages. Some of them had discontinued marketing of unprofitable items. More significantly, major directories of such tools exist, with well-organized taxonomy and regular updates. It was not reasonable to compete, so I dropped my list and referenced others. [Refer to good software directories, such as *Software Tools Directory* (published by Reifer Consultants, Inc., 25550 Hawthorne Blvd.; Suite 208, Torrence, CA 90505; Telephone 213/373–8728), the International Computer Programs directories (see the Bibliography) for COBOL aids, including preprocessors.] On the selling side it seemed that sales of the report paralleled the sales of some preprocessor packages. (There seems to be a correlation between size and success, and successful companies offer diverse products and services, not limited to tools.) The most successful preprocessor seems to be MetaCOBOL of Applied Data Research. One exception at a relatively low price is CBLSHORT of General Electronics, P.O. Box 79, Lyons, Illinois 60534.

How can the poor sales of the report (and the preprocessors) be explained? It appears that programmers are reluctant to change their work habits. Is it because they want job security, that they enjoy the routine work of COBOL programming, or simply that they are afraid to try anything new? Are they following a 'not invented here' rule at the personal or organization level? Finally, with so many COBOL preprocessors and aids available, each claiming dramatic increases in productivity, whose claims merit belief, and which packages deserve selection?

Choosing the right package for an environment may require study of all the packages available, and then the selection of the most suitable package to fit your budget. If possible, try appropriate packages (usually a free trial period of one month is available) in your environment before making a decision.

Adequate training in the effective use of packages is an absolute necessity. Before selecting a package, ask the vendor if a training program is available. If not, check the organization and readability of the manuals. Review the documentation. Consider setting up an in-house training program if the number and the turnover of programmers in the shop justify such a program.

The use of an appropriate COBOL preprocessor can dramatically increase programmer productivity. Management should investigate the packages that are available, and solicit feedback from programmers. If any of the programmers have used such a package before, talk with them. Encourage them to make suggestions. When programmers are involved in the selection process, they are likely to become enthusiastic users, and pass that enthusiasm on to others, resulting in broad-based productivity improvement.

Figure 4-1 shows how a preprocessor works in compiling a program.

## Acknowledgments

I thank Jon Cris Miller, then project manager, Applied Information Development (now president, The Catalyst Corporation, Brookfield, Illinois); William Hersh, Advisory Systems Engineer, IBM; and Gordon W. Terrill, then senior education specialist, Montgomery Ward Corporate Systems Division (now with Sysorex International, Cupertino, California), for reviewing the manuscript critically. For helping me in the research, I thank Margaret Milligan, the publisher of *Data Processing Digest*, and Peter D. Blainey, Manager, Circulation and Market Research, of Internatinal Computer Programs, Inc. In preparing the manuscript, my daughter Sharmila (now Mrs. Sharmila P. Houck) gave invaluable help.

We are heirs to all the good thoughts of the universe, if we open ourselves to them.

***Swami Vivekananda***
*Teachings of Swami Vivekananda.*

Taking a new step, Uttering a new word, Is what most people fear most.
***Fyodor Dostoyevski,*** *The Diary of A Writer*

Improving the art of programming offers the potential for huge dollar savings, as well as increased productivity. Bringing programming to a higher level will not only save money, it will also provide psychological rewards for the programmer who must bear the brunt of the work. This, in turn, should stimulate programmer productivity. And it will significantly aid the data processing manager and director who, being responsible for information services to the corporation, must be certain that programs continue to operate correctly and economically. Software tools, we hope, will open (or widen) their eyes to the potential of a more disciplined approach to commercial application development and maintenance.[1]

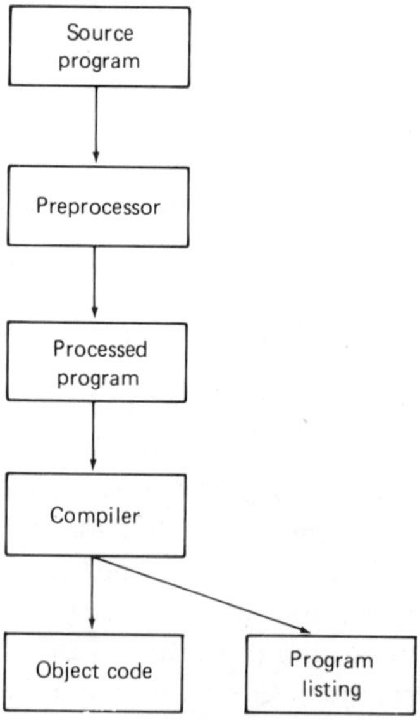


FIGURE 4.1 How a typical preprocessor (also called precompiler) works

[1]Martin A. Goetz, "New Software Tools Increase Productivity," *Infosystems,* February, 1977, p. 70.

Olin's Fine Paper and Film Group and its Ecusta Paper Division, Pisgah Forest, NC, found most of their COBOL applications already written and in use before today's COBOL standards came into widespread use. As a result, they found themselves with a large inventory of basically useful but non-standardized software. According to Nick Kaluger, Ecusta's manager, systems development, "It was an almost prohibitive expense to go back and re-do systems that had been running three or four years. But we had to do something about the accumulated problems we faced because of poor programming and lack of standards. So, we bought ADR's MetaCOBOL, mainly as a tool to clean up and standardize programs that were written over the years. These programs were assets, just like our plant building and paper—and cellophane-making machinery. These were assets that we thought could be salvaged. They were. And MetaCOBOL has been a tremendous help in that effort."

Kaluger doesn't believe that any preprocessing system such as MetaCOBOL can correct fundamental logic flaws. "But what you can do is make the programs more readable so that logic flaws and other errors are readily apparent," he says.

"For example, we had two relatively small non-critical programs with bugs in them that our programmers could not spot for two years. They had spent a lot of time looking but finally just gave up. After we got MetaCOBOL, we ran these two programs through for cleanup and standardization. We found the bugs in both programs the very next day—merely because the programmer could now follow what was going on," Kaluger emphasizes.

"MetaCOBOL helps the programmer get into a program faster. It helps us enforce details like alignment, paragraph numbering, level numbering, common names, etc. Until recently, we had various styles of programs. Each programmer would have his own little pattern. Some would do repeats at the bottom, others would do it in the middle. Some had little loops, others had giant loops. Things like that are still in the programs. But, superficially, they now look the same. We are now able to track down these different styles and get into the problems much more quickly," Kaluger explains.

Five years ago, 30 people were engaged in programming and maintenance. Today, with more work than ever, 15 people keep up with the whole operation. "With over 1000 programs in use, we're doing a tremendous amount of maintenance," Kaluger remarks. "We don't have as much time to devote to standardizing our programs as we would like. We have to have automatic tools to help us.

"We do know what our overall data processing budget has done in the last five years. It has stayed the same in spite of inflation and increased wages. We're asking fewer people to accomplish more. And they're doing it," Kaluger enthusiastically comments.[2]

Martha J. Cichelli, a partner with Software Consulting Services, who also markets precompiler SCOBOL, says: "We, and our customers, can tell you from personal experience that precompilers do contribute to dramatic increases in programmer productivity while creating a pleasant and disciplined programming environment."

I saved substantial time and money by completing several one-shot COBOL programs quickly by using a package called SCORE while working in a service bureau. Some programs were needed to handle crisis situations.

While contract programming, I used a simple shorthand, which had abbreviations for only 17 COBOL reserved words, such as #=SPACES, F=FILLER, P=PIC, V=VALUE, M=MOVE, $=PERFORM, etc. Use of the shorthand saved 25 to 50% in coding time alone, not to mention the keypunching and correction time. (The savings may vary from programmer to programmer and will obviously be less for complicated code. My test was small.)

## WHAT THIS CHAPTER CAN DO FOR YOU

This chapter should make you aware that COBOL programming productivity *can* be increased using a preprocessor. The Bibliography includes references for further study. With this information and a knowledge of your own environment, you can evaluate, select, and acquire an appropriate preprocessor.

### A Note To Programmers and Managers

The preprocessor does not replace the "thinking" that is necessary for a programmer to solve problems. It is only a tool to help him or her solve problems. To use the package most profitably will require training, experience, and thought. Usually, experienced programmers are able to make the most of a versatile preprocessor.

---

[2]The Olin story is extracted from "Non-Standard COBOL Programs Get Treatment (Users Report), *Infosystems*, July 1977, pp. 82–83, with permission.

Management commitment and support are necessary for successful use of preprocessor(s). Managers should not have the attitude: "We've given you a preprocessor. Now produce more [right away]!" It may take time because there is always a learning curve before the increased productivity is realized. Management must participate and monitor activities for preprocessor(s) to be successful. Also, management must continually evaluate results in light of company goals.

## PROGRAMMER PRODUCTIVITY

Programmer productivity is becoming important, as the cost of hardware is going down and programming cost is going up. In the next decade, programmer productivity will become one of the key issues in the data processing industry.

### The Four Kinds of Productivity

There are many kinds of productivity; the four important ones are:

*Program development productivity*: increasing the number of debugged program statements produced in a given period.

*Maintenance and enhancement productivity*: reducing the time and effort spent on maintaining and enhancing an application. Here, productivity is a direct function of the quality of the original program when it went into production.

*Production productivity*: decreasing the impact of program errors, inefficient code, and heavy utilization of computer resources as related to an operational program.

*Human interface productivity*: ensuring the ease of use and accuracy of all user documentation for those who must work with the operational programs.[3]

A COBOL preprocessor helps increase programmer productivity in new development, maintenance and enhancements, and in optimizing the programs. Improved productivity lends itself to meeting deadline and budgeting constraints.

---

[3]Martin A. Goetz, "New Software Tools Increase Productivity," *Infosystems*, February 1977, p. 66.

### How Do You Measure Programmer Productivity?

Programmer productivity may vary widely from programmer to programmer and from program to program. It may also vary from project to project depending on management philosophy. In new developments, the total debugged and maintainable output produced in a given period provides the data to measure productivity. In a maintenance environment, it is usually extremely difficult to measure productivity (see Parikh 1981a, 1981b, 1983).

### Increases in Programmer Productivity Using a Preprocessor

I asked several professionals and vendors for specific information on productivity increases. Here are the highlights of their replies:

> The improvement in programmer productivity has not been measured statistically. Most shops do not measure productivity at all—they just have a gut feeling about it. The gut feeling of the precompiler users has been that the precompiler is helping them.
>
> Programmer productivity increases vary greatly depending on circumstances and are very hard to measure.
>
> On the whole a good reformatting program will improve productivity among maintenance programmers by 10 to 50% and among developmental programmers by about 5%. There are, of course, diminishing returns for the maintenance programmer; after every program in the shop has been processed through the reformatting program, productivity will not continue to improve, but will remain at a constant level.

### Claims of Vendors of Preprocessors

In their literature, many vendors of COBOL preprocessors claim up to 50% reduction in coding time and substantial dollar savings to implement COBOL systems. The user should, however, test the product thoroughly to determine the cost/benefits in his or her installation.

## THE COST SAVINGS USING A PREPROCESSOR

> Cost savings are substantial. Aside from obvious, but hard to quantify, increases in programmer productivity, a precompiler pays for itself in keypunching alone.

Assume for illustration, a COBOL shop with 10 programmers, associated keypunch costs of 10 cent/card and a productivity of 300 COBOL statements coded per programmer per week.

If a precompiler is adopted and produces 50% savings, then, in effect, only 150 (instead of 300) statements are coded and punched for each programmer.

That is equivalent to a savings of 150 cards or $15 per week per programmer; $150 per week per staff of 10 programmers; or $7500 per year.

The $7500 figure—more than the cost of some precompilers—increases with the number of programmers and their productivity rate.[4]

## WHY COBOL AIDS ARE NEEDED

According to one estimate, COBOL is used twice as much as all other languages combined. Nevertheless, COBOL has its disadvantages, the most obvious being its verbosity. It requires a great deal of writing just to get out of the Data Division.

A review of changes to ANS COBOL is, of necessity, time consuming, because of possible implications to a wide variey of users. Some preprocessors provide COBOL enhancements that meet the needs of particular users now.

## THE GROUND WORK: COBOL SUBSET, MANUAL, AND EDUCATION

Let's identify the ground work necessary to use preprocessor(s) effectively:

A COBOL subset for your installation.

A COBOL (standards) manual adapted for the installation covering the subset.

Education in the use of COBOL subset.

Why should you have a COBOL subset? COBOL is a general-purpose business language. To use it most profitably, you must adapt it to your re-

[4]Rober T. Grauer and Marshal A. Crawford, "COBOL Precompilers Seen Lacking in User Popularity," *Computerworld*, April 25, 1977, p. S12. Copyright 1977 by Computerworld, Newton, MA 02160.

quirements. For a detailed coverage of the subject of "groundwork," refer to *Data Processing Digest*, (1971–1972), or Naftaly et al., (1972).

## AN OVERVIEW OF COBOL AIDS

Figure 4-2 provides an overview of COBOL aids. This chapter focuses on the use of preprocessors to increase programmer productivity.

### *Two Types of Preprocessors*

COBOL preprocessors can also be divided into two distinct types: *COBOL program genertor* (generates a complete COBOL program from programmer supplied parameters and specifications), also called a data (or file) management system (DMS); and a *COBOL (input) preprocessor* (uses abreviations and/or other conventions, retains the flavor of COBOL programming, accepts COBOL statements or an entire COBOL program, and outputs an expanded/reformatted or restructured COBOL program).

A preprocessor such as MetaCOBOL can be used as a COBOL (input) preprocessor; and using its powerful macro facilities, parameter-driven new programming languages can also be created (although it may be a tedious task), if desired. Such a preprocessor can be a synthesis of the two approaches.

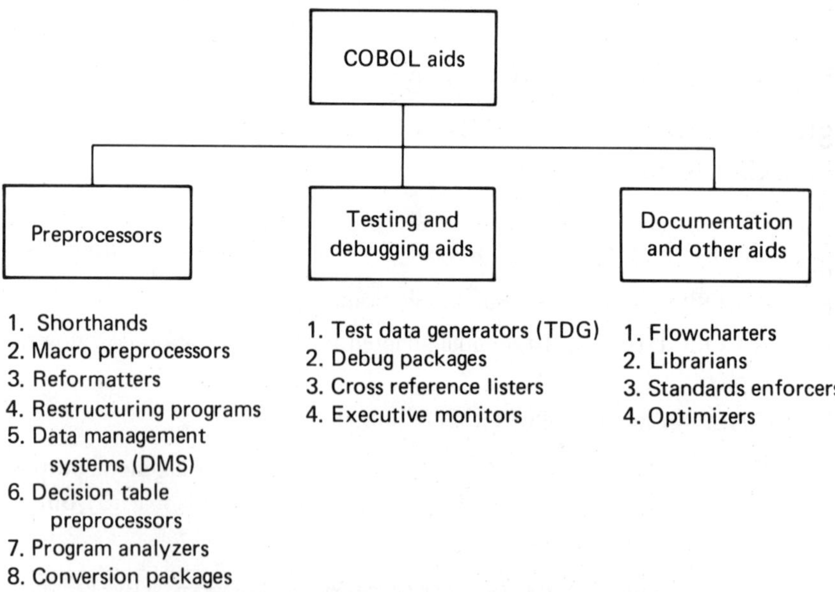


FIGURE 4.2 An overview of COBOL aids

### Some Preprocessors May Have More Than One Feature

Some COBOL preprocessors may have more than one feature. For example, a preprocessor may have shorthand and macro-preprocessor facilities. It may also have test data generation facility together with other features. Also, in a software package, some features may be standard, whereas others may be optional, extra-cost items.

### A Note on Terminology

Some technical words relate specifically to software aids. While discussing a particular preprocessor function, it is briefly explained. The words "preprocessor" and "precompiler" are used as synonyms, although I prefer the word "preprocessor."

## COBOL PREPROCESSOR FUNCTIONS THAT INCREASE PROGRAMMER PRODUCTIVITY

A preprocessor package may be named after its major or only feature. Let's take a closer look at preprocessor functions and how each can increase programmer productivity.

## Shorthand

A "shorthand" provides abbreviations for commonly used COBOL reserved words and phrases to reduce the physical coding effort. Some shorthands have the capability of accepting user-defined abbreviations for expansion. Shorthand is an invaluable tool of the COBOL programmer that reduces writing, improves documentation, and simplifies standards. Several estimates indicate that a good shorthand saves 30 to 50% time in coding effort. Also, program testing/debugging takes less time, because of fewer errors in the program.

While using user-defined abbreviations (if this feature is supported), documentation is improved, as shorthand abbreviations expand into standardized data names. For example, PMR becomes PAYROLL-MASTER-RECORD. Thus meaningful names can be introduced in the program any time. Some shorthand preprocessors also do syntax checking and error corrections.

Programmers think faster than they can code. Because of COBOL verbosity, sometimes they get bogged down. With fewer writing strokes, the logical thinking can be transferred into code quickly and correctly. For on-line application development and maintenance, shorthand reduces the size of messages and/or increases effective screen capacity, and improves the network throughput.

If you are considering any preprocessor, a simple shorthand may be the tool to start with. Some inexpensive shorthands are available, or you can write your own shorthand (reinvent the wheel!) and experience the benefits before getting into the multifeature preprocessor(s).

## Macro Preprocessor

A macro preprocessor analyzes and expands COBOL and/or non-COBOL source statements into standard COBOL output. Most COBOL program generators, also called data management systems (DMSs), which we shall discuss later, use nonCOBOL macros to generate standard COBOL programs.

A COBOL shorthand is usually a one-for-one translation of abbreviations, whereas a macro preprocessor generates phrases or whole COBOL sentences and sometimes whole paragraph(s). Macros reduce writing, improve documentation, and enforce standards. With powerful macros, savings can be substantial.

Macro instructions may have the option of providing paramenters. When parameters can be used, the macro instructions are like skeleton instructions generating the desired code using the values provided in the parameters.

The user can also code his or her own macros. Macros (and shorthand abbreviations) are usually stored in the library. (Hence a good source statement library is an important requirement for using these features effectively. Also, any program can use them, and standardization is maintained in the installation.)

## Reformatter

Reformatting a program improves its readability. The effect of better readability may sometimes be dramatic, as we saw in the case of the Olin Company in the beginning of this chapter.

The programmers in an installation may have different coding styles. It may be difficult and unpleasant to enforce the installation standards. A reformatter will provide readable versions of programs according to the standards, depending on the capabilities of the reformatter.

Some reformatters have built-in standards (with a few options), whereas others have more flexability, and allow the user to tailor them to his or her own standards. With the advent of structured programming, the indentation and formatting of code, such as nested IFs, 55-line-per-page convention, PERFORM statements, etc., have become increasingly important. A reformatter makes this formatting (and following conventions) painless. A missing or misplaced period in nested IFs can create a disastrous situation; such a situation becomes readily apparent when code is reformatted. The reformatter can also indent the new code according to the actual logic structure. The automatic indentation leaves no chance for indentation to be out of phase with the actual structure.

Another important feature of a reformatter is (if supported) paragraph numbering/renumbering. (Although it is sometimes called prefixing, prefixing has a different meaning, as we shall see in a moment.) The numbered paragraphs make it easier and faster for the programmer to find his or her way.

A reformatter is equally effective on new and existing programs. It eliminates the need for the maintenance programmer to make cosmetic changes in the vicinity of changed code.

Prefixing (if supported) works this way: When the same record format is to be used for input and output from a library, prefixing input/output formats by a preprocessor eliminates the need for qualifying data names. For example, an input record may be prefixed by IN-MSTR, an output record by OUT-MSTR.

## Restructuring Program or Structuring Engine

Restructuring of the programs goes beyond reformatting, so that the programs conform to the structured programming standards. Automated routines can be developed (their discussion is beyond the scope of this chapter) to do the following in COBOL programs:

ALTER removal

GO TO/PERFORM substitution

Closing subroutines

Highlight the control structures

The "structuring engine" is a package that transforms an unstructured program into a structured program.

## Data Management System

A data management system (DMS) is normally a program-generator type of preprocessor that usually accepts non-COBOL input parameters and generates COBOL programs. Many DMSs provide entry points for their own code. After the COBOL code is generated, the programmer may continue further development.

A proper DMS can complement the efforts of programmers by providing a tool to produce many small programs quickly. It is a handy tool for writing simple (one-shot) programs.

DMSs can also generate a skeleton of a more complex program. With the top-down program development approach, some DMSs may be helpful in generating the mainline and skeleton of the rest of the program, possibly with stubs. The DMSs have built-in logic for routine functions (invoked by parameters), such as file match/merge, sorts, detail and summary reporting, report headings, page spacing and numbering, record selection, etc. Program debugging time is reduced because of the pretested logic built into the DMS.

The built-in logic also has some disadvantages. When a programmer develops her or his own logic, he or she has no doubt about what is generated by a preprocessor and what is created personally. DMS is less flexible, and for complicated applications, it may be unsuitable, except for generating a skeleton program.

Some DMSs offer extensions to COBOL for accessing on-line data bases. ANS COBOL may eventually have such features, but a proper DMS may provide them now.

## Decision Table Preprocessor

A decision table preprocessor translates a COBOL-compatible table into COBOL statements. Most preprocessors analyze the table for accuracy and completeness. For further discussion of decision table preprocessors, refer to *Data Processing Digest* (1971–1972) or Naftaly et al. (1972). For available decision table preprocessors, refer to a software directory and/or service, such as the International Computer Programs software directory (see the Bibliography).

## Program Analyzer

A program analyzer analyzes source code for inefficiencies and produces analysis report(s) to help optimize the original program. The analysis report(s) can also help in program testing and debugging. A detailed discussion of a program analyzer is beyond the scope of this chapter. A program analyzer helps programmers to locate inefficient code, incorrect looping, etc., and helps increase productivity. A program analyzer, by flagging areas that are inefficient (if this feature is supported), alerts a programmer to areas where time can be spent most profitably.

### Conversion Package

A conversion package helps convert a COBOL program from one dialect to another. Conversion software, to translate programs from another language to COBOL, such as RPG/RPG II to COBOL, BAL to COBOL, etc., are also available.

## PROGRAMMER RESISTANCE AND ACCEPTANCE

### Why Programmers Resist COBOL Aids

Following are the common reasons why programmers resist COBOL aids:

1. The same reasons that software packages in general have not been widely accepted—Not Invented Here; need to learn something new; not tailored to company's specific needs.
2. Some packages do not save a programmer's time when first used, and in fact may require more of his time; savings come with repetitive use.
3. Some packages aim only at reducing coding time, which is not a large fraction of the total programming time anyway.
4. Using a new package requires learning something additional; user may still have to be proficient in COBOL. User may have to debug programs at the COBOL level, not at package input level.
5. Packages can introduce additional sources of error.
6. The department will have to set up and enforce new standard procedures when using these aids; this may involve quite new (to the installation) ways of doing things, such as the use of macros.
7. The department will have to train people in these new standards and in the use of the packages. Programmers will tend to fall back

on previous methods (1) if under severe time pressure, or (2) if bugs are encountered in packages when first used.

8. Many COBOL programmers resist decision tables, are unfamiliar with macros, and see no need for flowcharting COBOL programs. So they tend to look on these aids as of little value and hence a waste of time.
9. Decision tables may be looked on as a threat to the programmer.[5]

## How to Win Programmers

Have your best and most enthusiastic programmers initially use the package; they can subsequently act as highly effective in-house salesmen.

Convince your staff members that they are improving themselves professionally—i.e., appeal to their sense of pride in self-improvement.

Stress the importance of standardized approaches to problem solving.

Try to convince your personnel that many of the necessary clerical, noncreative tasks can be relegated to the programming aid—thus freeing them for the more challenging aspects of their positions.

Lastly, try to convey to your personnel that their company is dedicated to improving overall data processing operations, and that their installation, by taking advantage of the latest tools on the market, is among the more progressive members of the industry.[6]

# SELECTING A PREPROCESSOR

Many COBOL preprocessors are available, ranging widely in price, performance, and support. (One reason given for the unpopularity of COBOL preprocessors is the number of products available, which simply confuses the user.) Here are some suggestions for selecting and acquiring preprocessor(s):

1. Dollar return on investment should be the primary consideration in selecting a preprocessor.
2. Decide what you need and how you want to start using preprocessor(s) and lay out short-range and long-range plans, depending on the budget available.
3. Involve the user of the preprocessor—the application programmer.

[5]"COBOL Aid Packages," *EDP Analyzer, May 1972, pp. 12–13.*

[6]Martin A. Goetz, "Soup Up Your Programmers with COBOL Aids," *Computer Decisions*, March 1973, p. 9.

But select innovative, enthusiastic programmer(s) from your staff to help select a preprocessor.

4. Choose a package written in ANS COBOL, with source code, if available.
5. Investigate features and options to avoid duplication when considering and buying preprocessors.
6. Check the reputation and the background of the vendor before making commitments.
7. If not advertised, ask for a trial period, and test it as thoroughly as possible before committing yourself to it.
8. Draw a feature or product comparison chart to help select the best product for your environment. Refer to *Data Processing Digest* (1971-1972) or Naftaly et al. (1972) and Wooldridge (1973) for product comparison charts.
9. "The major considerations in the interest of the buyer are: adequate ownership; warranty, and financial transaction clauses; exemption from claims against the vendor; and a firm vendor commitment regarding enhancements, updates, and error corrections."[7]

## SOME SUGGESTIONS FOR IMPLEMENTATION

Instead of attempting to use a full preprocessing system, build gradually in phases. One suggestion is to start with a simple shorthand. The savings can be used to buy a macro package, and then a reformatter and a DMS, depending on your needs. An adequate training ranging from minutes or hours to a few days (preferably in phases if longer training is required) in the use of the package is also necessary.

## CONCLUSION

The preprocessor(s) suitable to your environment *can* increase programmer productivity, improve documentation, and enforce standards. The use of a suitable preprocessor also helps you meet deadlines and saves you money.

---

[7]Reprinted from *Computer Decisions*, March 1973, pp. 8–12, copyright, 1973, Hayden Publishing Company.

# How To Document Program Changes and Enhancements Internally

# 5

The importance of documenting program changes cannot be overemphasized, especially in a maintenance environment. The documentation may be external or internal. External documentation constitutes the external specifications, design, etc., for the changes made to the program; internal documentation is within the program itself. Internal documentation is easier to update, since most changes today are done on-line using a terminal under some form of a time-sharing system. Also, the internal documentation is easily referred to by the programmer, since it is easily accessible. This shows the importance of keeping it updated.

The commonly used internal documentation consist of program comments. Most programming languages have the commenting feature, and generally, the comments do not take additional memory.

The technique described in this chapter is an ingenious method for documenting the changes to a program internally. I have found it very useful in actual working environments. In fact, I developed it in response to problems I encountered in figuring out what changes were made in a program, and by whom. Although the technique is manual, a program can be written to extract all the change commentaries, and the change tabs, and list them.

You will appreciate the power of this technique when you use it in work. Apply it consistently to realize its benefits. First apply it as described in this chapter. Then modify it, if necessary, after you have some experience with it. You may have to modify the convention of numbering the changes depending on the standards in your environment. (Also see Chapter 12. RES-Q, described in that chapter, automatically separates or identifies program changes.)

When a modified program does not work, the changes are examined first, and usually the bug is found right there! But how do you identify the changes made in the program? That is not an easy task. If someone else made the changes, you would ask him or her, if available, about it. But who made the changes? Why? When? Unless the changes are properly documented, in some cases it may be almost impossible to handle the situation. Even the small bugs may take many additional, frustrating hours before they are fixed.

## WHAT THIS TECHNIQUE CAN DO FOR YOU

This new, tested technique provides instant identification of program changes comprising additions and replacements, and information about deletions. A concise, chronological record of the changes is also preserved. For further reference, it also includes identifications of the external specifications for the changes.

Although the examples used here are from BAL and COBOL programs, the technique can easily be adapted for almost any programming language on any computer system. Moreover, its use generally does not take any additional core storage. The technique can be used in maintenance as well as in new developments.

### Benefits in Maintenance

Programmers can easily retrace and recreate previous updating activities. The internal documentation also reveals how much and how often a program is changed, and who works most on it.

### Benefits in New Developments

While the new programs are being developed, the original specifications almost always change, requiring small or large modifications. By using this technique to tag the changes, a programmer will not only be able to control them better, but will also be able to justify the extra time taken to incorporate the changes. Once the program goes into production, the tags can be removed.

## THE TECHNIQUE AND HOW TO USE IT

The changes to a program usually start with a formal task assignment or an informal discussion of a problem or a proposed enhancement. The formal task assignment sheet (or a change notice) should include the external documentation of program maintenance, containing the short description, as well as complete specifications for this change. A task number should be assigned to it. (We shall see later that this task number used in the internal documentation provides identification of the external specification for this change.)

If the specifications for the change are not formally issued, the programmer should write it down from the informal discussions. It will not only help him or her make the changes, but will also serve as an external documentation. A short description of the change can be created from this write-up to enter into the "record of changes box." A task number should also be assigned. For the internal (within the source program) documentation, the "comments" feature of a programming language is used.

A step-by-step description of the technique follows (see Figure 5–1).

1. In the beginning part of the program, create a box for "Record of Changes Made in This Program." (Every time maintenance or enhancement is done, a record is inserted in the box.)
2. In that record of changes box, enter the following information for every task:

   A. Task number of the task assignment prefixed with T and suffixed with subtask or change number within the original task. *Example:*

   T00310

   where T = task

   0031 = task number from the task assignment sheet

   0 = subtask or change number within the original task

   How should the subtask or change number be used within the task? Generally, this number would be 0. Whenever an original specification for the task is changed, this number may be updated by 1 and the new entry may be made in this box, following the last entry for that task. For example, if specification for task 0031 is changed the first time, the new entry would be T00311.

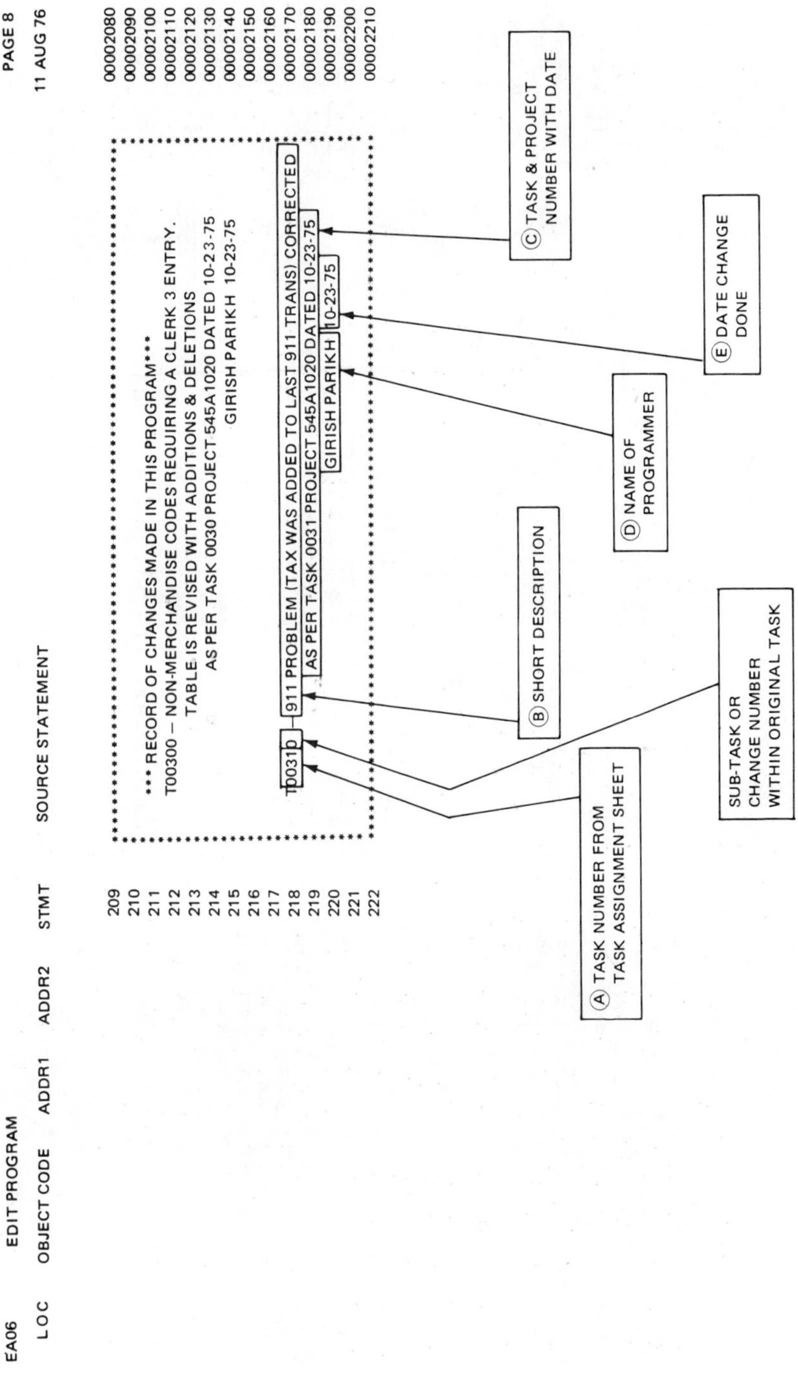


FIGURE 5.1 Internal documentation of a BAL program maintenance

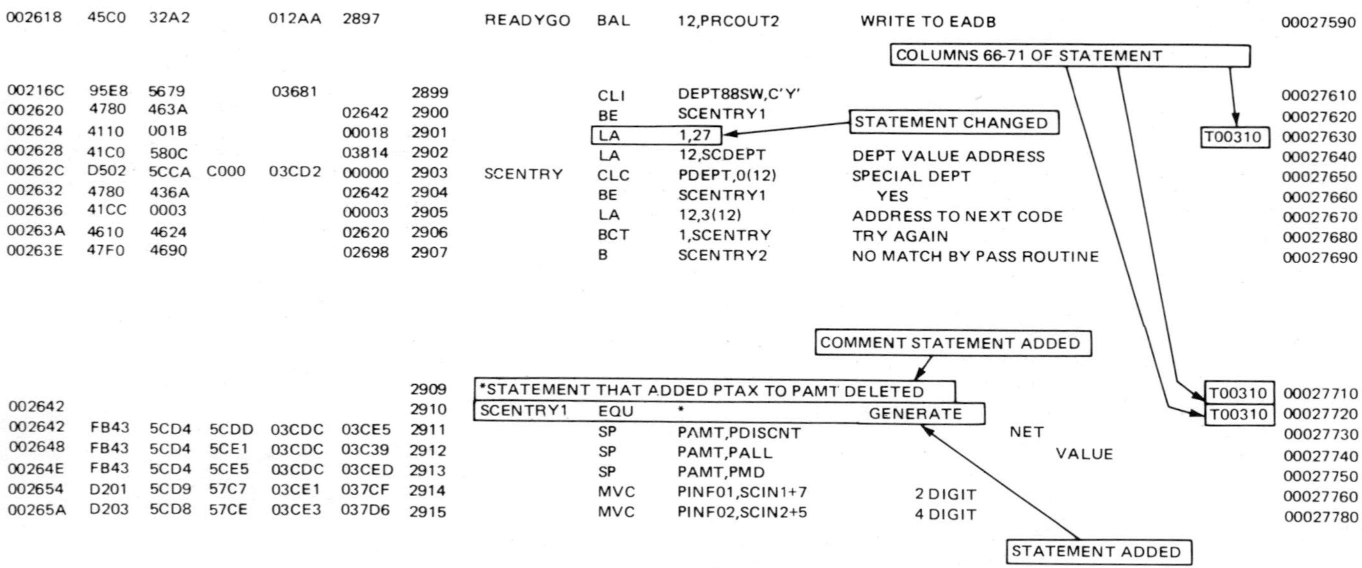


FIGURE 5.2 Internal documentation of a BAL program maintenance

```
000040 REMARKS      PROGRAM TO CREATE SALES AUDIT MASTER FILE
000050              UD. EE221201  REGISTER DISK.
000060               T00260   EE22 END CARD PROBLEM CORRECTED
000070                          AS PER TASK 0026 PROJECT 545A1010
000080                          DATED 10-03-75
000090                              GIRISH PARIKH 10-27-75
000100              NOTE ON CHANGE - CARD INPUT FILE IS ADDED (WITH)
000110               SELECT & FD- SO AS TO READ IT INSTEAD OF ACCEPT.  THE
000120               ACCEPT METHOD CAUSED UNENDING LOOP IF NO 'END' CARD,
000130               WITH THIS CHANGE, AT END OF CARD FILE IF NO 'END' CD
000140               MESSAGE WILL BE PRINTED & PROG WILL HAVE NORMAL END.
000150
000160  ENVIRONMENT DIVISION.
000170  INPUT-OUTPUT SECTION.
000180  FILE-CONTROL,
000190      SELECT REGISTER-DISK
000200            ASSIGN TO DA-I-EE221201
000210            ACCESS IS SEQUENTIAL
000220            RESERVE NO ALTERNATE AREA
000230            RECORD KEY IS KEY-IN-RECORD.
000240      SELECT SPOOL-FILE
000250              ASSIGN TO UT-S-EE220201.
000260      SELECT REGISTER-TAPE ASSIGN TO UT-S-EE221101.
000270 *                                                          T00260
000280      SELECT CARD-FILE ASSIGN TO UT-S-SYSIN.
000290 *                                                          T00260
000300  DATA DIVISION.
000310  FILE SECTION.
000320  FD  REGISTER-DISK
000330      RECORDING MODE IS F
000340      RECORD CONTAINS 60 CHARACTERS
000350      LABEL RECORDS ARE STANDARD
000360      DATA RECORDS ARE AD-RECORD, BD-RECORD, DD-RECORD,
000370                       DD-DATE-REC, LD-RECORD, ND-RECORD,
000380                       PD-RECORD, RD-RECORD, ZD-RECORD.
000390  01    AD-RECORD.
000400        02 RESERVED-PORTION          PICTURE X.
000410        02 AD-CODE                   PICTURE XX.
000420        02 AD-DATA-FILL              PICTURE X(51).
000430        02 AD-CREDIT REDEFINES AD-DATA-FILL
000440                                     PICTURE XXX   OCCURS 17 TIMES.
000450        02 AD-FILLER                 PICTURE XX.
000460        02 KEY-IN-RECORD.
000470        03 KEY-ALPHA                 PICTURE X.
000480        03 KEY-NUMERIC               PICTURE 999.
000490  01    BD-RECORD.
000500        02 FILLER                    PICTURE X.
000510        02 BD-CODE                   PICTURE XX.
```

(A) TASK NUMBER FROM TASK ASSIGNMENT SHEET

(A1) SUB-TASK OR CHANGE NUMBER WITHIN ORIGINAL TASK

(B) SHORT DESCRIPTION

(C) TASK & PROJECT NUMBER WITH DATE

(D) NAME OF PROGRAMMER

(E) DATE CHANGE DONE

(F) ADDITIONAL REMARKS

(G) COMMENT STATEMENT PRECEDING THE CHANGE (COLUMNS 66-71 IDENTIFY THE TASK & SUB-TASK)

(H) COMMENT STATEMENT FOLLOWING THE CHANGE (COLUMNS 66-71 IDENTIFY THE TASK & SUB-TASK)

FIGURE 5.3 Internal documentation of a COBOL program maintenance

The other use of this number may be for a big task broken down into subtasks. The subtasks are then numbered beginning from 0.

B. A short description of the change.

C. The task and project number with the date.

D. The name of the programmer who made the change.

E. The date the change was made.

3. Statements changed or added have the six-character number T00310 in columns 66 to 71, referring to the record of changes box. Note that, for deleted statement(s), the comment statement is added with six-character number in columns 66 to 71.

   If several statements are removed, the comment(s) should describe the function(s) that have been removed.

Figure 5–2 illustrates changes related to T00310. Changes related to T00300 are in other parts of the program and are not illustrated.

Figure 5–3 illustrates how this method could be used in a COBOL program. Instead of inserting comment lines to identify T00260, columns 73

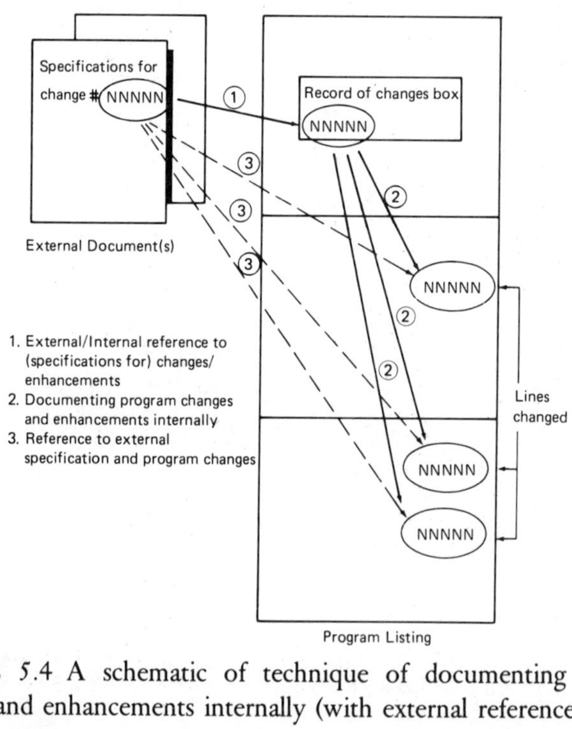


FIGURE 5.4 A schematic of technique of documenting program changes and enhancements internally (with external reference)

to 78 of the statement card, if they could be preserved and printed on the listing, might be used. The comment lines could be created when special comments for the change/additions/deletions are to be included.

Figure 5–4 is a schematic of technique of documenting program changes and enhancements internally (with external reference to specification). This technique can be used to document changes in the unstructured, modular, or structured programs. By documenting the programs this way, any changes made can be easily identified, and traced to the original specifications if needed.

## CONCLUSION

Although the technique looks simple, its consistent use by all programmers in a department generally helps increase productivity. Managers should let their best and most enthusiastic programmers use the technique initially. When these people are convinced of the worth of the technique, they will encourage and may even insist on its use by other programmers.

In necessary, management should enforce the use of the technique. Once programmers start using it, they will gradually come to appreciate its benefits. The first-line manager should periodically review programs to see that the technique is used consistently by all programmers in a department.

After using the technique for some time, it should be reviewed with the programmers. If it is found suitable to the environment, it should be made an installation standard after any necessary modifications have been made. Structured walkthroughs in development as well as in a maintenance environment can help ensure use of this technique.

# How To Make the Most of Top-Down Development

# 6

This chapter introduces the powerful concepts of top-down design, coding, and testing. It describes how the judicious overlapping of design, coding, and testing ensures smooth development of good-quality programs. It also includes techniques of top-down development, with illustrations. Top-down development of program enhancement is also covered. Numerous benefits of the method are described. Also included are the problems of top-down development, and how to solve them.

Frederick Brooks, considered the father of IBM System/360, in his classic book *The Mythical Man-Month* (Brooks, 1974) writes: "I am persuaded that top-down design is the most important new programming formalization of the decade." Harlan Mills, considered the spiritual father of structured programming states that the concept of top-down development is based on a mathematical foundation (Mills, 1983).

## WHAT TOP-DOWN DEVELOPMENT IS

The primary activities in program development are design, coding, and testing. With the advent of structured technologies, designing a program has become a prerequisite for program development.

In top-down program development, the three activities of design, coding, and testing are done in a top-down fashion. To understand the concept of top-down development, we should look at the three activities of development separately.

## Top-Down Design

Top-down program design begins from the top or the most abstract level of the program, and progresses hierarchically to more detailed levels of design.

Figure 6–1 shows both top-down and bottom-up design. (The traditional bottom-up design was done beginning at detailed levels and going to higher levels.)

Working from the top levels and gradually going toward more complexity prevents the designer from bogging down in too much detail. Thus he or she concentrates on one level of design at a time, and after getting that level settled in his or her mind, progresses to the next lower level.

However, top-down design is done in iteration. That is, after laying down the first version of the design, it is reviewed and any changes or improvements to it are made. This process of iteration is repeated until a satisfactory design emerges. This process of repetition helps produce a correct, and in some cases an optimal, design. Top-down system design is done similarly.

The hierarchy charts of HIPO, which represent functions in rectangular boxes, are very useful in developing top-down design. Other tools, such as pseudocode or the Warnier/Orr diagram, may also be used in developing a top-down design.

## Top-down Coding

As the name implies, top-down coding begins from the top function in the design and progresses to the lower levels. The hierarchical top-down design provides a road map for top-down coding.

The function charts may not provide the logic required in coding. They

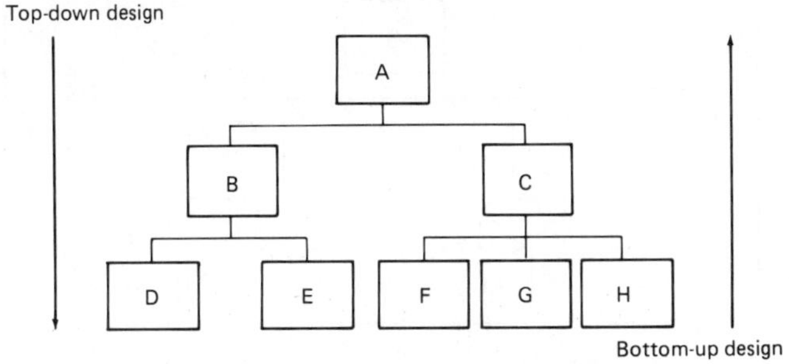


FIGURE 6.1 Top-down and bottom-up design

may also lack interfaces between functions. Thus if hierarchy charts of HIPO diagrams are used for the design, some additional work may be necessary before coding begins. [If IPO (input-process-output) charts are also used, these charts may sometimes include the logic and interface requirements, although IPO charts are supposed to be functional, as the principal characteristic of HIPO is functionality. See Chapter 2 for more information on this tool.]

Figure 6–2 illustrates top-down and bottom-up coding. (Note that a design done using top-down approach may be coded bottom up, and vice versa; however, the top-down approach usually becomes more effective when design, coding, and even testing progress in a top-down fashion. This is discussed further in the next section.)

## Top-Down Testing

Again as its name implies, top-down testing starts from top functions which are coded, and progresses toward lower-level functions. For top-down testing, normally the entire program is not coded. Thus coding and testing are done simultaneously. We will see how this works in more detail in just a minute. If the program is completely coded using the top-down technique, testing may be done on the entire program. If top-down testing is desired, lower-level functions would have to be replaced with stubs, which may not be desirable.

Combining top-down design, coding, and testing is done as follows. As the design progresses from the top functions to the lower-level functions, before the lower-level functions are detailed, coding and testing begin. The lower-level functions are not yet completely detailed; however, we should have a skeletal design, in order to see the overview picture of the program

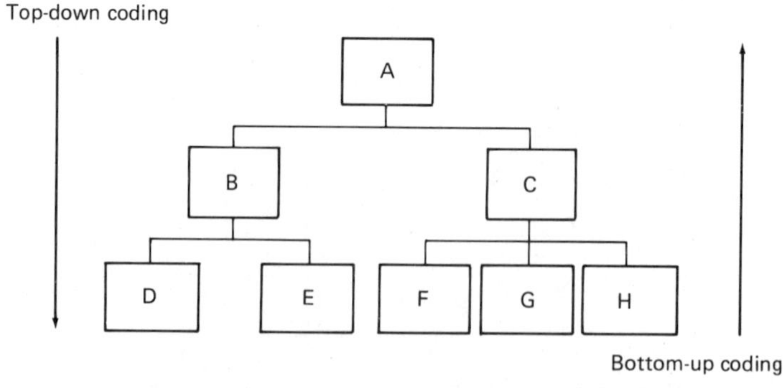


FIGURE 6.2 Top-down and bottom-up coding

design. First the top level of the program is coded, and the lower levels are included in the program as stubs. Thus we have a program that can be tested. The stubs may contain dummy code, or a short routine to display entering into that function, or provide random data to the high-level function. After this program version is tested, the stubs at the level immediately lower are replaced with code. The functions below the stubs now become new stubs, and the process is repeated until the program is completed and there are no more stubs. See Figure 6–3.

When top-down design, coding, and testing overlap, the keypunching or data entry of the source program can also be scheduled effectively. For example, the functions designed can be coded and sent for keypunching while other functions are being designed. When the functions sent for key punching are finished, they can be tested while the new coded functions can be sent out for key punching. Thus the activities of design, coding, keypunching, and testing overlap, providing better utilization of programming, keypunching, and computer resources. However, the programmer should prepare a plan of top-down development and keep track of progress. Figure 6–4 details the sequence of events for top-down development using the Warnier/Orr diagram (see Chapter 3 for material on this powerful tool).

How should top-down testing progress? In the beginning it is good to follow a rule such as to develop beginning with the top function and progress one level at a time. Either you may code one function at a time at the level you are working on, beginning from the left, or you may code all the functions at that level. Then work on the remaining levels progressively, in the same way, that is, one level at a time. This will give you some feeling for this method. After some experience you can vary the sequence of top-down design (still hierarchical and top-down), coding, and testing to achieve some of the benefits described later.

In the array of structured programming technologies, where does top-down development fit? Top-down development is one of the techniques in "improved programming technologies" (a collection of six techniques; the other techniques are structured programming, HIPO, development support library, structured walkthroughs, and chief programmer teams). Top-down development is also an important technique in Constantine-Yourdon structured design. In general, this technique can be used in functional methodologies. Yourdon has suggested that the top-down technique be used to overlap the various activities of a software development life cycle. He calls a cycle in which the activities of analysis design, coding, and testing overlap, a "structured life cycle."

In top-down development of a program, top-down design, coding, and

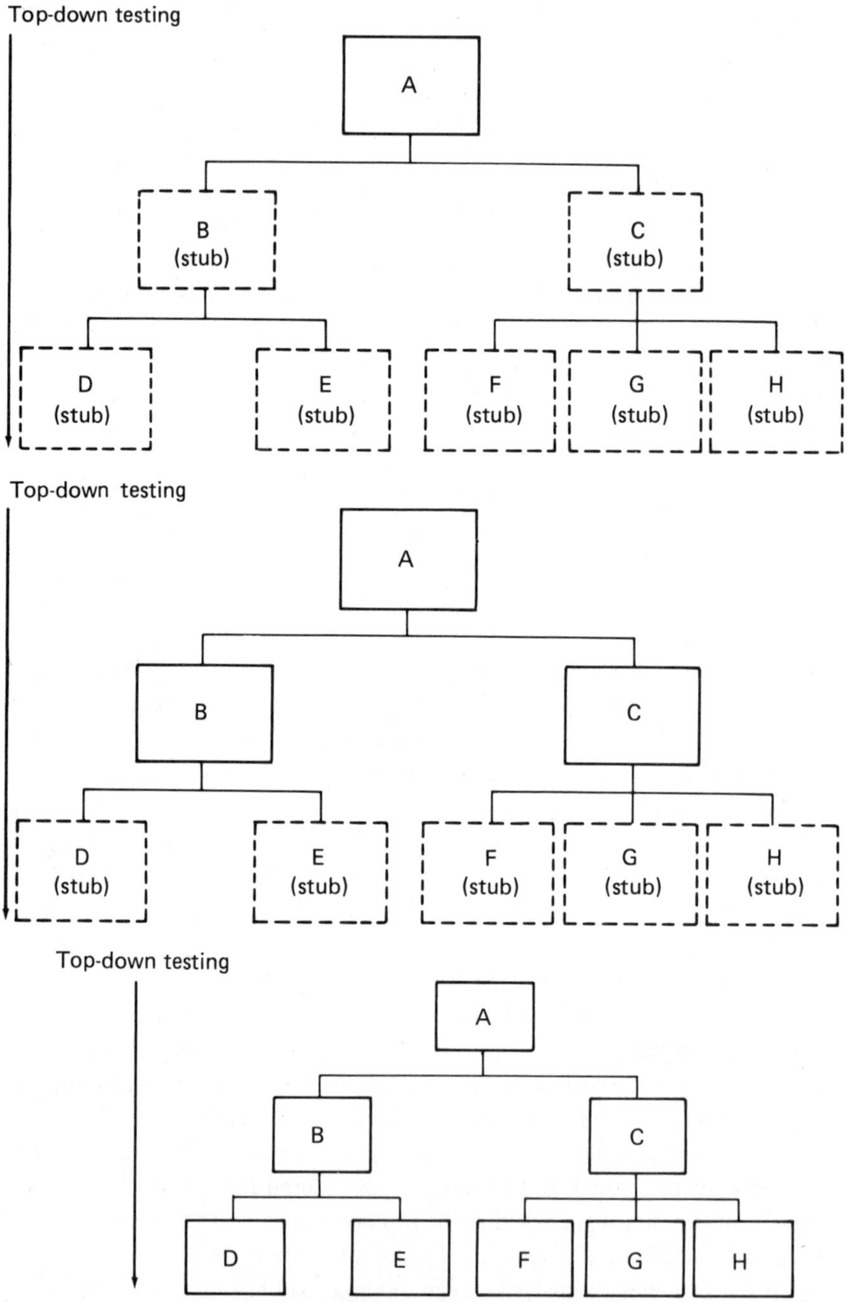


FIGURE 6.3 Top-down testing (stage 1); (b) top-down testing (stage 2); (c) top-down testing (final stage)

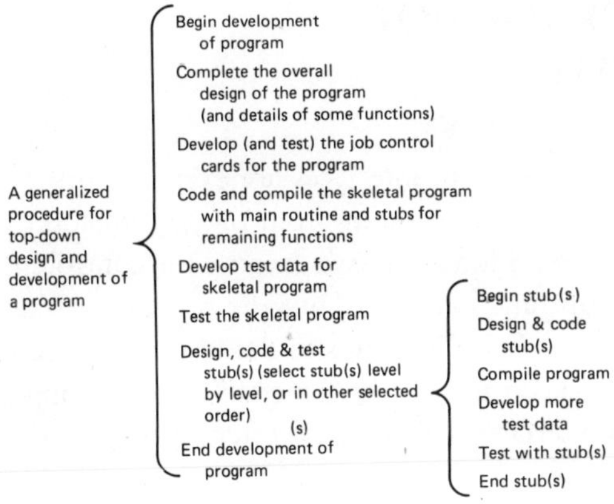


FIGURE 6.4 The Warnier/Orr diagram showing a procedure for top-down design and development of a program (see Chapter 3 for an explanation of this diagramming technique)

testing can overlap. The degree of overlapping may vary. (Almost) complete overlapping is sometimes called a radical approach, and no overlapping [i.e., first top-down design is completed, then top-down coding is completed, and only after that testing (of the whole program) begins] may be called a conservative approach (see Figure 6–5).

In between the radical and conservative approaches, there can be several approaches. Depending on the environment, the volatility of design, and the fickleness of the users, the appropriate approach can be selected. If the user thinks that the design will be stable (i.e., not too many changes are expected while the development is in progress), the conservative approach may be used. If there are chances of changes coming in, a variation of the radical approach should probably be used.

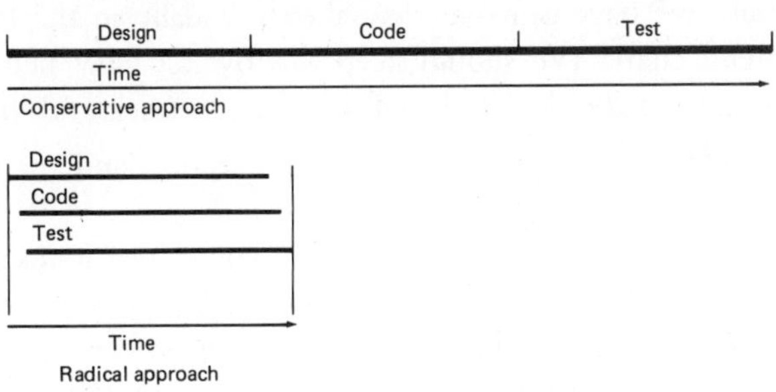


FIGURE 6.5 Conservative and radical approaches of (top-down) program development

## BENEFITS OF TOP-DOWN DEVELOPMENT

1. The major program interfaces are exercised first.

    Since we start testing from the top function and use stubs for the lower-level functions, we exercise the control interfaces provided by the top function first. Thus the program remains under control all the time. As we progress to the lower levels replacing stubs with code, we keep testing the program as it is being developed. Thus the top interfaces are executed often, providing thorough testing of the program.

    Since the testing starts from the top level, we do not need a test driver. If we progress from a bottom level to a higher level, as in bottom-up testing, we would need a driver to provide the controlling function of the higher-level module.

2. A working demonstration of the program is developed quickly.

    Strategic top-down testing can produce a working model of the program quickly. The results may not be complete; however, users can get a good picture of the outputs. Thus they can see that what they are getting is what they wanted. Since we developed the program from the top down, it would not be very difficult to make changes in the program if users change their minds.

3. Overall control of the system can be maintained.

    Since we develop the overall design (i.e., a skeletal design) of the program before doing the detailed design of the top function to be coded and tested in a top-down fashion, we can maintain overall control. We have a road map of our program. Like an artist drawing an overall sketch of a painting on canvas before working on the details, we have our overview sketch, usually in the form of a hierarchy chart. We should keep this overall view before us while working on the details. It will keep us on track and in control.

4. Major problems can come into focus earlier and there should be sufficient time to resolve them.

    Major interface problems may come into focus earlier. This aspect may be particulary useful while working on hardware components from more than one vendor. If a problem cannot be identified in a multivendor system, the tendency on the parts of vendors is to blame each other, but such finger-pointing does not help the user. Top-down development may help detect the errors in a particular component.

Other problems related to results created in other programs and used in the particular program may also be detected. I remember one instance when I started top down testing of a large program as soon as I developed the overall design. It was only a week or two after starting work on the program. The test data used by my program comprised the output of another program in the system. Testing only the top function of my program, with that data revealed an incompatibility between the design of the data and my coding to that point. When I told the developer of that program, he at once realized the defect and corrected the program. When completed, my program was of several thousand lines, and took a few months to complete. If I had waited to code the entire program before starting tests, I would have found that defect much later when deadlines to complete the system would have been very tight.

5. Testing time can be distributed throughout the development process.

   In a bottom-up environment, testing becomes hectic as deadlines approach. All programs are now completely coded and need to be tested. First they are tested individually in unit tests, then they have to be integrated and need system testing. Large blocks of testing time are requested, and programmers forget to look at the clock—they work day and night to get the system running.

   The miserable situation described above can be avoided by following the top-down approach. The test time is evenly distributed under top-down development. It begins early, as soon as the overall, and some detailed design of the top function(s) are finished. Thus the use of hardware resources is evenly distributed. The testing continues at an even pace as top-down development progresses. System testing is almost eliminated, as system integration begins when testing starts, when system development is also done in top-down fashion.

6. The approach enables improved programmer utilization.

   Since coding and testing start early, programming resources are used effectively. Under the bottom-up approach, while the system design is being done, the time of programmers may be wasted if they are dedicated to this system and do not have other assignments. Also, programmers see the results early under top-down development—they do not have to wait for a long time to see results, as in the bottom-up approach. This improves programmer morale. Most programmers really love programming (otherwise they would not be programmers in the first place)—and the top-down approach provides what they love to do throughout the development cycle.

7. More thorough testing of the system can be done. Critical parts can be tested thoroughly.

   Since testing starts early in the development life cycle and continues throughout the cycle, testing is more thorough. Major interfaces are exercised early, as we saw before, and the high-level control functions are tested more often.

8. Top-down approach work may go relatively faster.

   With practice in top-down development, the work may go faster. Whatever work is done will be thorough and of high quality if it is done correctly using the top-down approach. With sufficient test time distributed evenly, the work may go faster than with the bottom-up approach.

9. Test data for a lower-level program (or another program) in the system can be created early.

By judiciously selecting a branch of top-down development in a hierarchical design, input required by a lower-level program in the system, and

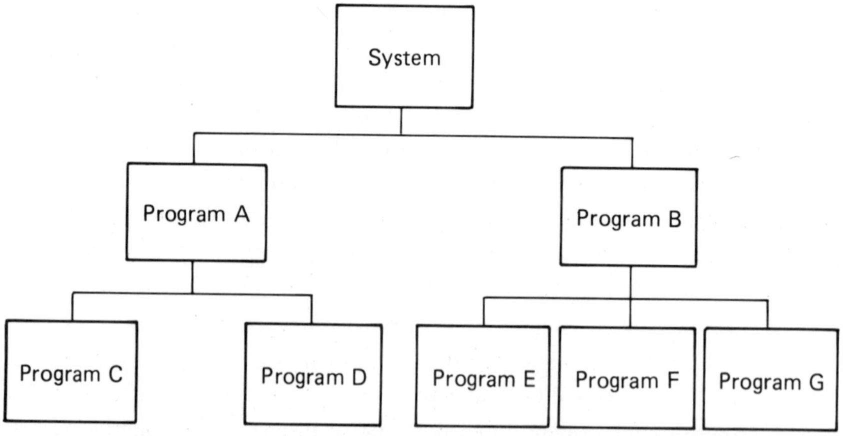


FIGURE 6.6 A system design, after packaging it into programs

created by this program, can be generated early. Thus the testing of the lower-level program does not have to wait for the completion of the higher-level program. It can also begin early if it is also done in top-down fashion.

In Figure 6–6, suppose that the output of program D is used as input by program B and that program D is being developed by programmer p–d while program B is being developed by programmer p–b, working as a team. Both programmers are committed to top-down development. Programmer p–b wants input to start her program as soon as possible.

Suppose that Figure 6–7 represents the overall design for program D. In the design of program D, suppose that function D2.3 creates output for program B. Programmer p-d can follow the top-down development pattern shown in Figure 6–8 instead of the normal way of following level by level as described previously, and create the input for program B first, and then do the other stubs. (Note that in the figures, for simplicity, the same number of lower-level functions are shown; however, in practice, the designs may have different numbers of functions at each level, and the number of levels to which the designs are carried may also vary.)

Suppose that the top-down path leading to function D2.3 cannot create the complete record (data for some fields in the record may be created by other functions which are still stubs)—the skeletal record can still be useful for testing program B. You might argue that programmer p-b may create temporary data to test her program. But under a top-down development environment, why do this extra work when program D, which is to be done anyway, can create test data early?

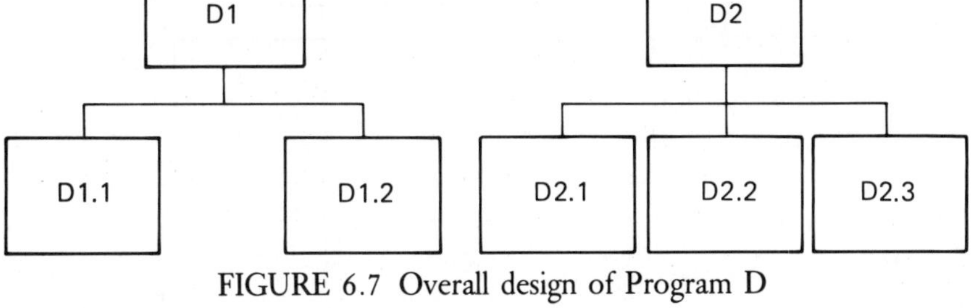


FIGURE 6.7 Overall design of Program D

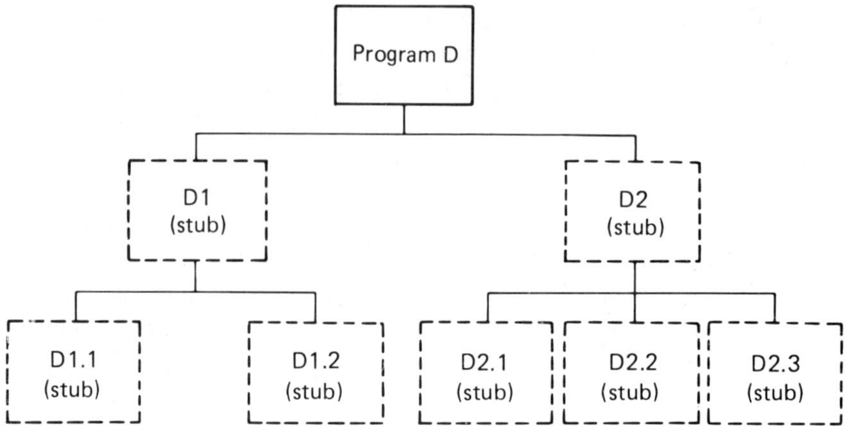
Program D
D1
(stub)
D2
(stub)
D1.1
(stub)
D1.2
(stub)
D2.1
(stub)
D2.2
(stub)
D2.3
(stub)

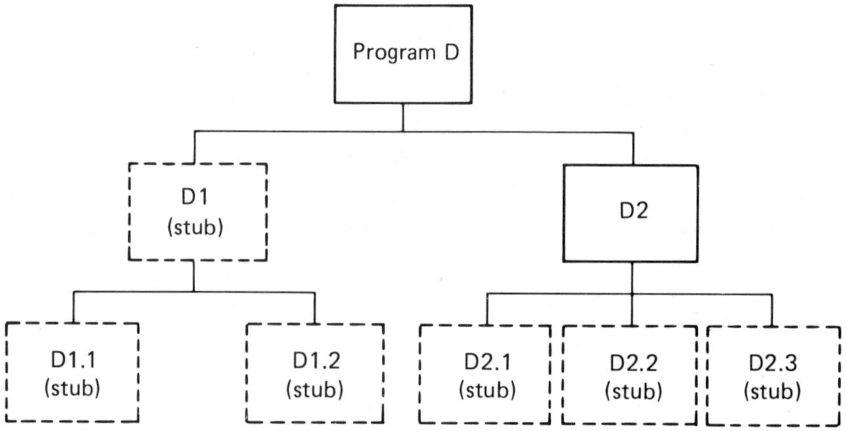
Program D
D1
(stub)
D2
D1.1
(stub)
D1.2
(stub)
D2.1
(stub)
D2.2
(stub)
D2.3
(stub)

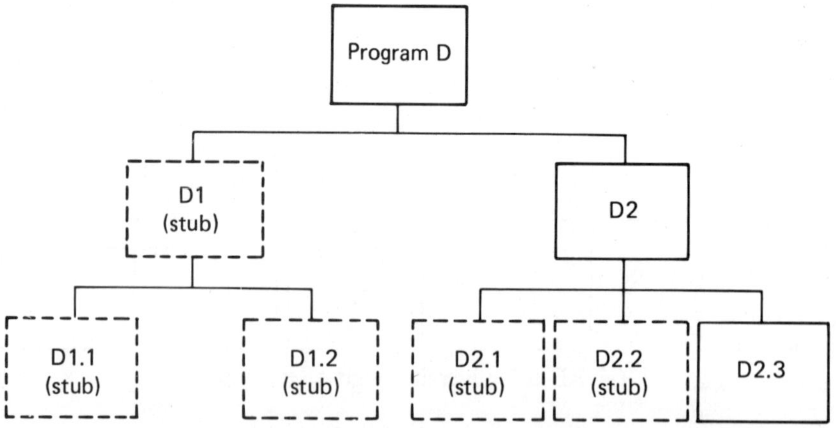
Program D
D1
(stub)
D2
D1.1
(stub)
D1.2
(stub)
D2.1
(stub)
D2.2
(stub)
D2.3

## DEVELOPING PROGRAM ENHANCEMENTS USING THE TOP-DOWN APPROACH

In a maintenance environment, program enhancements can be developed using the top-down approach. Especially large enhancements can be undertaken using this approach. Once the specifications for enhancement are available, study the existing program to get familiar with the outputs produced by it, inputs used, and processes. Once you decide where the enhancements will fit in the existing program, start designing the enhancement, preferably as a separate routine to be performed by a higher-level function in the program. Trace the hierarchical documentation of the existing program, if available, and fit the higher level of enhancement function in it. Then develop the overall design of the enhancement separately.

Then you may start testing the main program, with the enhancement functions done incrementally. However, this can be justified if the enhancement is large, say running to several thousand lines. If it is a small enhancement, it can be completely coded, and then the program tested. The enhancements can, of course, be designed and coded using structured techniques.

## PROBLEMS WITH TOP-DOWN DEVELOPMENT AND HOW TO SOLVE THEM

There are several problems with top-down development. Some of them are described below, and possible solutions are given when available.

---

FIGURE 6.8 (a) Top-down development of Program D (stage 1); (b) top-down development of Program D (stage 2) [to generate input for Program B (see Figure 6.6) first] (note that function D2.3 generates data for Program B); (c) top-down development of Program D (stage 3) [to generate input for Program B (see Figure 6.6) first] (note that function D2.3 generates data for Program B)

## How to Do Top-Down Development When Test Turnaround Time Is Restricted

Top-down development is difficult when test turnaround time is restricted. Sufficient test turnaround time makes top-down development easier and smoother. When test turnaround time is restricted, programmers tend to finish up coding, to make the best use of their time; however, top-down development can be done in this environment.

One technique that will enable you to use top-down development when test turnaround is restricted is to set up different sets of JCL (job control language) cards, and different versions of a program for testing. Testing different versions of the program at the same time will help you make the most of the available test time.

When test turnaround is bad, coding may go ahead, and testing may lag, or more functions can be coded at a time and submitted for testing. Thus a compromise may be reached to make the most of the test time and programmer's time available. The available test time should, however, be used wisely. It should not be wasted or let go. Each meaningful test would help you progress, and lead you to the successful completion of the program. However, you should thoroughly plan your strategy for top-down design, coding, and testing. Also, you should think about what you will be testing in the next few test runs. Since you have more time between test runs, you can work out the expected results of the current and forthcoming test runs. Also, you can desk check the code thoroughly.

Figure 6–9 gives a suggested form for planning and recording the results of top-down development of a program. It can also be used when test turnaround time is adequate. The hierarchy chart of the program can be attached with the plan, and the functions in progress can be shaded in different colors for design, code, and testing. A simple but suitable visual scheme can be devised to keep track of progress at a glance.

## Lack of Hardware

When hardware is not available for testing, naturally we cannot do top-down testing; however, top-down design and coding can still be done. The code can be walked through and thoroughly checked before the hardware arrives. This will save time in testing.

If an arrangement can be made to rent machine time for similar equip-

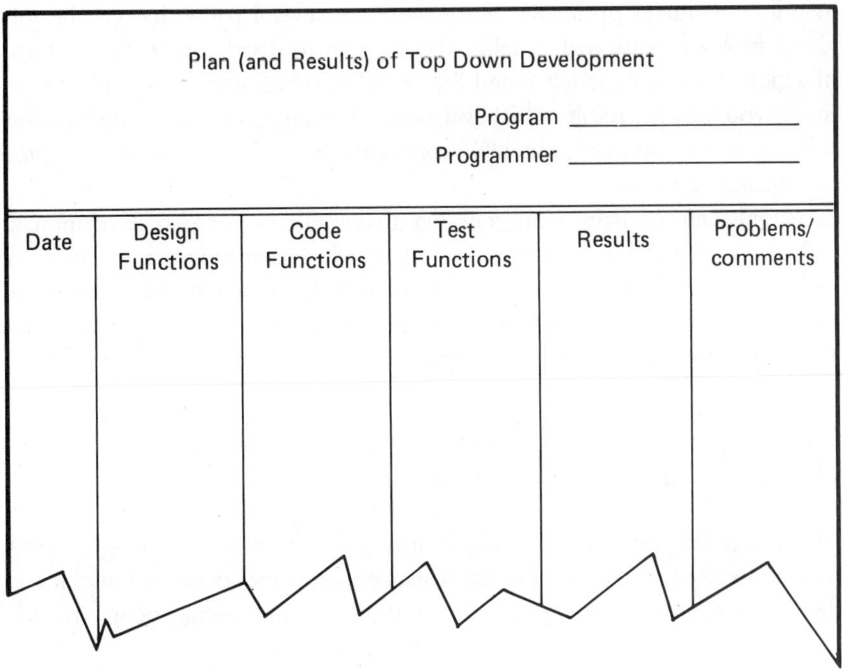
Plan (and Results) of Top Down Development

Program ______________

Programmer ______________

| Date | Design Functions | Code Functions | Test Functions | Results | Problems/ comments |
|---|---|---|---|---|---|
| | | | | | |

FIGURE 6.9 A suggested form for recording plan (and results) of top-down development

ment from a local service bureau or other company, it may be worthwhile to do this. Any testing that can be done, preferably in top-down fashion prior to the arrival of hardware, will put you ahead. If several terminals are on order but will not arrive until later, it may be a good idea to arrange to get at least one terminal, so that you can start testing.

## Problems in Visualization of Top-Down Development

To be effective, the process of top-down development needs clear visualization. The visualization can also be called "imaging." You have to image in your mind the various overlapping activities of design, coding, keypunching, and testing taking place in a certain, best possible sequence to get results and to utilize resources optimally. Since there are several paths that can be followed to reach your goal, it takes visualization to decide on the best course of action. It takes experience and judgment to arrive at the best path. Eventually, you may get results whichever course you take; however, which course will utilize the resources optimally, achieve the results smoothly, and produce high-quality software?

One way to help a programmer to visualize top-down development paths is to provide him or her with the help of a senior programmer, or even an outside consultant well versed in top-down development. The consultant can help chart the path, and the programmer can then follow it. After practicing on a few programs, the programmer can work on his or her own.

## Changes at Lower Levels May Need Revisions at Higher Levels

This is another fear that may sometimes prevent uninitiated programmers from using the top-down approach. Changes sometimes occur at lower levels that need revision at higher levels. However, if the overall design is well thought out and discussed with the users, such occurrences can be reduced, if not totally eliminated. Higher functions are usually control functions, and so the better control functions are designed, the better your chances are that most changes will occur at the lower-level, detailed functions. Changes in lower-level functions would be easy to accommodate, since most of these functions are still stubs in the program. Only on paper are they represented as boxes, and not much detail work on design is done yet. As we shall see a little later, such changes are relatively easy to make.

The technique of design iteration can help reduce revisions at higher levels. Usually, several iterations may be necessary before a design is approved for development. Again, this process can be done in top-down fashion; that is, after laying down the overview design, the details can be filled in. However, the higher controlling functions may be given special attention to reduce revisions later.

## Users May Ask for More Changes When They See That It Is Easy to Change

When changes are easy to make, users may ask for more changes. This is usually the fear of programmers. Using the bottom-up approach, they can say that the program is now completely coded and users will have to wait for changes until the program is finished. Then the work of making changes is transferred to the maintenance programmer.

However, under the top-down approach, changes should not be hard to make, as the lower-level functions are still stubs, not yet coded, as we saw earlier. But another fear of programmers is that the schedule may be upset. However, under top-down development, certain work will go faster. So some change in activities can usually be accommodated. Still there may be a need to renegotiate the schedule. When the programmer can produce visible results early using the top-down approach, his or her chances for successful negotiations increase.

To achieve maximum benefits from the top-down development approach, system design and development should also be done top down, together with the development of component programs in a top-down fashion. Although programs can be done top down, and systems can be developed bottom up, this approach may create problems in system testing and integration. Under top-down development of system and programs, the work of integration of systems begins in the early stages of development and continues during development. Thus when testing of the last program is done, system testing is also done. In addition, the system is well tested and well integrated. This approach, however, will need perception, and visualization at the systems level. The chief programmer, or supervisor in charge, should be trained in these concepts. The work will progress smoothly if well planned.

## TOP-DOWN DEVELOPMENT AND SPECIFICATION CHANGES

During development, the requirements and/or the program specifications often keep changing. The programmers may be in a process of either coding or testing. If they are following the top-down approach properly, the changes may have less impact on their work, whereas if they follow the bottom-up approach, trying to finish coding before starting the testing, they may have to do major alterations to the program under development. However, to evaluate the programmer's approach may not be easy. Again, each change in requirements/specifications may be unique. No two programmers are working on the same changes in the same program. So there is no comparison. How, then, do you judge that the approach followed by the programmer was optimal? Again, there is more than one strategy for top-down development, as we saw earlier. Was the approach chosen most effective?

Before selecting a strategy, a programmer can ask the analyst and/or users how many changes are expected in the specifications. "Probably none!" may be the answer, and then several surprises may pop up. To judge "how firm the specifications are" is not easy. But with experience one gets a feeling for it.

So the qualitative aspect comes into the picture. This will have to be judged by the managers and programmers. I think it can be done best if both discuss it frankly. They may include a peer who is good in top-down design and development technology. (Such a meeting and discussion can be very useful for future use of what is learned, so they should be encouraged.)

## TOP-DOWN DEVELOPMENT AND PRODUCTIVITY

### Top-Down Developer Versus Bottom-Up Developer (Is a Fast Coder More Productive?)

The measure of productivity should not be based only on the number of lines coded. However, when only coding is in progress, the number of pages coded becomes the measure of productivity.

Consider the case of two programmers, working on separate programs. One programmer is coding the entire program, whereas the other, following top-down methods, codes the skeletal program and starts testing with stubs. The coding process of the latter is obviously slower. However, the top-down developer following the techniques properly may be ahead of the programmer using the traditional bottom-up approach.

It is not easy to see the productivity of the top-down developer while the work is in progress. The productivity and better quality of the top-down developer usually become visible only at the end. The walk-through during development where strategies are usually discussed may not help, since managers generally do not attend them. Even peers participating in the walk-through may not be able to appreciate the top-down approach.

I recall an instance where a top-down developer, going slowly but producing solid, tested code incrementally, was kicked out for not keeping up with the progress in coding compared to another programmer (bottom-up developer) who did full-time coding! He argued his case with management (he had kept productivity data) and fortunately was called back after a few days. Only in the last days of the project was the output of the top-down developer found to be superior to that of the other, whose code needed more work to debug and test.

The moral is: The productivity measurement of programmers should consider the overall aspects of the programmer's work. Under top-down development, the completed testing of the code should be considered. Also, when programmers follow different development approaches, comparisons should be made with extreme caution. If you find disparity in productivity between programmers, the one with apparently less productivity should be given a chance to explain and, if possible, the case reviewed by a technician competent in the programmer's approach before taking any corrective action.

## CONCLUSION

Thus the techniques of top-down design and development have many benefits. Although requiring some training and experience, once learned, these techniques can be applied to advantage. The management and programmers should digest this chapter and use the appropriate techniques in their work.

Top-down techniques are considered useful primarily in functional structured methodologies. However, they can also be used to some extent with data structured techniques. Study the tips, techniques, guidelines, and ideas presented in this chapter, and make the most of top-down development.

# *Techniques of Measuring Programmer Productivity*

# 7

This chapter overviews the state of the art and evolving techniques of programmer productivity measurements. It also describes a new technique of measuring programmer productivity (based on Tom Gilb's MECCA method) called "Parikh productivity metrics." The technique is based on several factors, and combines quantitative and qualitative measurements. It can be used to measure productivity in development as well as in maintenance environment. An example of the use of the technique is included.

## Acknowledgments

I am grateful to Gerald M. Weinberg, as the idea for developing productivity metrics flashed into my mind while attending the Technical Leadership Workshop (TLW), sponsored by Ethnotech, Inc., and led by Weinberg in Lincoln, Nebraska, in June 1980. Further ideas on productivity metrics were suggested to me by the writings of Tom Gilb in *Software Metrics* and his book *Design by Objectives*.

Programmer productivity has become one of the key issues in data processing. It is becoming more critical as hardware costs plummet and software (especially programming) costs skyrocket.

An article in *Computerworld* by J. Daniel Couger (Couger, 1980) put it dramatically: "What is the time comparison for writing vs. processing a programming instruction?" The ratio of processing to coding is more than 100 million to 1!

The issues of programmer productivity and its measurement have also become important as the emerging and now rapidly spreading structured technologies (structured programming, structured design, structured analysis, and the related productivity techniques) claim to improve programmer productivity in development as well as in maintenance.

But how much productivity is increased and against what? Percentage increases do not make much sense, and increases in lines of code per day are meaningless unless qualified, as we shall see later. On most projects, no historical data have been kept—so there are no past data against which to compare.

Unless we have systematic methods to measure programmer productivity, "productivity" becomes merely a buzzword. What exactly do we mean by programmer productivity? And how do we measure it?

Programmer productivity is generally defined as the quantity of work produced by an individual programmer in a unit of time. The definition implies the speed of programming, including the related tasks such as program design, coding, testing, and documentation. The definition can be modified to use an expense or cost unit instead of a work unit. In addition, the definition should be extended to include program quality measurements.

The quantity and quality measurements of programmer productivity can be integrated using Parikh Productivity Metrics, as we shall see later.

Managers need quantity and quality measurements of a programmer's output for several reasons, among them the following:

1. To assure that the company is getting its money's worth
2. To appraise and reward a programmer properly
3. To estimate programming resources for scheduling a project

Programmers, too, should be aware of their productivity. By being objective and evaluating themselves, they get to know their true worth. A person may intuitively know how good or bad he is, but the productivity data may speak louder.

## UNITS OF MEASUREMENT

For measuring programmer productivity, we need units of measurement. The most commonly used are work units. Cost units have been proposed as a better alternative by T.C. Jones in his numerous articles (see, e.g., "Measuring

Programming Quality and Productivity," *IBM Systems Journal, vol. 17, no. 1, 1978;* included in Jones, 1981). However, it seems that they are not widely used.

Work units generally measure the speed of programming. Examples of work units are lines of code (LOC) per programmer-day, documentation pages per documenter-month, CPU hours per programmer-month, and test cases developed and executed per programmer-month.

The most common unit is LOC per programmer-day. Since the final product of a programmer's work is a working program, the ratio of lines of code produced and time expended may indicate his productivity.

However, there are several problems with this unit. For example, what does LOC mean? Does it mean all the lines a programmer coded during the development of a program (including the throwaway code, if any, and the code that was added, changed, or deleted because of specification changes), or just the lines in the final product? Does it include data definitions and comments, or just the executable statements?

Unless LOC is precisely defined, productivity measurements do not make much sense, and productivity comparisons are misleading.

## COMPARISONS DIFFICULT

Work units, though widely used, are paradoxical and even misleading. For instance, LOC per programmer-day penalizes high-level languages, such as COBOL and favors the lower-level languages, such as BAL, making it harder to compare productivity from program to program and between programmers.

I recall one large project in a major midwestern corporation that used COBOL and BAL. The project manager tried to spur on a COBOL programmer by telling him about the productivity of a BAL programmer.

"Look, your buddy is producing 84 lines per day!" the manager said.

"But he programs in BAL," the COBOL programmer reacted sharply. Naturally, he was turned off!

Similarly, the work units of program quality measurements, such as cost per defect, favor older methods of software development. Consequently, they delay the acceptance of modern methods.

Thus work units should be used cautiously—and with precise definitions.

## COST UNITS

Units for measuring programming cost concern themselves chiefly with the central product (e.g., 1000 lines of a program), not the human activities that go into developing it.

The following are examples of cost units: programmer-days required per 1000 LOC; CPU hours per 1000 LOC; cost per documentage page; cost per defect for maintenance.

Because of inflation, the costs per unit do not remain stable for a long period. Perhaps it would be better to estimate effort in man-hours or man-days necessary for different activities to complete a unit of work. Then, based on the current programming rates, the cost per 1000 lines can be worked out to get cost estimates.

## MEASUREMENT BY FUNCTION

With the advent of structured technologies, especially with the function-driven approaches, function may become a basic unit of the system or program. With progress in these methodologies, it may be possible to estimate the effort needed to design a function. After the (logical) design, the coding and testing effort can be estimated depending on the language used.

For most of the common functions, reusable code may be available. For others, effort can be estimated using tables on productivity (containing data such as type of function, effort needed, and a language factor) developed from past experience.

LOC data, with proper qualifications, for each function may also be collected and included in the table. Such tables, built and updated over time with estimates and actual experience, may prove to be valuable references.

## EXTERNAL DOCUMENTATION

External documentation (as opposed to "internal" documentation, or comments within a program) is an important programmer job function. A program is *not* considered complete until it is documented. How do you measure programmer productivity in documentation?

In work units, the unit is documentation pages per unit of time. In cost units, it is cost per documentation page. However, cost per page will be lowest for documentation pages with more white space. Generally, cost goes down with a greater number of pages. The cost per page is not a good unit since it penalizes compact, tightly written documents, as the cost per page is more compared with that for longer documents; however, the total cost may be less. Thus cost for documenting 1000 lines of code may prove to be a better unit.

Effort needed to document 1000 lines of code may prove to be a relatively stable unit of measure for a particular language, application and programmer.

## PARIKH PRODUCTIVITY METRICS[1]

Parikh productivity metrics integrates quantity and quality measurements and can be used with the consensus of programmers. The metrics can be used for individual programmers or for a team. The productivity [or productivity index (PI), if you will] will be more comprehensive than any single measure, such as LOC. However, several attributes in the metrics are subjective and need the judgment of more than one expert in calculating average ratings.

Parikh productivity metrics is based on the MECCA (Multi-Element Component Comparison and Analysis) method developed by Tom Gilb, an independent consultant based in Kolbotn, Norway. The MECCA method has been successfully used in various applications, such as hardware evaluation, software package evaluation, and so on.

Parikh productivity metrics combines the quantitative and qualitative aspects of productivity measurement. Because several elements are used, the result is likely to be more accurate than with a single method of measurement. The attributes to be measured are determined by the programmer and manager whenever possible, so the results tend to be more objective. A sample form for programmer productivity metrics is shown in Figure 7–1 and an example of measuring development programming productivity is given in Figure 7–2.

The overall productivity index in the example in Figure 7–2 is 0.84. This is how it is worked out: The first column lists the elements or attributes

[1]Most of the material in this section is excerpted from a text of the video course "Measuring Programmer Productivity," developed by Girish Parikh (1983) with DELTAK, Inc.; copyright © 1983 DELTAK, Inc.

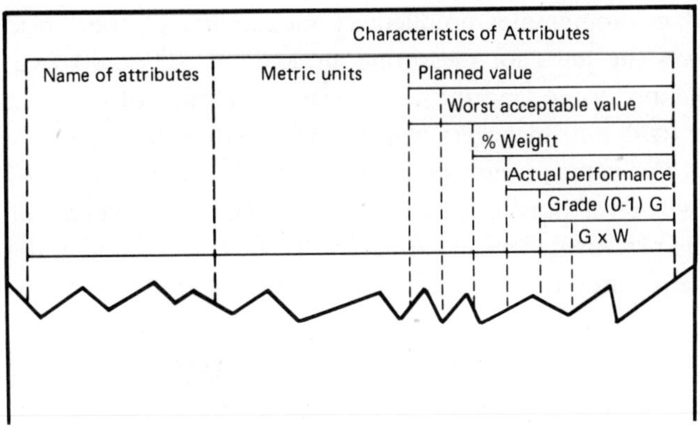


FIGURE 7.1 Form for Parikh productivity metrics

| Name of attributes | Metric units | Planned value | Worst acceptable value | % Weight | Actual performance | Grade (0-1) G | G x W |
|---|---|---|---|---|---|---|---|
| | | Characteristics of Attributes | | | | | |
| 1. Quantity of work | Lines of code per day | 60 | 30 | 5 | 45 | .5 | 0.25 |
| 2. Errors found after inspections | Errors per 1,000 lines of code | 5 | 10 | 10 | 10 | .0 | .0 |
| 3. Documentation quality | 7 for best quality<br>1 for worst quality | 7 | 1 | 15 | 6 | .80 | .12 |
| 4. Correctness of test cases/ Quality of testing | 7 for totally satisfactory<br>1 for totally unsatisfactory | 7 | 1 | 10 | 6 | .80 | .08 |
| 5. Number of compilations for effective testing | Number of compilations | 10 | 20 | 5 | 18 | .80 | .04 |
| 6. Maintainability | 7 for best maintainability<br>1 for worst maintainability | 7 | 1 | 25 | 5 | .7 | .18 |
| 7. Completed on schedule | 7 for before schedule<br>1 for after schedule | 7 | 1 | 10 | 4 | .5 | .05 |
| 8. Completed within estimated budget | 7 for less than estimated budget<br>1 for estimate exceeded | 7 | 1 | 10 | 5 | .7 | .07 |
| 9. Execution efficiency | 7 for maximum efficiency<br>1 for minimum efficiency | 7 | 1 | 5 | 5 | .7 | .04 |
| 10. Memory used | 7 for minimum memory used<br>1 for maximum memory used | 7 | 1 | 5 | 2 | .2 | .01 |
| | | | | | | | TOTAL 0.84 |

FIGURE 7.2 Example of measuring development productivity using Parikh productivity metrics

to be used in programmer productivity measurement. The "metric units" column gives the units for measuring an attribute. The next two columns give the planned value, and the worst acceptable value of the attribute. For qualitative attributes, managers will determine what these values will mean in practice. Percentage weights are assigned (with the agreement of the programmer whenever possible), based on the relative importance of each attribute. The percentage weight should add up to 100%. Note in the example that qualitative aspects are emphasized. Managers may change the weights based on their goals. Management may also change, delete, or add new attributes with the agreement of the programmer when possible.

The actual performance for a given assignment is recorded in the next column. The grade is an interpolated value of the actual performance based on the planned and worst acceptable values. The planned value is assigned numeral 1. The worst acceptable value is assigned zero. The actual performance can then be assigned a value, usually a fraction between 1 and 0. This interpolated value of actual performance is called a *grade.* The following examples illustrate the calculation of grades for the first three attributes. The first two are quantitative and the last is qualitative. Determining the grade for the first attribute, quantity of work:

| | Grade | |
|---|---|---|
| 1 | 0.5 | 0 |
| 60 lines of code/day (Planned value) | 45 lines of code/day Actual performance | 30 lines of code/day (Worst acceptable value) |

Determining the grade for the second attribute, errors found after inspections:

| | Grade | |
|---|---|---|
| 1 | | 0 |
| 5 errors/ 1000 lines (Planned value) | | 10 errors/ 1000 lines (Worst acceptable value) Actual performance |

(In the above, the unit is "errors found *after* inspection," for instance, in the unit tests, systems tests or in the first few production cycles.)

Determining the grade for the third attribute, documentation quality:

| | Grade<br>0.80 | |
|---|---|---|
| 1 | | 0 |
| Quality = 7<br>(Planned value) | 6<br>Actual performance | Quality = 0<br>(Worst acceptable value) |

(Note: For simplicity, the figure above shows the worst acceptable value as zero. In actual practice, the lowest acceptable value might be 2 or 3.)

Then the grades are multiplied by the weight percentages to get an index for each attribute. The indexes are totaled to get an overall productivity index.

Productivity data collected by the programmer, reports from walk-throughs, and outputs of programmer productivity tools (such as a source library management system or source code auditor) provide performance data for the assignment of grades.

Management determines the worst or lowest acceptable value for any attribute. If a programmer scores below the worst acceptable value, he or she has failed to perform that attribute adequately. That particular attribute does not receive a grade. If the attribute is critical, for example, completing an assignment on time, the programmer may not receive a grade for the entire assignment.

Parikh productivity metrics can be used for measuring both development and maintenance productivity. In maintenance, it can help combine the quantitative and qualitative aspects of productivity measurement.

Attributes that may be used to measure maintenance productivity include programmer experience, structure of software, correctness of test cases or quality of testing, and quality of change (e.g., design of code). Some of these attributes are quantitative and some qualitative.

## PRODUCTIVITY IN DESIGN

Programmers are normally responsible for designing a program from specifications. How do you measure their productivity in designing?

Design productivity depends on many factors, such as the quality of specifications, the tools used (such as Warnier/Orr diagrams, HIPO), the complexity of the functions, guidelines and standards, individual abilities, and management attitude and constraints.

Using cost units, the cost for designing a unit of lines (such as 1000 lines) can be determined. Designing costs may be different for different parts of a program, depending on varying complexity. For a large program, the costs of overall design can be distributed equally and added to the cost of designing its parts, each comprising unit number of lines.

Here is a rule of thumb for measuring programmer productivity in designing, based on work units. First, decide on a unit of measure based on the design tool used—for example, for HIPO, the "function box"; for pseudocode, the number of lines; for a Warnier/Orr diagram, the number of braces. If HIPO is the design tool, the productivity can be measured as follows.

The number of completed function boxes per day in a hierarchy chart may be a rule-of-thumb measure of system and program designers' productivity. However, remember that many factors are involved in the design, such as complexity of the system or program, support of the users, and quality and completeness of specifications. The measurement and comparison of design personnel's productivity in different situations may not be accurate. Use this method with great caution.

Such a unit of measure may encourage creating more boxes, so some standard, such as equating each box to an average of 50 lines of structured code, might be established.

Experimentation with this unit of measure in a particular environment may lead to some useful results.

## PRODUCTIVITY IN MAINTENANCE

In a maintenance environment, it is usually extremely difficult to measure productivity. Here are some suggested guidelines.

### Number of Requests Handled by a Programmer

Number of change requests handled by a programmer (or a team) in a period of time may indicate productivity. However, some change requests may be big and complex, while others are simple. Complexity and magnitude factors can be used to come up with the units of maintenance work done. Also, number of lines added, deleted, and changed for an assignment can be recorded to assess productivity.

## Lines of Code Maintained by a Programmer

The number of LOC maintained by a programmer can roughly indicate the maintenance programmer's productivity. However, this measure depends on the structure of the system, programs, and documentation. The programmer's experience and application knowledge may also be a factor.

For a well-documented, reliable software package, a large number of LOC (if source code is supplied) can be maintained by one programmer. The same would be the case with systems software. If vendor support is adequate, a programmer can handle considerable LOC. In contrast, the applications software, if unreliable and poorly documented, would be hard to maintain, and the number of lines of code maintained by a person would decline drastically.

## Bebugging Technique

Bebugging means artificial insemination of bugs in a program. The time taken by a programmer to correct a bebugged program may indicate his productivity. (Productivity of different maintenance programmers can also be compared.) The technique can be extended to measure productivity in enhancing a program. After an enhancement assignment is completed, the same program (before enhancement) can be given to another programmer to do the same assignment. The time he takes may indicate productivity.

## Breakdown of an Assignment into Required Functions

Breaking down an assignment into required functions, then estimating time required for each function and keeping track of the time spent for each function may give some idea about productivity. Time required can be reasonably estimated, based on experience, for routine functions, such as getting a dump of a file, updating the documentation after completing a maintenance assignment, testing a job or job streams. They could be like constant functions—not all constant functions identified will be necessary for a particular assignment, but guidelines can be developed for all such functions once they are identified.

Examples of variable functions include diagnosing the problem and locating the place in the program where changes should be made. A technically oriented manager may be able to qualitatively assess the productivity of a programmer, based on his experience and knowledge of the system. However, such assessment may not be accurate and objective, since each problem may be different. The comparison of programmers for such activities may be inaccurate and unjustified.

Programmer productivity also depends on "structuredness" and the quality of documentation of a system or program.

## MAINTENANCE FUNCTIONS

The following is a list of functions (excerpted from Parikh, 1982a) into which a maintenance assignment can be broken down. The list is not complete. But it can also be used for estimating and then as a checklist for the work on a maintenance assignment. The following steps may not all be necessary for every assignment.

1. Review the requirements or specifications of the assignment.
2. Talk with the involved persons, such as an analyst, user, or the boss. This may be a continuous function throughout the assignment.
3. Take an inventory of the affected program and documentation.
4. Investigate the affected program.
5. Locate the spots in the program where changes should be made.
6. Check the side effects of the proposed program changes on the other parts of the program.
7. Code the changes. Have them keypunched and verified.
8. Make the changes and get a clean compile.
9. Walk through the changes marked in the program. This can also be done after coding the changes.
10. Create test data, if not available.
11. Set up test JCL, if not available.
12. Test the program.
13. Do the system test, if necessary.
14. Review the results.
15. Move the program to production.

16. Update the affected documentation.
17. Conduct posttest reviews.

## FUTURE DIRECTIONS

A news item titled "Beyond Measuring Lines of Code, New Gauges of Programmer Productivity Set" (*Computerworld*, July 28, 1980) summarized the talk on programmer productivity given by T. C. Jones to the New England Productivity Information Exchange Round Table and indicated some future directions in programmer productivity measurements.

More attention should be paid to the design and analysis stages of program development and measuring the benefits user departments obtain from software.

According to Jones, two methods of measuring productivity across languages, though not yet widely used, are attracting more and more attention: Halstead metrics and functions metrics.

"Instead of lines of code, Halstead metrics, now widely experimented with at universities, counts the number of action statements (operators) and data elements (operands) in a program.

"Experimentation has found there is a correlation between the sum of number of operators and operands in the error rate and productivity of a program. Larger companies such as IBM and ITT are experimenting with the method.

"Function metrics, also under study by IBM, attempts to quantify the cost per function rather than lines of code and assign a benefit to the function."

The author feels that in the future, mathematical methods of productivity measurements, such as Halstead metrics and function metrics, may become popular. However, he feels that, in the functional method, effort per function may be used instead of cost per function. Using effort instead of cost would give relatively stable figures, since cost figures change with inflation and rising programming costs.

Even tables for the effort needed for different programming functions and standard functions (or function integration using reusable code) within a program for a semiskilled to skilled programmer may be developed for estimating purposes. The costs can then be extended using the programming rates.

Parikh productivity metrics may also be used. The lines-of-code methods of measurements will continue to be used, but the line counting rules will be defined and published with the productivity data, to make it meaningful. Research may continue with this method also.

Using the guidelines presented here, management can develop a method of productivity measurement. There is no one perfect method. Several approaches are available and evolving.

Being a human activity, programming may not be measurable with mathematical accuracy. There are just too many factors affecting productivity. However, systematic methods can allow reasonable assessments of productivity, and as methods are refined, accuracy will improve.

# *Software Tools and Programmer Productivity*

# 8

**The resources available to help increase productivity include software tools. However, it is essential to keep track of the use of software tools. Since software tools are, in fact, programs, automated periodic reports indicating their use can be produced. Such reports could include the percentage increase/decrease in use of software tools compared to the previous month. The sample form (Figure 8–1) illustrates the kind of information that can be reported.**

Data on the use of "productivity tools" would indicate, to some extent, productivity status. The increased use of productivity tools does imply an increase in productivity, since tools generally increase staff effectiveness dramatically. Also, the number of uses of tools would indicate the effectiveness of the training material on productivity tools. This approach would indicate the productivity of a department or installation. For individual productivity, use the individual account number(s).

Also, the number of uses of each tool, as well as the total number of uses of tools, can provide useful statistics. Is the number of uses for each tool increasing or decreasing? By what percentage? Is the total number of tool uses increasing or decreasing, and by what percentage? Which tool(s) are widely used, and which tool(s) are least used? Are there different users for different tools, or do the same users use most of the tools?

The data above can reveal if the number of users are increasing or decreasing. If a certain tool is used more than other tool(s) among tools having similar features, an analysis can be made of why that tool is used more. What aspects of a tool, such as ease of use, training material, or available feature(s),

Use of Programmer Productivity Tools

During February and January 19 84

| Software Productivity Tool | Number of Uses in February 1984 | Number of Uses in January 1984 | Increase/ (Decrease) in February 1984 | Percentage Increase/ (Decrease) in February 1984 |
|---|---|---|---|---|
| (Tool 1) | | | | |
| (Tool 2) | | | | |
| (Tool 3) | | | | |
| (Tool 4) | | | | |
| | | | | |
| | | | | |
| Total | | | | |

FIGURE 8.1 A sample form of the use of programmer productivity tools with the months of February and January, 1984, used as examples

make it more popular? Such data may give useful information for the future selection of tool(s).

If a particular tool is not popular, action may be taken if appropriate to provide more training documentation on pertinent defaulting of parameters. Such feedback also provides vendors with important information on which to base the direction of their enhancements.

Such a productivity measurement facility can help in making decisions as to whether a tool should be purchased/leased after a trial period (if the trial period of the tool is included for data collection). Of course, the use factor should not be used as the only criterion for making a decision.

## OTHER OBJECTIVE MEASURES OF PRODUCTIVITY

The results of the use of productivity tools, such as quality and quantity of added/changed/deleted code [made visible by a source code auditor, such as RES-Q (see Chapter 12)], can be used to make certain decisions. It can provide data for assessing qualitative productivity.

Certain kinds of problems, such as redundant code, may go away in the due course of time. Walkthroughs and qualitative productivity assessments, aided by the use of software tools, may become instrumental in accomplishing this.

## MEASURABLE ASPECTS OF PRODUCTIVITY TOOLS

The productivity tools can help indicate (personal) productivity. Especially when structured walkthrough is used with the output from the productivity tools (such as RES-Q), together with the necessary source code and other documentation, the concepts become much powerful.

For example, RES-Q makes the cumulative changes to a program easily available, providing a measure of the quantity of changes. The structured walkthrough can indicate the quality of work. Thus, combining the use of productivity tool and walkthrough gives a good measure of productivity.

All productivity tools are useful in assessing productivity throughout the life cycle. For example, in subsequent walkthroughs during development, are the changes suggested in prior walkthroughs done? RES-Q can isolate the changes and make the data available for review. Thus structured walkthroughs can become more powerful by combining the use of productivity tools.

Although RES-Q is cited above, other productivity tools can also be helpful. For example, a static analyzer such as SCAN/370 helps detect dead code and perform range violations, among other things. A preprocessor (see Chapter 4), among other things, improves the visual aspect of a program. Refer to good software directories, such as International Computer Programs directories (see the Bibliography).

## SOFTWARE RELEASE AND SOFTWARE TOOLS

While releasing programs to production, the use of software tools can help detect any flaws. A walkthrough can be used before moving a program (either newly developed or maintained/enhanced) to production. The purpose of this walkthrough is different from the development or maintenance walkthroughs. The productivity tools may make the "production release walkthrough" (i.e., walkthrough before releasing a program to production) easy. For example, RES-Q will indicate changes made to a program. Such changes will be easy to review before moving a program to production. The person in charge of production may hold a walkthrough meeting with the programmer/analyst before accepting the program for production.

# How To Be Egoless

# 9

**Gerald M. Weinberg, in his classic *The Psychology of Computer Programming* urges programmers to be egoless. But how do you become egoless? Can you erase ego altogether, or can you only reduce it? How do you control ego? The most humbling activity: maintenance programming. Vedanta shows the way! This chapter provides guidelines for reducing ego, seeing through the problems clearly, and solving them without involving ego. The chapter also shows how to prevent the waste of millions of dollars by reducing ego at the higher levels of management, and preventing ego trips. It discusses dangers and illusions of ego trips as well as ego clashes and how to prevent them.**

> Accompanying you constantly will be one of three platoon drill sergeants. His job is to insure that, at the end of camp, you possess the skills required to enter the ROTC Advanced program. You won't get hollow praise or undeserved criticism from him. He will be honest in his comments, usually in very blunt and concise language. Your ego may be somewhat bruised after a direct confrontation with him, but normally you won't have a question about your error and you probably won't let it occur again."
>
> from *Army ROTC Basic Camp Guide,* 1979

The concept of "egoless programming" was popularized by Gerald M. Weinberg in *The Psychology of Computer Programming* (listed in the Bibliography). Egoless programming has become a buzzword in data processing, and is indeed a worthwhile goal to attain, unless one becomes egotistic about being egoless. The problem remains: how to become egoless? I don't know of any guidelines in the computer literature. This chapter, drawn primarily from the Eastern Vedantic philosophy, provides some practical guidelines. Although in this chapter a programmer is used as a guinea pig (poor programmer!), the concepts can be applied profitably by managers and other nonprogrammers.

The following material is based on an interview with Arvind Vasavda, an eminent psychologist and a student of Carl Jung.

> One should try to be completely free from the past, then new thoughts come. One should not be a prisoner of the past.
>
> Leap into the unknown.
>
> Intution is needed. Intution comes by humility, listening to others, and not having an intoxication that "I know."
>
> To be egoless is to be free from prejudices, and preconceptions, and being prepared to look at the new; also, listening to others, keeping aside one's knowledge and preconceptions, and having humility. Total receptivity helps to develop egolessness.
>
> An egoless person does not say "I did." Egolessness is built on purity.
>
> Identification with past knowledge is ego. The past knowledge provides the superstructure. An egoless person does not misuse past knowledge. His attitude is: "I don't know everything, the other person also has knowledge." He accepts the joys and sorrows of life without being disturbed. He knows the relative importance of everything. The universe is an integrated living whole. Even a company is a living whole. He sees every one in equal partnership with what is going on. We are all equal as human beings. The terminology of subordinate or hierarchy should go away; relative importance is okay. We are all equal as human beings. Egolessness can help a lot in life, including in business situations.

Narsimh Mehta, a famous poet from Gujarat, India, says:

> "I am doing everything" is ignorance. It is like a dog walking under a cart pulled by a bull, and the dog claims he is pulling the cart!

Also have a feeling that you are not serving merely a company but that you are serving the universe.

## WHAT IS EGO?

Can you describe ego? You may say that "I" is ego. What is that "I" that you keep repeating? Is it your physical body? Is it your hands, head, or feet? Or is it your mind? or your brain? You see, it is hard to pinpoint what ego is. But we know that ego is associated with "I"ness, and me. (But remember, ego may also be of a group, or a race, or a country.) Ego pertains to the "self," with a small "s," for we shall see later that there is another "Self," spelled with a capital "S." You identify yourself with self, your vision gets clouded, and you suffer from limited vision. You cannot get a total picture or an objective view. In other words, your ego becomes an obstruction to clear thinking.

For example, if you are a gifted programmer with unusual programming capability, you may not listen to suggestions coming from an average programmer. "Who is he to make suggestions to me? I know!" you may think resentfully. Thus you may dismiss the suggestion, even if it might have saved you a substantial amount of time and effort.

If you are a manager, you may not discuss problems with your programmers, but go to other managers to discuss them. Or a programmer suggests solutions, and you may simply give them lip service and not think about them seriously. If you like a certain way of doing things, you may insist on that approach, mainly because "It's *my* approach," and disregard another person's approach, even if it is a better one.

The examples cited above are instances of ego. I do not know of any statistics on how much ego costs business, but I would bet on a figure of several million dollars a year.

## WHY BE EGOLESS?

You may say, "I am happy in my own small world. I am proud of my work. My ego gives me good feeling." But what happens when your ego is hurt? You feel upset. When you see someone with talents superior to yours, regardless of color or sex or race or nationality, you may feel jealous, or try to disregard him or her. And if you are a manager, you may even try to get rid of the person. But eventually such actions hurt you alone. If you want self-fulfillment and success, the way is to be egoless. Also, merging your small ego in a larger, absolute ego will not only relieve you of many problems, but will also liberate you.

## HOW TO BE EGOLESS

Let me give some practical guidelines for becoming egoless. You can be proud of your work and humble at the same time. It sounds contradictory; however, I believe it can be done. We will also explore whether you can eradicate ego completely, or only partially.

In modern programming techniques, also called structured programming techniques, walkthroughs can be very useful in reducing egos. Even if you have long programming experience, when your program is subjected to an intensive scrutiny for errors even by novice programmers, it will be a challenge to come out of that grueling session with an unbruised ego. (Such a session may also show that experienced programmers are not necessarily more productive. This may be a revealing experience, hurting your ego.) But try to look at it from an objective point of view. Your program will be more reliable and better with a good walkthrough.

Do not take the criticism personally. In other words, keep the ego away. Be open to suggestions. Strive to improve within practical constraints.

You also realize, maybe painfully, that the program you call "my" program is not your program at all—it is public property within the organization. Thus you expand your thinking, or rather you are forced to expand your thinking. Now if you can expand your thinking in this instance, you can also expand it further. Maybe you can cover your city, the country, the world, the universe—see, there is no limit. Your ego becomes limitless. If your small ego can give you pleasant feelings, how about stretching your ego to envelope the universe?

Another humbling experience for a programmer is to work on software maintenance assignments. Probably, maintenance programming on old, unstructured existing programs is one of the most humbling experiences in data processing. And it may not be your fault, although management may think that you are incompetent. When you are unable to make a simple change (from the management or user point of view) correctly, or fast enough, you will fall down in the eyes of management, however capable you may be in new development. (And once in a while you may totally fail to make a change correctly, however competent you may be. I know from experience that it can crush your ego, as well as depress you.)

## CAN WE ERASE EGO ALTOGETHER?

If we want to continue living physically, it seems to me that we may not be able to erase ego completely. To write with a pencil on a paper, for example, we need friction; without friction we cannot write. So possibly we cannot live without a trace of ego. In the same way, we are generally not able to remove all the bugs from a program. Let's debug the ego from us but know that some trace of ego may remain.

## HOW TO CONTROL EGO

Ego may sometimes become uncontrollable. Especially when you become successful, for example get a promotion or a hefty raise, it may be hard to control your ego. How do you control ego? Before the ego controls you, you should control the ego.

### Vedanta Shows the Way

Vedanta is an ancient Hindu philosophy based on the world's oldest set of books, known as Vedas. Vedanta is a Sanskrit word meaning "end of knowledge." It implies that there is nothing further to know once you reach the end of knowledge. In other words, we should try to reach the absolute. This is not emptiness. It is not possible to describe the end of knowledge in words, as words cannot reach that stage. It is a matter of experience.

Egolessness can help you to reach this stage. Vedanta can also show you the way to control ego. In essense, Vedanta teaches you to merge all ego in the larger ego. Following is a story from one of the Upanishads, the ancient books from India.

There are two birds on a branch of a tree, one on the lower side, and another on the higher side. The lower bird is scratching its beak and seems to be restless, while the upper bird seems to be happy and contented. The lower bird makes faces and seems to be dissatisfied with itself, whereas the higher bird enjoys itself. The higher bird is quiet and peaceful. The lower bird looks up and sees the happy bird, and jumps up and merges with the higher bird. Both birds become one. In reality, there were not two birds; there was only one. The lower bird was the lower self of the same bird, and the higher bird was the higher or real self of the same bird. When the birds merge, the ego of the lower self merges with the ego of the larger self.

## SOLVING PROBLEMS WITHOUT INVOLVING EGO

You will be able to solve problems better if you do not involve the ego. Let's see why. You will be able to see through things when your thinking is clear and not deluded with ego. See through the problems clearly and solve them without involving ego. Yes, you *can* solve the problem; however, do not be proud of your ability and do not be overconfident. Do your best, and then leave it to the higher force. Leave the data about the problem with the subconscious, meditate, and in due course of time, you should get a solution.

## LET THE EGO GO

Like Goto-less (or less Gotos?) programming, let the ego go, or be egoless. Probably that should be the new slogan of programmers and managers alike. Egolessness may not be completely possible, but any degree of less ego can be beneficial. When the ego goes, true judgment comes. The vision becomes clearer.

## MILLIONS OF DOLLARS WASTED BECAUSE OF EGO

Management sometimes wastes millions of dollars because of personal egos. I have heard of a large midwestern corporation in which millions of dollars were wasted because of the ego of a manager. The technicians tried to convince the manager of the error in one decision; however, the manager acted on his decision. In a talk with me, the technicians declared it a case of pure ego. Such instances may rarely be recorded; however, if we had statistics, I believe their rate of occurrence would be startling. Such waste can be reduced by controlling or reducing ego.

## EGO TRIPS AND EGO CLASHES

Ego trips can cost a company millions of dollars, as we saw above. How do we distinguish persistence from an ego trip? We can find this out from the previous track record of the worker. If the previous record is okay, you need not worry.

How about ego clashes? Two staff members may fight over egos. Both may not be willing to give up, even when they have been convinced that it is their ego they are holding on to! How do we prevent ego clashes?

Ideas from this chapter may be helpful in preventing ego clashes. Encourage your staff members to be egoless. Harmony will prevail with egoless employees. Instead of fighting ego clashes, fight the ego and try to remove it. Structure your environment on the foundation of egolessness, for better profits and productivity. Also, when management does not get involved in egos, the lower-level staff, including programmers, will have a good example to emulate.

It might seem that we have gone on a philosophical tangent in this chapter. However, the material is essential in understanding the concept of ego and how to control it, and primarily, how to be egoless for self-fulfillment and success in your professional as well as your personal life.

Being egoless can be beneficial to your well-being and general health.

# *The Three T's For Increasing Programmer Productivity: Techniques, Tools, and Training*

# 10

**The key to improving programmer productivity is in the three T's: techniques, tools, and training (see Figure 10–1).**

The productivity techniques (the first of the three T's) are not only for programmers, but also for managers. The managerial techniques include developing standards and guidelines, evaluating programmer performance, motivating programmers, and so on.

The programming techniques include better ways of performing the job, and making the most of time and technical resources. The techniques would include the best utilization of the software tools available. The programmer may also be involved in modern techniques such as structured programming based on functional or data structured approaches, top-down design and development, on-line programming, and fourth-generation languages. Programmer should be familiar with the techniques associated with these methodologies.

The training for programmers should include learning new methodologies, and improving on what has been learned. Training is an ongoing process, especially when the data processing field is changing so rapidly. Going to a school or taking in-house courses does not mean that a programmer is not knowledgeable. It means only that the programmer wants to keep updated.

Training for managers should include an overview of modern techniques, motivating technicians, technical leadership concepts, problem-solving

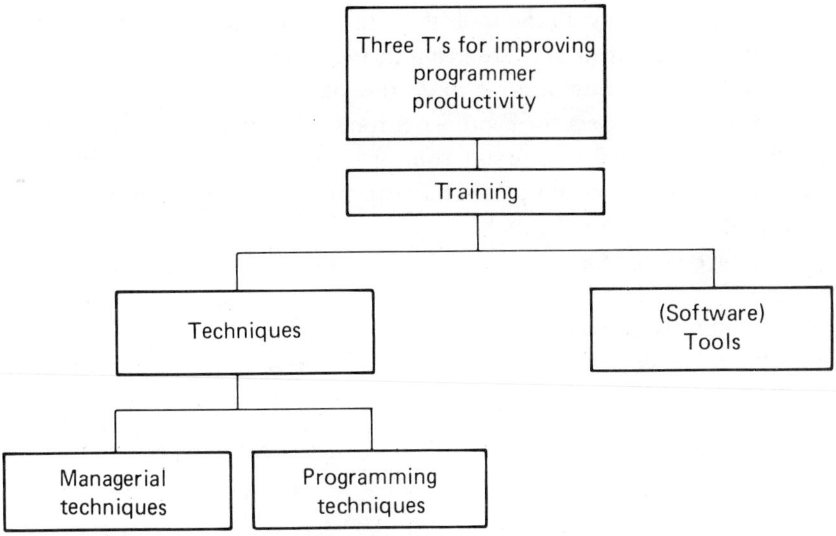


FIGURE 10.1 The three T's

ideas, software maintenance management seminars, and so on. The training should also involve information on available tools to increase programmer productivity. Measuring and improving quantitative and qualitative productivity of programmers should also be the subject of management training.

The third T for increasing programmer productivity is tools. Software tools are software packages that aid programmers in their jobs. (The documentation tools, such as HIPO and the Warnier/Orr diagram, are also sometimes called software tools. Here we are talking about software packages that help programmers.)

There are numerous software tools available. Refer to a good software directory, such as the International Computer Programs directory (see the Bibliography) for the variety of software tools available. Tools can be general purpose or programming language oriented. Tools can also be classified according to hardware that they support. Your selection may be restricted depending on your hardware.

Examples of general-purpose tools are: source statement libraries, source code auditors (source compare programs), file compare utilities, and test data generators. Examples of programming language-oriented tools are: COBOL preprocessors and COBOL structuring engine (to restructure an unstructured program automatically).

It seems that most managers and programmers are not using tools; they are not even familiar with the tools that are available. As one tool developer remarked: "Many managers are living in the stone age." When a hammer is available, they still use a stone to do the job.

How do you select the appropriate tools? One way is to study software directories. Another way is to ask your programmers if they have used software tools in their previous jobs. Their experience with tools can be an asset for you in selecting a right tool.

Involve your programmers in the selection of tools. Review their feedback carefully. When programmers are involved in the selection of tools they become enthusiastic users.

A productive programming environment *can* be created by the effective use of the three Ts: techniques, tools, and training.

# *Productivity Improvement Through the Use of Software Tools*

*By Jon Cris Miller*[1]

# 11

Productivity is always an issue for serious business and professional people. Remaining competitive in the domestic and international marketplace depends on continuous and significant improvements in productivity. Today, computer software is the vehicle for implementing most corporate business practices and many manufacturing activities. It increasingly provides the same kind of support for the engineering community. There is no option to back away from software and remain competitive. If software systems are unreliable, or modifications to them are delayed as well as unreliable, an organization suffers.

Over the past three decades, data processing personnel have brought about major improvements in software. Most such improvements have been products of intellectual brute force. Uneconomically, most mental activity has been spent on sequencing, cross-referencing, consistency-checking, duplicating, and other essentially mechanical activities. This activity has been at the expense of time necessary for the uniquely human capabilities to investigate, infer, intuit, and integrate.

The productivity tools are as basic to a modern software environment as hammers, saws, pliers, screwdrivers, wrenches, and rulers are to construction. Whether you are a manager or programmer, there is a message for you: productivity must improve, and tools are keys to such improvements.

The objective of this chapter is to raise consciousness about the potential within an organization to raise productivity directly in terms of data processing performance, and indirectly to the user community, through faster development, greater reliability, easier operation, and more timely maintenance and enhancement. The focus is on multiplying human capabilities by providing quality tools and the training to employ them effectively.

## BACKGROUND: THE SYSTEM (DEVELOPMENT) LIFE CYCLE

The System (Development) Life Cycle is one mechanism for plotting the creation of computer software applications. The typical phases identified are:

Requirements Definition

System Design

Coding

Testing (unit)

Testing (integration)

More sophisticated treatments recognize that these activites represent only a part of the total picture, and add:

Conversion

Operation

Maintenance (routine)

Enhancement (major)

Audit

Indeed, even excluding the operation component, this latter group expends two-thirds of the expenditures of time and money of data processing departments. One can, of course, treat enhancement as new developments, and achieve corresponding adjustments to activity. However, there are very different risks and consequences to applying changes to systems in production from systems not in production.

What is at issue is that each of these activities has traditionally been a labor-intensive activity. Consider the time spent on:

Interviewing during requirements gathering

Writing documentation

Typing and keying activities
Coding
Preparing test data
Reviewing test results
Scheduling job submissions
Converting files
Estimating
Analyzing failures
Documenting changes
Accounting for time spent on the above

Indeed, when one considers that on average, a good programmer writes fewer than 25 lines of program code per day, it is clear that something other than writing instructions to the computer is going on.

In most cases, habits from a pre- (or emergent) electronic era govern our activities. For example, in documentation:

We write instead of dictate.

We type instead of using electronic word processing or text editing.

We prepare nominal lists of indexes, figures, and glossaries instead of producing them mechanically.

In short, we limit our minds to the speed of our extremities. The Industrial Revolution freed our bodies. The Electronic Revolution has provided the means to free our minds. We must, however, free ourselves.

Fortunately, we have options. To understand them, we must review the underlying issues.

## ISSUES

The issues underlying productivity in modern business organizations are:

Productivity and the human machine interface
The strategic application of technology
The pervasiveness of computing

Let us review each turn.

Productivity, from an Economist's standpoint, is measured by the value of the output attributed to the last dollar expenditure on the factors of production: on land, labor, and capital. It is the task of management to continually deploy financial resources among these factors to maximize returns on investment. Our attention here is on labor. Management faced with higher labor costs with falling output must do one of these things:

Cutback on (or replace) least productive workers until those remaining can produce at a pace consistent with their pay level.

Hold labor constant while increasing expenditures on marginally superior land and capital until reaching a new equilibrium.

Upgrade the "human capital" by supplying the appropriate training techniques, and tools to stay ahead of labor costs.

This chapter addresses the implications of the latter option. Frequently, recurring short-term crises short-circuit the training which could eliminate many of the crises themselves. Many staff people believe that managers consider any training (particularly company-sponsored) as a boondoggle. Sometimes, that belief is well-founded.

Management habit patterns, however, have focused on the traditional definitions of tools—tangible extensions of the land.

In recent years, there have been many attempts to minimize the problems, particularly scheduling, inherent in formal classroom situations. "Programmed Instructions" texts, as well as audio and video tapes, have provided some relief, but are still subject to scheduling and mailing. Further, they often do not address local situations.

A good computer-based training program can follow a different strategy.

Each session can be based on an electronic document, viewable or printable on request.

Information specific to a company (e.g., accounting codes and libraries) can display generic information.

The session focuses on strategic issues—how to get the most benefit from defaults of options.

The session operates in the same environment as the material being presented.

For optimum benefits, schedule *a regular* time (e.g., each Monday, 3 to 5 P.M.) as the training slot. Such scheduling allows each topic time for digestion without disrupting normal workloads. In other words, there is no time or expense allotted to off-site training or imported trainers. More important, while the training should follow a normal pattern, disruption of any one person's schedule (illness, vacation, emergency) does not affect anyone else's schedule.

Technology is a strong word. It frightens many people, often concerned about "keeping current" in dead-end assignments. On-the-job training has proven a powerful attractant in recruiting, and even more effective in holding quality staff. Reasons for training are many, but include:

Preparation for more demanding assignments.

Developing skills to handle current assignments more effectively.

Raising consciousness about issues with predictable needs but an unpredictable timetable.

In regard to the latter, there is a story of the retiring dean of a medical school delivering the graduation speech who said: "Half of what we taught you is erroneous; unfortunately, we don't know which half."

Most of the time, most tasks we address consist of many mechanical subtasks, with few opportunities for mental manipulation.

It may be true that we need the tedium to let the brain rest, but there is no clear evidence to that effort. Since management cannot easily control one's mental activity, there is an undue emphasis on the manual. This results in asking people to spend increasing amounts of time on that which they are even less competitive vis-à-vis machines. Automation has been concentrated on the tangible aspects of manual activities, rather than on the mental ones. CRT, local printers, and even desk calculators are visible evidence of automation. Software tools aiding the mind are visible only by reflection.

The key to the effective application of technology is to recognize that new technology:

Disrupts previous equilibrium, making current staff less secure and less effective in routine activities.

Operates on simplyfing assumptions, and depends on the current staff to fill in the gaps left by these assumptions.

Over time, ill-defined human experience can be identified, catalogued, defined, and frequently, incorporated into new technology. Indeed, freeing people from handling the mundane norm provides both the time and the measure to address the exceptional. In short, management must resist the temptation to assume that anything lacking definition either doesn't exist or is without value.

When the technology involves computers, there is a special problem in this area. A computer solution bears no physical relation to the process underway. In this respect, old Tab or EAM [electronic accounting machine] equipment had an advantage. One can observe a card sorter in operation, identify with it, and recognize its relationship to manual activity. No such analogy applies to the computer. Unsorted transactions go in and sequenced reports come out, "by magic." When the magic fails, the supplicant cannot take action directly, but must go to the data processing priesthood for more magic. Magic, however, is not predictable.

This leads to our third point: Software is pervasive. The move to automation has been relentless—sometimes taken out of fear, often out of a failure to understand the merits of the human mind and heart. No secretary would address a letter: "Dear Mr. Addressee Unknown." An electronic replacement would do so until someone translated human experience into machine experience, via editing criteria.

The issue is that computers and computing are not equivalent. Computers have declined in cost per unit of capacity. Computing has not, largely because of the unappreciated variation in pre-electronic systems, held together with "human glue." In the first and second generations of computer users, experienced staff remained to cover for the shortcomings of computer software.

Reassignment, retirement, resignation, and reorganization have dissipated that organizational resource. In its place, we have computer systems which behave consistently, if not always intelligently. Unfortunately, in the mean times to repair between a request for maintenance enhancements and a proven response, has been lengthening, despite massive budgeting increases. In fact, efforts to control the situation have tended to worsen things by increasing burdensome overhead on those directed to act upon the requests. In other words, organizations are trapped.

Human resources do not understand the magic within the computer system. The technicians do not understand the functional characteristics, and the users do not understand the technical. Consequently, changes are time-consuming and expensive.

Consequently, innovative organizations which have led the way in automation now find themselves depending on software which does some things very well, but which is steadily losing its adaptive capacity. This is the situation which leads us to our subject: software tools. Software tools are those computer programs which provide data processing personnel with the means to improve the quality, reliability, performance, and maintainability of computer systems.

## OPTIONS—TOOLS FOR EVERY NEED

Some concepts are so distasteful as to discourage conversation. Software maintenance, until recently, was one. Indeed, now people may talk about it, but may not seriously present battle plans for controlling it.

The point is, someone must take the first step. Some companies have put a priority on productivity increases. Data processing is not exempt; indeed, given the pervasiveness of computing software, productivity in other areas is often keyed to that in data processing. Otherwise, solutions in other areas can not get off the ground.

The first step is to develop or acquire and then exploit tools. To some degree, the selection sequence is event-driven.

Consequently, follow this strategy when forced with a technical problem:

1. See if there is currently a tool to address it.
2. Check your own experience and circle of professional acquaintances to see if they have a tool solution.
3. Review the literature for alternatives.
4. Request the technical services group in your company to follow up on your need/findings. Quantify your needs as much as possible.
5. Follow through.

Remember, personal—or trusted—experience is a powerful aid in evaluating packages.

## CONCLUSION

Productivity is a serious subject. Computer hardware and software are integral to corporate processes. Software productivity gains have not kept pace with hardware. A class of software, i.e., software tools, provides a means of automating many processes in software development, operation, maintenance, and enhancement, thereby improving human productivity.

It is important to learn about both the concept and the availability of tools. It is also important to offer training in tools—and other productivity measures—on a routine and continuing basis.

Feedback on the material (tools, training, and texts), as well as open needs, are essential to ongoing productivity gains.

Productivity is important, but depends on management support, effective training, current materials, and continuing feedback.

# *Automated Auditors Aid Maintenance Programming Productivity*

# 12

You have been burned by a midnight programmer who made changes to a program without letting you know.

You are a maintenance programmer, and have worked several days on a program. How can you demonstrate to your boss what you have done? In other words, can you show what changes you have made to the existing program?

You are in a second walkthrough of the same program. Several changes have been made in the previous walked-through version. You keep mumbling: What changes have been made? Is there an easy way to know this?

How do you achieve the changes to your program for audit purposes? A good source auditor can help improve productivity in attacking such problems.

An automated auditor is a software package that audits source code (or other kinds of data) against a previous version of that program (or data). There are two kinds of automated auditors: file-compare utilities, and source-code auditors. File-compare utilities (such as IBM's IEBCOMPR) compare two files of data, and they are normally used for demonstrating that two files are identical, and any difference between them is considered an *abnormal* situation. A file-compare utility can also be used to compare results of parallel runs.

In comparing previous and new versions of a program, a maintenance programmer needs to know what has been changed. Differences between two files (old and new program, in this case) are a *normal* situation here. A source-code auditor is a source-comparison program primarily designed for this purpose. (Some source-code auditors can handle data and JCL files also.) The identified changes comprise added, deleted, and changed lines of code.

(Note that change-date-stamps of source library management systems like Panvalet from Pansophic Systems Inc. or Librarian from Applied Data Research, Inc. do not show *what* changes have been made.)

A source auditor is thus a software tool that makes tracking program evolution easy and reliable. It is a programmer productivity tool in software maintenance. It can also be productively used in new development. For example, program changes because of design and specification changes during development can be tracked with an automated auditor. Its effective use can improve productivity in DP audits and security, management of programming, quality assurance, updates/modifications of vendor packages and software conversion.

This article outlines how a source-code auditor helps improve and evaluate maintenance programming productivity. We will look at three examples: with Res-Q from Quality Systems Development Corporation used primarily for References and capsule descriptions of some other source code auditors, IBM's 5796-PDF (DOS) and 5796-PDH (OS), and SRCCOMPR (Source Compare) of Harlan S. Hersey, Inc. are included.

## SOURCE AUDITORS

A source auditor automatically generates statement-by-statement audit trails for every change made to a program.

It serves as a research tool—saving many hours of manual review. Res-Q especially works with any source library management systems and any online system.

Some other uses of Res-Q include:

Integrating changes made separately to two or more copies of the same program;

Reintegrating field maintenance into a changing base;

Combining similar, but slightly different "special" programs, or eliminating them as obsolete;

Reviewing modifications made when an "updated" program product version comes out.

The unique capacity of Res-Q to produce an update deck based on any library management system facilitates the above functions; with some manual work, the other source auditors can also be used to perform the above functions.

Normally, a source-code auditor compares code on context rather than sequence numbers which are often obliterated. Usually, there are no restrictions on the size or complexity of program updates. Generally, other kinds of data can also be compared.

With a good source auditor, program changes can be documented in three time frames.

As changes are proposed, it supplies in-context contrast of lines to be added and/or deleted.

As changes are implemented, it supplies documentation for ready reference.

As changes are discovered, it can supply audit trails to track down the sources and reasons. (For example, the maintenance history preserved by Res-Q can reveal what has changed, when it was changed, and by whom it was changed.)

One approach to assessing maintenance programming productivity is to measure the quantity of changes made to a program. However, it does not consider quality of work.

A source auditor makes the changes easily available, for objective, quantitative, and qualitative assessments. Output of a source auditor can be used in a structured walkthrough, or for management review.

It also provides an excellent training tool for new and back-up programmers, in that it provides a listing of changes.

## OUTPUTS

Res-Q has two output files, both optional (see Figure 12–1):

1. *In-context transaction register:* A concise but detailed and easily-used in-context list of the differences between two files (File A and File B) in groups of records. It gives data regarding matched, inserted, and deleted lines, as compared in two programs.
2. *Update deck:* This unique feature of Res-Q is the library-based (e.g., Librarian) data set, generated while comparing old and new programs. It can be directly used on an old program, when necessary, to generate an updated, new program.

RES-Q OUTPUT

1. Control Card listing — documents run options.
2. In-Context Transaction Register — shows differences clearly.
3. Update Deck output in optional LIBRARIAN® format — with Deck ID feature shown.

```
QUALITY SYSTEMS                     C O N T R O L   C A R D   L I S T I N G                        PAGE    1
RES-Q  C VERSION, RELEASE  1.0                                                                      05/28/80
                                                                                                    00:47:06

RESQ-000    COBOL,LIBRARIAN,LINECNT=60,MARK=73,MARKSTR=MMC80149
```

```
QUALITY SYSTEMS                  I N - C O N T E X T   T R A N S A C T I O N   R E G I S T E R                     PAGE    2
RES-Q  C VERSION, RELEASE  1.0                                                                                      05/28/80
                                                                                                                    00:47:06

RECORD NUMBERS            1         2         3         4         5         6         7         8   SEQUENCE FIELDS   FILE STATUS
FILE A  FILE B  123456789+123456789+123456789+123456789+123456789+123456789+123456789+123456789+   FILE A   FILE B   FILE A FILE B

   1       1            IDENTIFICATION DIVISION.                                                  000100   000100      * *
   2       2            PROGRAM-ID. MILPROOF.                                                     000200   000200      * *
   3       3                                                                                      000300   000300      * *

           4        ********************************************************                               000400        *  INSERT
           5        *                                                      *                               000500        *  INSERT
           6        *   04/19/80  MMC, SYSTEMS & PROGRAMMING               *                               000600        *  INSERT
           7        *                                                      *                               000700        *  INSERT
           8        *             MODIFIED TO CHECK FOR DUPLICATES,        *                               000800        *  INSERT
           9        *             PRINTING PHYSICAL RECORD LOCATION        *                               000900        *  INSERT
          10        *                                                      *                               001000        *  INSERT
          11        ********************************************************                               001100        *  INSERT
          12                                                                                               001200        *  INSERT

   4      13            ENVIRONMENT DIVISION.                                                     000400   001300      * *
   5      14                                                                                      000500   001400      * *
   6      15            CONFIGURATION SECTION.                                                    000600   001500      * *
   7      16                                                                                      000700   001600      * *
   8      17            INPUT-OUTPUT SECTION.                                                     000800   001700      * *
   9      18            FILE-CONTROL.                                                             000900   001800      * *

  10                        SELECT CARD-FILE ASSIGN TO UT-S-CARD.                                 001000               *    DELETE
  11                        SELECT PROOF-FILE ASSIGN TO UT-S-PROOF.                               001100               *    DELETE

                                                                                                           001900        *  INSERT
                                                                                                           002000        *  INSERT
                                                                                                           002100        *  INSERT

                                                                                                  001200   002200      * *
                                                                                                  001300   002300      * *
                                                                                                  001400   002400      * *

                                                                                                           002500        *  INSERT
                                                                                                           002600        *  INSERT
                                                                                                           002700        *  INSERT
                                                                                                           002800        *  INSERT
                                                                                                           002900        *  INSERT
                                                                                                           003000        *  INSERT
                                                                                                           003100        *  INSERT
                                                                                                           003200        *  INSERT
                                                                                                           003300        *  INSERT
```

```
-INS     00000003
       ********************************************************             MMC80149
       *                                                      *             MMC80149
       *   04/19/80  MMC, SYSTEMS & PROGRAMMING               *             MMC80149
       *                                                      *             MMC80149
       *             MODIFIED TO CHECK FOR DUPLICATES,        *             MMC80149
       *             PRINTING PHYSICAL RECORD LOCATION        *             MMC80149
       *                                                      *             MMC80149
       ********************************************************             MMC80149
                                                                            MMC80149
-REP     00000010,00000011
             SELECT CARD-FILE        ASSIGN TO UT-S-CARD.                   MMC80149
             SELECT PROOF-FILE       ASSIGN TO UT-S-PROOF.                  MMC80149
             SELECT SORT-CARD-FILE   ASSIGN TO UT-S-SORT.                   MMC80149
-INS     00000014
                                                                            MMC80149
         SD  SORT-CARD-FILE                                                 MMC80149
             DATA RECORD IS SORT-CARD-RECORD.                               MMC80149
                                                                            MMC80149
         01  SORT-CARD-RECORD.                                              MMC80149
             05  FILLER                  PIC 9(1).                          MMC80149
             05  SORT-NUMBER             PIC 9(6).                          MMC80149
             05  FILLER                  PIC X(73).                         MMC80149
             05  SORT-SEQUENCE           PIC S9(4)    COMP.                 MMC80149
                                                                            MMC80149
-REP     00000029,00000029
             05  PROOF-DUPLICATE         PIC X(19).                         MMC80149
             05  PROOF-SEQUENCE          PIC ZZZZZ9.                        MMC80149
             05  PROOF-LINE              PIC X(107).                        MMC80149
-REP     00000033,00000033
         01  WS-MISCELLANEOUS.                                              MMC80149
             05  WS-EOF-FLAG             PIC X(1)        VALUE LOW-VALUE.   MMC80149
             05  WS-SEQUENCE             PIC S9(4) COMP  VALUE ZERO.        MMC80149
             05  WS-NUMBER               PIC 9(6)        VALUE ZERO.        MMC80149
-REP     00000066,00000067
             05  FILLER                  PIC X(11)   VALUE                  MMC80149
                 '  CARD #:'                                                MMC80149
-REP     00000074,00000075
             05  FILLER                  PIC X(12)   VALUE                  MMC80149
```

FIGURE 12.1 RES-Q's update deck output LIBRARIAN format (shown), with the Deck Id option.

IBM's Source Auditor produces output as described in the capsule presentation later.

The simple output of SRCCOMPR (Source Compare) consists of sections of difference between old and new code, followed by match line(s) which signals the end of a section of difference. The lower the matchcount, the more detail is presented. The higher the matchcount, the more inspection of the printout is needed for differences.

Currently, no statistics are printed at the end of the run, but this feature is currently being developed.

A good source code auditor can help rescue managers and technicians from crisis. It helps improve and evaluate maintenance programming productivity. Software professionals should understand and use such a productivity tool.

## VENDOR INFORMATION

Audit-Source Code Compare for S/370 DOS/VS (5796-PDF)

Audit-Source Code Compare for S/370 OS/VS (5796-PDH) [General documentation number: G320-5532-0]

IBM (Installed User Program), installed at:

IBM Corporation
Corporate Information Systems Department
Armonk, New York

This audit/control tool analyzes the differences between two versions of a program's source code. The variations detected are highlighted on a message listing.

The features include: Complete listing of both versions of source code; appended messages to both listings indicating variations; synchronized page and statement numbers between the two listings; and statistics summary of number of input statements and of number of matches, deletions, additions, and changes.

Res-Q is available from
Quality Systems Corporation
875 N. Michigan Ave., Suite 2510
Chicago, IL 60611
(312) 266–6060

Available for IBM/OS, IBM/DOS, or for any other mainframe that supports COBOL.

SRCCOMPR (Source Compare) is available from

Harlan S. Hersey, Inc.
106 Quaker Drive
West Warwick, RI 02893
(401) 822-0176

This is a source compare utility for IBM OS and DOS uses. The features include: Comparison of only certain columns of the input record; detection of inserted or deleted records; changes made on a line shown by old and new version; control over match line count; optionally ignore blanks when comparing records; optionally ignore comments when comparing.

Contact the vendors for current information, including prices. Other source code auditors are also available. Refer to a good software directory for a comprehensive list.

# *How To Pick A Winner: A Look at Software Methodologies*

# 13

Let us perfect the means; the end will take care of itself . . . .

*Swami Vivekananda*

One industry guru reveals that annual software maintenance costs worldwide are over $30 billion. Several other studies indicate that maintenance is two-thirds (67%) of the software life cycle; the remaining 33% is development. Taking 10 years as the average life of a software system, the total worldwide software maintenance costs would be $300 billion, and development costs (one-third of the total life-cycle cost) would be $150 billion. The total life cycles cost a stunning $450 billion!

By using the right methodology, if you save at least 10%, the savings would be an overwhelming $45 billion! The potential for savings with the correct methodology is staggering! Proper training and experience in such a methodology will also result in a solid increase in programmer productivity.

But the catch is: the "right" methodology. How do you select such a methodology? Especially when so many are available, and almost every vendor claims that his or her methodology is number one! The debate over methodologies rages on, and there seems no way of deciding what is best . . . until now! This chapter describes a definite plan to help you pick a winner. And the chances are that it wouldn't cost you anything! On the other hand, the right methodology may save you a fortune in the long run. Let me give you some thoughts on software methodologies.

The industry thinking on methodologies ranges in two extremes: some give all credit to people, saying "people design systems, not methodologies," whereas others follow a methodology religiously. There are half-truths in both extremes—the fact is, people and methodologies are both important. However, this chapter emphasizes methodology. People,if willing to learn, can be trained in the right methodology.

A word about the so-called "fourth-generation methodologies," such as data base languages, nonprocedural languages, and program generators—1000 percent productivity gains are sometimes touted with such methodologies! Whenever such a methodology *fits* into your development and maintenance work, consider using it. If you can use such a methodology, by modifying the design without sacrificing the objectives, try it. However, you will still need to design the system and most of the programs—that is, you need a design and development methodology.

Most professionals are confused over the commonly used classification of software methodologies: functional and data structured methods. The methodologies that use data flow diagrams (DFDs), such as structured analysis and design according to DeMarco and Yourdon-Constantine, respectively, are sometimes confused with data-driven methodologies. However, these methods are essentially functional. Eventually, we derive functions from the data flow diagrams. The data flow diagrams describe processes (most of which become functions in the structure charts), and the flow of data to and from them. Thus the data flows tie the functions together. Essentially, the process of drawing data flow diagrams during analysis stage is to partition the processes.

The approach in a data structured method is quite different. The basis of design is the logical structure (not the physical structure, i.e., the layout of fields in a record).

To understand the differences in functional and data structured approaches, one needs some training, study, and experience in using both kinds of methods. Which type of method is better—functional or data structured? There are strong arguments for both types of methods. Is there an objective way of picking a winner, not only among the kinds of methods—functional or data structured—but a particular method? The method is described later in the chapter.

The method proposed to select a methodology includes the use of a methodology with [when tool(s) are available] and without tools. Fortunately, there are only a few *major* methodologies to choose from.

Here are some methods traditionally used for selecting a methodology, and my reflections:

1. Hire a consultant to prepare an extensive report on the best methodology for you.

   The consultant may be presenting the same report (with a few variations) to several companies which are looking for a magic method! The ideas in the report may have been borrowed from several sources—the consultant may not have actual experience in methodologies.

   If you want to use a consultant, make sure that he or she has actual experience in several methodologies, is objective, and can support the recommendations with solid data.

2. Attend seminars or classes on each method, then use your judgment.

   A high-key instructor may sell you a method. If you have to use this method, investigate each methodology further. Ask for a list of users, and contact some of them. Try a promising methodology on a pilot project, described next.
3. Do a pilot project for a potential methodology.

   Use the methodology on a medium-scale, noncritical, actual project, and keep accurate records. Analyze different aspects of methodology, such as training, design, coding, testing, and so on.

   Usually with this method, the methodology tested is likely to be selected. If you do not have any method now, the methodology tested would almost always increase productivity. After investing effort and time on the pilot project, it is unlikely that you would turn it down. Unless you do a series of pilot projects with different methodologies, you may be a loser in the long run!
4. Randomly select a methodology, and pray!

I believe that the method of selecting a methodology can be precise and as objective as possible. Moreover, as mentioned earlier, it may not cost you anything—on the contrary, it may save you a fortune in the long run!

In this chapter I discuss the following four methodologies, listed alphabetically (however, you may add other methods, or replace one or more with other methods):

1. DSSD (Data Structured Systems Development)
2. Jackson methodology
3. LCP (Logical Construction of Programs) of Jean-Dominique Warnier
4. Yourdon-Constantine methodology

(Also seek the help of the original developers of the methods—Ken Orr, Michael Jackson, Jean-Dominique Warnier, Ed Yourdon and Larry Constantine—on a volunteer basis, if possible. They may agree, as their fortunes are also at stake!)

Our focus in the method is on program development and maintenance, that is, design, coding, testing, maintenance, and documentation in each activity. (However, the scope of some methodologies may extend to systems analysis and systems design.)

We also consider training—the transferring of techniques. Other aspects include: ease of use, maintenance savings, preserving the quality and integrity of a program, and "programmer portability"—how well other programmers not involved in the original development can maintain it.

The highest-ranking methodology may be adapted as a standard method in the shop. Programmers trained in other methodologies will also be helpful when the need arises. The second best method may also be used in some cases. A method rated best for a particular application and organization may not necessarily be the best for all applications and environments.

Hardware technologies also affect programmer productivity. Software technologies, which include methodologies and people, also affect environments. Accurate records should be kept on an ongoing basis. The right methodology will go a long way toward increasing programmer productivity. The claims of the various methodologies can thus be evaluated objectively. The winner can make you a real winner, in the long run.

Why use an independent consultant as an observer on the project to select a methodology? Some may argue that an internal consultant can do the job. However, following are the considerations for selecting an outside consultant.

To shield the project from company politics

To provide objective viewpoints

To use the knowledge of the consultant in software methodologies

To help in the objective evaluation of the project

To help resolve disagreements

This brings us to the selection of an ideal consultant for this kind of project. Following are some suggestions:

1. He may be expert in one or two methodologies; however, he should have an overall understanding of other methodologies.
2. He should be a good technical consultant as well as a leader. Although he will not be leading this project, his qualities of leadership will be an asset in the evaluation of the project, especially its managerial aspects.
3. He should be open minded.
4. He should be willing to work hard and long hours if necessary.
5. He should be prepared to undergo the training that is given to the programmers in the project, when appropriate.
6. He should be a good observer and recorder of the progress of the project.

7. He should be innovative to suggest kinds of records useful for the evaluation of the project. Also, he should be flexible to suggest improvements during the progress of the project.

The project team consists of 14 members: 12 programmers, a supervisor, and an independent consultant. The project may take over one year. The additional costs may include training, purchasing/leasing methodologies, computer time, travel, and secretarial support. This may amount to substantial costs. How to justify them?

I believe the costs are only in the front end. The selection of a right methodology would save substantial money in the maintenance costs of the program. This may offset the front-end costs and may even save a fortune. The other programs done with the winning methodology would further increase savings.

The team consists of 12 programmers; however, during the maintenance phase, the program developers may work on other assignments. During development the maintenance programmers can do other work. Thus all programmers would not be needed all the time.

In the following chapter I have given an outline of a suggested method for selecting a programming methodology. The method can be adapted according to the requirements and the available resources. The method can also be used to compare fourth-generation languages, software tools, and the data base management systems. Of course, the methods and/or products to be evaluated should first be selected for a particular environment.

Who should do such a project? I believe such a project should be done in an industrial environment. Then the results would be valid. If industry is not willing, it may be done jointly by industry and an academic organization. Possibly a government agency might fund such a project. Initially, it can be done on a very small scale, preferably in an industrial environment. If the results are promising, a medium- to large-scale project may be considered.

The following excerpt from a letter to me by Ben Shneiderman, Associate Professor, Department of Computer Science, University of Maryland, supports the plan of selecting a best methodology described in this chapter.

> Thank you for your letter of February 23, 1983 and your article with the outline for an experimental comparison of programming methodologies. I think it is a fine idea and I have suggested similar "clinical trials." The difficulty in carrying out such a study is ensuring adequate experimental controls. It is possible for a commercial development organization to gain useful experience from carrying out such a study. An even

> more exciting prospect would be to conduct enough concurrent studies so that adequate validation is ensured. I think that a grand national clinical trial of methodologies would be a terrific notion. It would require substantial investment and coordination and would have to be funded by NSF or DoD. I think the work of Basili and Reiter (*IEEE-TSE* and *IEEE Computer*) serve as a good basis for such studies.

Peter Freeman and Anthony Wasserman have proposed a similar plan to compare designing methods in connection with the Ada programming language (see the Bibliography).

But how about fourth-generation methodologies, which have been found by some users to help increase productivity dramatically? The fourth-generation methodologies can also be compared using a plan similar to the one described in this chapter. Also, methodologies are needed to build and maintain the fourth-generation languages and tools.

Methodologies are also used to develop software packages.

---

Selecting the "right" software methodology may save you a fortune in the long run. Consider these figures: Several studies indicate that maintenance consumes 67% of the software life cycle; the remaining 33% is development. Once a software system becomes operational, it may be used for five to 20 years (some IBM 1401 programs are still around).

Consider the result if a methodology helps you save at least 10% in total life-cycle costs. This savings may result in different ways. For example, depending on the methodology, you may spend more on the front-end development cycle (in the design stage) and save 20% on the subsequent maintenance, including repairs and enhancements.

Keep an open mind when choosing a methodology. Be willing to learn and discover no matter what your position—president or programmer. Remember that a highly promoted or well-known methodology is not necessarily the best.

Professionals should learn more than one methodology, since one may not be suitable for every application. To save on training costs and to standardize, organizations may select one major methodology and use another when an application demands. When possible, methodologies may be judiciously combined. Large companies may have methodology specialists, while

FIGURE 13.1 Four software methodologies in front of the race track ready to run the race

small companies might use outside consultants specializing in the appropriate methodology.

Most methodologies can be divided into two major groups: functional and data-structured. With the first type, data flow analyses (for instance, data flow diagrams) are ultimately transformed into functions.

The major function-oriented methodologies include improved programming technologies (top-down development, structured programming, structured walkthroughs, development support libraries, team operations and HIPO); DeMarco's structured analysis; Yourdon-Constantine structured design; and SADT (Structured Analysis and Design Technique, trademark of SofTech).

Data-structured methods derive design structure based on the logical structure of data—both input and output. The major data-structured methodologies are Logical Construction of Programs/Logical Construction of Systems (LCP/LCS), developed by Jean-Dominique Warnier; Data Structured Systems Development (DSSD) of Ken Orr and Associates; and Jackson methodology (developed by Michael Jackson).

Some methodologies have automated tools available. For example, DSSD has Structure(s) for automating the Warnier/Orr diagrams during design and a code generator for outputting Cobol code from detailed program structure charts.

Should you select a methodology that has automated tools? Effective use of appropriate tools would increase programmer productivity substantially. On the other hand, a manual methodology may be more elegant.

Consider the following in making a decision:

Can the use of tools be extended in the maintenance phase?

Are the vendor-supplied tools adequately supported?

Are the tools well-documented and easy to use? Is training available?

Are the tools cost-effective?

If a manual methodology is selected, can it be automated in whole or in part at a reasonable cost? If yes, who will automate it—vendor, user or a third party? Make sure there is a definite plan for automating.

To make the most objective choice possible, test a few candidates (both with and without tools) yourself.

The following discussion is restricted to program development and maintenance, but the same testing process can also be used to evaluate systems analysis and design methods. It can encompass all activities from analysis to system maintenance.

First, select a typical program (2000 to 3000 lines of code) from the design of a system currently being developed. The system itself may be designed with any method. The selected program should be noncritical.

If you are not currently developing a system, select a stand-alone program or an existing unstructured program for rewriting.

Assume you are evaluating four methodologies. Select four programmers with equivalent capability and experience. They should have no knowledge or experience in the method they will be using.

These programmers, designated A, B, C and D, will develop the program. Assign a programmer to learn and use each method.

Using the same criteria, select another four programmers (a, b, c, d) with less experience than the first four. These programmers will serve as backup and will do maintenance when programs are installed.

For each method that has automated tools, select a programmer, using the same rules. In our example, we need a programmer for DSSD and Jackson methodology. Call them programmers $a_t$ and $b_t$. These programmers will develop the same program using tools. For maintenance with tools, two more programmers, $a_{tm}$ and $b_{tm}$, will be needed.

Next, assign each programmer to a methodology. Let each one select the method with which he would like to work. (If more than one programmer wants to work on the same method, flip a coin.)

If programmers have selected methods in sequence, the distribution may work out as in the table [see Fig. 13–2].

Thus, we need 12 reliable programmers.

For one week, give each programmer the best training available in his method. If possible, use the same kind of training for each method—for example, classroom or video courses.

Select an open-minded person to supervise these programmers. He should get an *overview* training in all the methodologies and should collect management and technical data during the project.

Appoint an independent observer, preferably an outsider consultant who is knowledgeable in the methods. Ideally, he should also take all four training courses.

Let programmers A, B, C, and D start working on the same program *separately*. Four versions of the program will be developed, using four methodologies. Backup programmers may be called in when the original programmers cannot work further. When not needed, backup programmers may work on other assignments.

Programmers $a_t$ and $b_t$ should develop the same program using tools and the appropriate methodology.

Programmers

| Method | Development | | Maintenance/modifications | |
|---|---|---|---|---|
| | Manual version | Tools-based version | Manual version | Tools-based version |
| DSSD | A | $a_t$ | a | $a_{tm}$ |
| Jackson methodology | B | $b_t$ | b | $b_{tm}$ |
| LCP | C | | c | |
| Yourdon/Constantine methodology | D | | d | |

Sample methods and programmer assignments

FIGURE 13.2 Sample methods and programmer assignments

Record progress data on a daily basis. Also, make sure that the methods are followed correctly. A consultant can guide, if necessary. It may even be possible to get help, on a voluntary basis, from the original developers of the methods.

Determine which data is to be collected and develop forms before the project starts. During the project, these forms may be modified, if necessary.

Examples of data that can be recorded are:

Time spent on different activities, such as program design, coding, testing, and documenting.

Daily progress, including progress in design, coded lines, tested lines, and so on.

Number of test runs and errors found after walk-throughs (if walk-throughs were conducted).

Use of automated tools and programming aids.

Other help used and time spent during such help.

Program completion date (when a program goes into production).

Any other pertinent data.

The real race begins when the programs go into production. Of course, the performance of the winner during development should be considered when selecting a methodology; however, the long, expensive maintenance cycle will probably decide the race. (The maintenance/modification cycle is like a "hurdles" race.) Let all programs be completed before beginning the maintenance race.

Next, change the programmers' assignments. Let a, b, c and d take over the maintenance of each manual version of the program and $a_{tm}$ and $b_{tm}$ take over the tool-based version. As we saw earlier, a, b, c, d, $a_{tm}$, and $b_{tm}$ served as backup programmers for programmers A, B, C, D, $a_t$, and $b_t$.

If any of the backup programmers had to work during development, he already knows the program and has an advantage. However, when he worked in development, there must have been some time elapsed in communicating—which may offset the advantage.

During maintenance, A, B, C, D, $a_t$ and $b_t$ are given other assignments; however, they should be available as backup programmers for maintenance.

If at any time backups are needed, deduct some points for that program, since the backup programmer already knows that program.

Give the same maintenance and modification assignment to each programmer.

Record the kinds of maintenance handled. The major classifications may be corrective (to correct problems), adaptive (to adapt to changing environment, such as operating system or hardware) and perfective (to take care of changing user requirements).

Record such data as quality of work, time taken and so on. Especially note the condition of documentation. It *must* be updated as the maintenance work is done.

The race may continue for one year after the programs go into production. Note that not all programmer time will be spent on maintenance during that period. If an existing program was redeveloped, maintenance may continue on the old program, to estimate savings resulting from redevelopment. However, the old program might have changed while the new versions of the program were being developed.

After the one-year maintenance race is completed, analyze the data. Rank the methodologies. Then, continue to use the highest ranking program. The program ranking second may be used as backup (i.e., a spare program, like a spare part in a system's machinery).

But how does one justify the cost of such a project? It will probably only be a front-end cost. Assuming the life of the program is 10 years and the best method saves at least 10% annually on maintenance, imagine the savings over a period of nine years. And the progam may last longer than that, especially when it is maintainable and well-documented.

But what if the highest ranking method is the one you might have selected anyway? This method confirms your choice.

In addition, you will also know the second best method and will have programmers who are trained and experienced in other methods, just in case.

The project may be repeated with different kinds of applications and environments.

Such projects may be conducted periodically, perhaps after a couple of years, but especially when the time comes to rewrite a system.

The method can be extended to include systems analysis and design methodologies. Some methods can be used in the entire software life cycle.

By selecting the best method for you, imagine the savings in all your new programs.

# *Unpaid Overtime: An Impediment To Increasing Programmer Productivity*

# 14

The custom of unpaid overtime for data processing (DP) professionals is sometimes called "a time-honored system." Most companies do not pay overtime to DP professionals. The only exceptions seem to be data-entry people and operators.

Programmers are generally considered professionals and as such usually do not qualify for overtime. I believe the unpaid overtime to programmers may be an impediment to increasing programmer productivity. Let us see how.

Unpaid overtime, as it does not cost management anything, may cause slackness in management. Managers take it for granted that programmers will be available seven days a week, around the clock, when required (or even when not required!), as programmers generally make themselves available for overtime. In some environments it seems to be a norm to work overtime. Believe it or not, it is often considered as part of a good performance and attitude!

The practice of unpaid overtime is usually unfair to the highly productive programmers. They tend to be penalized for their high competence!

However, working overtime does not necessarily mean that a programmer is more productive. In fact, presuming that the unfinished work can be done in overtime may reduce productivity during the working hours. Thus increasing productivity may become a moot point. How can this situation be corrected?

Perhaps the best way to correct this problem is to pay overtime to programmers. When costs are substantially increased by using programmers beyond normal working hours, management will attempt to make the most of the regular time of programmers. This cost consciousness will open the door for increasing programmer productivity. When overtime is paid, most programmers would be pleased to work extra hours. Some programmers may even stretch the work to create overtime. (When overtime is not paid, programmers stretch the work to do in overtime for different reasons, for example, to show that they work long hours and expect a good performance evaluation. In some cases they may even intentionally make errors so that they can correct them at night! Also, the management should plan better and use software engineering disciplines for managing projects, and make better estimates.

Nonetheless, the first step in increasing programmer productivity is to know their true worth which requires measurement. Unless we measure accurately, we have no way of evaluating performance fairly. When overtime is really necessary, it can be justified if we are sure that the programmer's productivity was optimum during the working hours. Such information will help in justifying overtime pay.

But how do we measure programmer productivity? There are several techniques available, and new methods are evolving. Chapter 7 gives some ideas. For further information refer to *How to Measure Programmer Productivity* (Parikh, 1981a), the video course "Measuring Programmer Productivity" developed by Parikh with DELTAK, Inc., and other references listed in the Bibliography. The video course texts include lists of selected readings.

Another point raised in regard to overtime payment to programmers is that programmers, as professionals, do not qualify for overtime. Are programmers really professionals? In some companies, when management wants programmers to work unpaid overtime, they call them "professionals"; but do not otherwise treat them so. This management attitude is negative. The debate over the work of programmers—whether it is an art or science—goes on.

My view is that at the present time programming is a craft. It involves the art as well as the science of programming. The advent of structured programming and software engineering technologies indicates that programming is on its way to becoming an engineering discipline. With the work of eminent systems scientists such as Jean-Dominique Warnier and Harlan Mills, the discipline may even approach a science, drawing fundamentals from mathematical disciplines such as set theory, Boolean algebra, and function metrics. Systematic programming discipline will help measure programmer productivity precisely, and programming will become a profession.

Also, when maintenance programmers are paid overtime, high maintenance costs will spur managers to develop maintainable software in the first place. This will help improve software development as well as maintenance productivity.

Another reason programmers are called on to put in overtime relates to mistakes of management in estimating projects. Sometimes the deadline, based on imagination alone, is handed down from higher-level management. Lower-level management accepts this without question and, without asking the opinion of programmers, imposes this deadline on them. Most programmers recognize an impossible deadline, and the futility of arguing with the boss. In some cases they may be asked to estimate, but this is just a routine to appease programmers. Most technicians are over optimistic and cannot develop realistic estimates. They tend to come up with an estimate that management would like to see, or agree with management's estimate. Thus they may be digging their own grave. The inevitable result is 80-hour workweeks for several months.

The other aspect of unpaid overtime is related to social considerations. I do not know of any statistics regarding unhappy, broken marriages because of unpaid overtime. Unpaid overtime does not show up on the paycheck. The spouse has no way of knowing whether it was a genuine overtime or rampant infidelity. This creates social tensions. What does this have to do with programmer productivity? Social instability and tensions do affect a person's productivity, but the subject needs further research and social study.

Another aspect of unpaid overtime is the stress it causes. It may demand working under pressure, sometimes unfairly. For example, when a programmer is called at midnight to fix a problem in a program that abends, and the results are required immediately (e.g., paychecks to be delivered in the morning), the stress on the programmer may be traumatic. His job may be at stake. To add insult to injury, the program may not have been developed by him. He is being punished for the sins of others (possibly the sins of his own manager!), who developed an unstructured, unreliable program.

Data processing professionals thus work under stress. Under stress, productivity sometimes gets diminished. Stress and productivity usually do not go together. However, a few programmers may be most productive under stress, but they may be an exception. (Maintenance programmers, under present unstructured environments, are required to work under stress. The subject of measuring and improving their productivity under such situations is an interesting subject of research.)

This brings us to the topic of going an extra mile. When a programmer does not agree to work unpaid overtime, the management may label it as bad attitude. I believe that it is a question of how much unpaid overtime a programmer should be willing to work. If he considers working overtime occasionally as going the extra mile, it is a commendable part of a programmer's performance. However, expecting that he will work unreasonable hours of overtime is too much to expect. I was a programmer for many years and I usually avoided overtime by being more productive during working hours. I did work overtime, but only occasionally. As a programmer, I accepted the need to go the extra mile—it was a good policy to work a little more than what I was paid for—but it is bad business to go extra *miles* all the time. As the company is in the business of making money, so am I to sell my services at the best possible price. To make myself more valuable to the company, which should profit both parties, I definitely kept myself continually improving; that is, I looked for ways to keep educating myself to increase my productivity. Management should also provide the necessary means, including training, to increase one's productivity, and benefit both parties.

Think over the subject of unpaid (and paid) overtime. If you are a manager, and are convinced that paying overtime to programmers may help increase the productivity of your programmers (and thereby yours as well), give me a call. I might be interested!

# Programmer Productivity Tips

# 15

## A PRODUCTIVE PROGRAMMER IS A READING PROGRAMMER

"A professional is known by the books he reads!"

It is claimed, or rather "complained," that dataprocessing professionals don't read books! And professionals who do not read (professional) books do not remain professionals long—their knowledge becomes obsolete. They become outdated and less useful to their employers. Especially in a rapidly growing field such as the computer field, it is almost mandatory that computer professionals read books and trade periodicals in their field.

I recall one incident. I called a local member of a consulting association. He was a senior data processing professional with many years of experience. When I mentioned that I had written books based on my experiences, he advised me, "When you look for a contract programming assignment, don't ever say you've written a book. You may not get work!"

For more thoughts on this vital topic, read (I hope you are a reading programmer) Chapter 19 if you are a programmer, or Chapter 20 if you are a manager.

## BE A THINKING PROGRAMMER

Are you only a "programming" programmer? Be a "thinking" programmer also. A thinking programmer is a more productive programmer.

What does a thinking programmer do?

1. A thinking programmer, of course "thinks."
2. Because he thinks, he designs his solutions before coding.
3. He thinks over the design—or the conceptual design sits in his mind, as his subconscious is working on it. His thoughts are: Will that solution work? Is it the best one? What are the alternatives? How can it be implemented? What could be the further problems or benefits?
4. The thinking programmer thinks over the code.
5. The thinking programmer thinks over the testing process and results.
6. The thinking programmer thinks over the maintenance process.

It may seem that a thinking programmer thinks all the time. When does he work? Programming is one of the most intellectually challenging activities, and thinking is an absolutely essential part if you want to be productive. However, the process of thinking can be disciplined. Training can even be given in thinking.

### Logical Thinking

If you are familiar with Jean-Dominique Warnier's work, you have heard the term "logical." Logical design is the heart of Warnier's approach—even his approach is called a "logical" approach. The process of logical design does need thinking; however, it is disciplined thinking, and I believe programmers can be taught this way of thinking.

## TIME MANAGEMENT FOR PROGRAMMERS

### How to Make the Most of Meetings

Meetings can be a great time waster. Some programmers, being introverted, dislike meetings. They prefer to work on their own at their desks once they are given the specifications. However, most managers and supervisors do ask the programmers to attend meetings. In a few cases even the design work is done by meetings.

Sometimes managers hold meetings periodically to evaluate the progress on a project. Programmers are asked to attend the meetings in order to discuss schedules and other problems. Then there are performance evaluation meetings—perhaps the most important meetings for programmers. I will offer tips about them later.

From my experience I have found that most meetings waste the valuable time of programmers. (If you consider walkthroughs as meetings, well-conducted walkthroughs certainly help improve the quality of a programmer's work.) Long discussions may be necessary before any decisions are made. When decisions are not reached, more meetings may be necessary, wasting more time.

Once I worked in a group where the supervisor preferred to design a system in meetings. It took most of the day to come to some design decisions. Although I was expected to attend such meetings, I generally prefered to work at the desk and liked to get a summary of what happened in the meetings. I believe I progressed faster this way.

Then there are unscheduled meetings. The boss comes to your desk, and asks "Have you got a minute?" You are concentrating on a problem, you stare at your boss for a few seconds, then leave what are you doing and go with your boss. Instead of a minute, you return to your desk after several hours. You cannot say no to your boss, and you waste a lot of time. Whenever possible, insist on scheduling a meeting.

Following are general guidelines to make the most of meetings:

1. *Know the subject of a meeting in advance*. Try to get the agenda of the meeting.
2. *Do your homework*. Preferably write down points briefly so that the points of discussion are highlighted. When you have an agenda or list of topics to be discussed in a meeting, you will be able to prepare for it.
3. Stick to the subject so that all issues can be covered. During the meeting try to focus on the subject that is being discussed.
4. Resolve all issues within, at the most, three meetings.
5. Keep the duration of the meeting reasonable. Informal meetings may last for 20 to 30 minutes, while formal meetings should not take more than one hour. About one hour is the time in which concentrated discussions can be held; if it stretches beyond that, concentration wavers.
6. Take notes and summarize immediately. While points are being discussed, take notes of relevant points. It may be a good idea to make one person responsible for noting the highlights and summarizing them later for distribution to the participants.

7. When certain discussions in subsequent meetings supersede those in previous meetings, this should be indicated clearly in the summary.
8. After a few meetings make a master summary of previous meetings related to all topics.
9. Alternate the persons who make the notes and master summaries in meetings.
10. Schedule the next meeting, if one is needed, before ending the meeting.
11. On each page write the date of the meeting and the initials of the participants.
12. Try to be frank and honest. However, depending on the situation, you may have to be diplomatic.
13. Circle or underline the key words in meeting summaries.

## Performance Evaluation Meeting

Here are some tips to make the most of the performance evaluation meeting.

### *Tips for Programmers*

1. Do your homework. Prepare for the evaluation meeting. Make a list of the assignments completed during the evaluation period (see Figure 15-1). If you keep a list of work done on an ongoing basis, you will already have such data in your hands. (You may use the handy form shown in Figure 15-1. I have used such forms while I was a programmer. In fact, I once managed to get a better raise by listing what I had done on such forms!) The lists of work done may be broken down into: completed new program assignments, completed maintenance/enhancements assignments, new program assignments under progress, and maintenance/enhancement assignments under progress. Do not forget to list the courses completed or under progress, list of professional books read, conferences/seminars attended, and suggestions made for improvements in your environment.
2. Analyze yourself before, and after, the evaluation meeting. Be honest with yourself. What are your goals? What do you want to accomplish? What are your strengths and weaknesses? To achieve your

Programming/Maintenance/Enhancements Assignments Record

During ________________ Through ________________ Programmer: ____________

Department: ____________

| Number | Assignment No. | Project No. | System | Program(s) Involved | Short Description | Comments/ Completed On |
|---|---|---|---|---|---|---|
| | | | | | | |

FIGURE 15.1 Form for recording programming assignments

goals, do you want to build on your strengths, or would you like to correct the weaknesses?

3. Write down your goals. When you put your goals on paper, they become clearer. In putting goals on paper, you are forced to think. You also get a sense of commitment that is required to achieve the goals.
4. Collect your own productivity data. If your company does not have a programmer productivity measurement program, design your own measurements while working on assignments. Such data can also be helpful for self-analysis. Start with simple measures and refine them with experience.
5. Be pleasant and diplomatic in the evaluation meeting. However, if you think you are right, be forceful and persistent. Do not get intimidated.

### *Tips for Programming Managers*

1. Do your homework. Review your notes about programmer performance. If your company has the programmer productivity measurement program, you can access these data. (Unfortunately, many companies do not have such a program. In that case you will have to depend on your own data.)
2. Be as objective as possible. This is difficult. You may have prejudices. You either like a programmer, or you don't. Or you may be indifferent. The programmer might have argued with you. In spite of all this, just remember: You are evaluating the programmer's work, *not* the programmer. Try to keep personal matters out of your evaluation.
3. Make evaluation a two-way street. Let the programmer present his side. Encourage him to speak out and listen carefully from the programmer's point of view. If possible, let the programmer fill out the evaluation form before the meeting.
4. Focus on the accomplishments of the programmer. Make it a positive evaluation meeting. Don't play on the weaknesses and mistakes of the programmer. Everyone who *works*, or tries new techniques, may make mistakes. Bring the strengths of the programmer into focus.
5. Be constructive in your critique. How can the weaknesses be corrected? What can be done so that the mistakes will not be repeated? How can the performance be improved upon?
6. Also discuss the goals and aspirations of the programmer. What does he really want to do? Does he feel a sense of accomplishment? How can you make the best use of his talents?

## TIPS FOR ORGANIZING

A well-organized programmer uses his or her time more effectively and productively. With rising programming costs and scarcity of resources, it is imperative that programmer time be used wisely.

However, programmers are rarely taught to organize themselves to make the most of their time. Managers are concerned about their time and may attend seminars on time management; however, programmers are usually not given this opportunity. Programmers also have to manage their time, and need discipline and training in this vital area.

Programmers well organized in their personal life may also be organized in their programming work. They can also use productive organization techniques to achieve further improvement.

Now picture in your mind a disorganized programmer (see Figure 15-2). Probably you will not have to stretch your imagination. You may be such a programmer (be honest; I wouldn't be candid if I didn't say that at one time I was such a programmer), or if you are a manager, you certainly have seen one. However, the discipline of organization can be learned and applied. It may need training.

Often we see the desk of a programmer crowded with several feet of listings, a bundle of dumps, scattered manuals, a bunch of coding sheets, scratch pads with illegible (even for the programmer!) scribblings, and of course a cup of coffee. To find a particular paper the programmer may nervously search the drawers, the desktop, and even the garbage can!

A disorganized desk may reduce the effectiveness of even the most productive programmer. In a hectic environment it is inevitable that his desk will get disorganized occasionally. He may also have a habit of saving almost everything as a back up or for his protection.

Sometimes there may be organization in disorganization. This seems to

FIGURE 15.2

be contradictory; however, if a programmer is able to find what he needs quickly, he is naturally organized, although to others he may seem disorganized. Sometimes a programmer may intentionally remain disorganized, while at the same time he may know where things are and may be able to find out quickly. The reason for this kind of (dis)organization may be to protect himself, or to make his knowledge a secret, or to increase his importance, and have a feeling of job security—although "job security" is a myth.

When the programmer is sick or goes on vacation, others who may have to work on his assignment will have a difficult time. Does this indicate that we should have standards of physical organization? We have all kinds of standards in data processing—why not organization standards as well?

This brings us to the method of physical organization of the programmer's work environment. In every department there is usually at least one programmer who is very productive. Study his work habits and organization methods. Try to use a similar method with other programmers. Improve on it and document it. Try this as a pilot project on one friendly and cooperative department. Measure the productivity of programmers before and after the pilot project. I believe the same programmers, when organized, will become more productive.

While I was working as a programmer for many years, I took time occasionally to clean up my desk. If I did this work after a long time, naturally it took more time to clean up. But after cleaning up, I always felt more productive and self-assured.

How can a manager know that a programmer is well organized? He can ask for certain paper and see how long it takes for the programmer to find it.

A programmer librarian can help programmers get and keep themselves organized. In addition to helping in light technical areas, a librarian can act as a technical secretary to programmers. A good technician may be a poor organizer (although this habit can be changed with discipline and training) and may need help.

Why do managers ignore this important aspect of programmer productivity? They probably consider it to be a personal matter and let the programmer organize in the way he wants. However, like training in other technical areas, most programmers also need training and discipline to get themselves organized.

How do you get and *keep* yourself organized, and make the most of your time? One excellent book on organization is *Making Time Work for You: A Guide Book to Effective and Productive Time Management* by Harold L. Taylor (Taylor, 1981). It contains excellent tips and techniques to control time and get yourself organized. This book should be mandatory reading for every programmer and every programming manager.

Taylor's book gives guidelines for organizing yourself for effective use of time. It strongly urges you to take action. Unless you take action, reading books may not make much sense.

Incidentally, programming is considered one of the more stressful professions. Maintenance programming, especially, can be extremely stressful. If you are well organized, it may help reduce stress. Also, the organized material will help you solve problems more effectively. (Tips for dealing with stress are given later in this chapter.)

One good system of organizing your documents and files is "mNemoDex," developed by Robert M. Gordon. A computerized mNemoDex system (for a microcomputer) is available from Robert M. Gordon, P.O. Box 4874, Irvine, CA 92716. The following column written by Robert B. Forest in *Infosystems* magazine includes a capsule description of mNemoDex.

## GETTING ORGANIZED[1]

**by Robert B. Forest**

For some reason there is etched in my mind a scene from a W.C. Fields movie, the name of which I have forgotten. Fields is an employee of a bank, where his sole value is that he knows everything about every key transaction and every client the bank has ever had, even though his desk looks as if the cleaning person has been casually dumping the contents of several large waste baskets on top of it for several weeks.

### Losers Weepers

On the screen in my head, Fields is asked to locate some key document. He saunters over to the desk, and almost in a trance allows his hand to hover over the mess. Then, with a delicate, darting movement, he reaches into the pile and comes up with the piece of paper his manager has asked him to retrieve.

This was before the days of automated information retrieval systems, of course. But most of us still don't make use of those gadgets at all. We

[1]Reprinted from *Infosystems*, August 1978; © copyright 1978 by Hitchcock Publishing Co.

have filing cabinets, and book shelves, and rotary files, and little files full of business cards. And smart assistants. Then there are those stacks of papers on our desks.

We get a piece of information, and we jot it down. Into the stack it goes. Someday we'll file it in an appropriate place. You bet. What was the name of that consultant who specializes in DP audits? Somebody has published a check list of security precautions. Saw it around here somewhere just the other day. Wonder where I put it? Where's the latest version of our organization chart, Charlie? Did we file that report on programming productivity under the name of the company that did it...or by subject matter?

There's a lot of talk about the need to know. I claim that the problem is the need to *find*. Most of us see enough papers cross our desks in one day to justify a personal shredder. There's always enough time to glance at most of these, make a mental note...and never enough time to do more than put off figuring out what to do with them.

One approach to solving this problem is to establish a filing system. In this column in December of 1976, I described one such system devised by consultant Bill Helgason.

I guess the column had an effect on one reader, at least. Because several months ago I heard from an old friend of mine named Bob Gordon, who had had a visitor who mentioned that column and wondered how Gordon kept track of his stuff. Gordon, who was probably born in the stacks of a university library, obliged by showing him his filing scheme. Later, he showed it to me.

## Seek and Ye Shall Find

What Mr. Gordon has done is to develop a very general and simple system that allows you to enter information (about objects or information or people or...) in a random, sequential manner, then label it or cross-index it any way you want for later retrieval. You don't have to construct a big metaphysical filing scheme, labeling ahead of time all the boxes into which you may conceivably someday put things in.

He calls his system mNemoDex, a combination of mnemonic and index, or "a system for aiding memory and facilitating access to members of a collection." It's pronounced knee-mow-decks.

It consists of two kinds of notebooks, filled with carefully designed forms. In one notebook, you enter, in sequential fashion, descriptors of the items or information you want to be able to look up. You assign to each entry an identifier number. Gordon uses identifiers YY.NNNN, where YY is the year the item is recorded, and the Ns are the serial accession or entry numbers. You also jot down the index terms for this item, a brief summary or abstract, and any comments you want to include...like where you put the dadblamed thing.

Now, for each index term, you turn to the alphabetized index notebook, and create an index entry that lists the identifier numbers of the pages where you'll find the original entry in the descriptor notebook.

## Personal or Public

I don't have space here to go into all the other features of mNemoDex, but as a proud owner and user, I can tell you that it is both flexible and easy to use. It's helpful, too. If you want to use it primarily as a personal retrieval system, you can index quite casually, knowing that you will always look for an organization chart, for instance, under that heading. If several people are going to use it, you'll want to be more thoughtful—more formal and thorough—in the way you index things.

One problem that most people anticipate when they first hear about mNemoDex is how they are ever going to transfer into it all the information they now have. For most of us, that would use up more time than we have, or are willing to spend.

What I'm doing is starting by cataloguing all of my personal possessions. As I get information—or have to look for something—I mNemoDex it right away. Eventually, I'll get organized. In the meantime, I know where the deed to my house is, and my insurance policies. I know what stocks I own, when I bought them, what I paid for them, and where the certificates are.

mNemoDex is, I am happy to report, available to the general public. To expedite matters, I suggest that if you want to know more, you go straight to the head mNemoDexer, Bob Gordon.

Let's see. It's right here in my mNemoDex under "information storage and retrieval," and "filing systems"—Robert M. Gordon, P.O. Box 4874, Irvine, CA 92716.

## LET'S GET AWAY FROM MACHINES!

With the advent of microcomputers, we are becoming even more machine oriented, but we should always remember that machines are our servants, not our masters. We should control machines; not let machines control us.

To keep this perspective on machines which serve us, and problems which face us, it is helpful to get away from them regularly. When I say "Let's get away from machines," it sounds like a crazy idea, doesn't it?

Let's see how getting away from machines temporarily might be beneficial to productivity.

We are usually too close to machines. A terminal is so handy that we normally rush to it to solve the problems. The more hours spent on the terminal, the busier one seems. However, we should consider whether we are losing the art of thinking. Thinking through a problem at mental speeds permits investigation of several possible solutions before going to a terminal. There, we are constrained by keyboard speed. So outline the solution before implementing it. (At implementation stage, the outline keeps our minds from wandering during the tedium of transcription.)

We also need to develop the discipline of thinking logically, that is, thinking independently of hardware and programming language.

In short let's get away from computers for a while, develop our reasoning, and think logically!

## TIPS TO REDUCE STRESS

Programming is considered to be a stressful profession, with maintenance programming an extreme. As we saw earlier good physical organization can help reduce stress. Here are some other tips for reducing stress:

1. Do the best you can and then forget about it. This is easier said than done. However, practice may lead you to that kind of behavior. (Candidly, I must confess that I have tried without success at achieving that state of mind. Most of the time I have carried the problems with me in my mind, and have brooded over them. However, this has one advantage. I have found solutions to some problems by contemplation; for others, I have been able to outline the actions that I would like to take. In this sense I can be accused of working countless hours of unpaid overtime! I suspect that many programmers do the same thing.)
2. Imagine the worst that can happen. If worst comes to worst you may have to find another job. It may not be bad; on the contrary, it may even be better.
3. Meditate. Meditation not only helps you to relax but also helps to improve concentration which is essential for productive program-

ming. Regular meditation helps you focus your attention, gives you a better perspective on your work, and gives you strength. After a time your own mind becomes your teacher and guides you.

4. Relax. Take a break from work. Perform another activity, such as cleaning your desk or reading a fiction, or nonfiction book. (Be aware of the attitude of the management on this. They may not like reading at the desk other than the programming manual. However, during your break, you may read other material or even take a nap.)
5. Develop a hobby. Search within yourself to discover what else you really enjoy doing. Develop that hobby and devote yourself to it in your spare time.
6. Exercise. Proper exercise can not only help to keep you healthy, but it can help you to get relieved of stress. I have found walking to be the best exercise. I believe it is an ideal exercise for sedentary professions like programming. After a walk of a couple of miles, blood will circulate more freely in your veins, and you will feel refreshed and ready to attack problems.

I urge you before it is too late to read the essay "Personal Chemistry and the Healthy Body" by Gerald M. Weinberg in his book *Understanding the Professional Programmer*. [See the Bibliography.]

## INTELLECTUAL PRODUCTIVITY

The subject of intellectual productivity is not well understood. What is intellectual productivity, and how can it affect programmer productivity?

The conscious and unconscious activities associated with programmer productivity can be called intellectual productivity. The programmer may not seem to be productive while engaged in an intellectual pursuit; but his productivity may be affected by these activities. For example, a maintenance programmer may spend almost an entire day turning pages of a program listing, or keep scrolling the program on a terminal, or keep shuffling the documentation pages. He does not seem to be producing any useful work, but subconsciously he is getting absorbed in the product and the related material. This familiarity is valuable while working on that product.

How can a manager be sure that the programmer is engaged in an intellectual activity and not simply relaxing? If the manager knows the productivity of the programmer, that is, his track record, he need not worry.

## STRUCTURED WALKTHROUGHS, PROGRAMMER PRODUCTIVITY TOOLS, AND OBJECTIVE/ SUBJECTIVE PRODUCTIVITY MEASUREMENTS

Structured walkthroughs detect

1. Errors
2. Omissions
3. Misunderstandings

Programmer productivity tools (also called software tools—software packages that aid productivity) provide objective measures. The objective measures help the subjective measures.

For example, if 1500 lines are added in a program, RES-Q (see Chapter 12) makes these new lines readily available for a walkthrough. Arrange the required number of walkthrough sessions (e.g., three, to review 500 lines in each review).

In summary:

Use objective measurement data provided by productivity tools.

Then apply subjective measures to assess productivity.

Use objective and subjective measures to get the productivity measures: faster and more accurate.

Why do objective measures make productivity measurement faster and more accurate?

The productivity tools provide the objective measures automatically and fast.

The productivity tools also provide standard, consistent, and reliable output.

You can evaluate productivity faster when supported by data from productivity tools.

## JOB HOPPING

According to one survey, programmers change jobs every one and one half years. There are several reasons for job hopping—job stagnation, obsolete technologies, and so on.

During my 16-year programming career, I changed jobs every one and one half years, like a typical programmer. In my early career, I also had a stint of freelance programming—also, coincidently, for one and a one half years. I was almost always looking for better and easier ways to do things. My frustration increased after I came to know about structured programming. At that time, unfortunately (or fortunately), I was stuck in almost impossible maintenance work. The only reason I stayed on in that job was that the system was to be redeveloped using improved programming technologies, including structured programming, and I wanted to have firsthand experience with the new technologies.

At another place, reluctance to adopt better techniques turned me off. I demonstrated the power of the Warnier/Orr diagram; however, management refused to give up HIPO!

I have been searching for better methods of program development and program maintenance most of my career. In order to try emerging technologies, I kept changing jobs. (I usually do not believe in a technique until I try it myself.) I found the consulting environments more challenging than the user environments.

Depressing maintenance work may be one of the instigators in promoting job hopping. Money may be another reason. Sometimes new hires earn more money than that earned by a senior programmer in a company. If that is the result of staying longer with a company, job hopping is the sensible way to keep up in salary.

Nonetheless, before job hopping, do a self-analysis. Why do you want to change jobs? What are your goals? Discuss this frankly with your boss. If that does not help, consider going to higher-level management. In most cases, higher-level management may be more understanding. If there is nothing (or very little) to lose, and everything (possibly) to gain, by all means try!

Try to stay at least one year in a single job. One programmer I know always started looking for another job the day he started a new one! After some time, even in a big city like Chicago, he had difficulty in finding any job.

## Programmer Turnover: A Management Problem

High programmer turnover, frequently higher than 30%, costs the DP industry heavily. Nonetheless, not all turnover is bad. In a few cases turnover is even desirable to get new programmers on board. How can you solve the problem of high turnover? Here are some suggestions:

1. Give incentives, raises, etc.
2. Improve and measure programmer productivity. Reward productive programmers. Train less productive programmers.
3. Keep current, if not ahead, of technologies, within budget and constraints. Especially, use modern software technologies.
4. Treat programmers as human beings.
5. Give comp time (equivalent time off) or preferably, pay overtime. But make the most of the working time of programmers. Measuring programmer productivity can help.
6. Set up productivity circles to discuss productivity issues and other problems.
7. Improve maintenance environments. (Maintenance may be your most vulnerable area.) Set up training programs for maintenance programmers. Use logical retrofit concepts outlined in Chapter 16.

## POLITICS AND PROGRAMMER PRODUCTIVITY

Politics is a touchy subject. Not much has been written on the political aspects of data processing environments. It is an important factor when considering improvements in productivity.

Whenever two or more persons come together to work, politics is present. How can programmer productivity be increased in spite of politics? This section presents some ideas.

Generally, programmers are not very political. If an experienced programmer working many years in the same company remained a programmer, it may be for one of two reasons: he loves programming, (technical problems) and dislikes management (people problems), or he is not political.

Being political involves working with people. Programmers who prefer working with machines rather than with people may consider people unpredictable, and machines reliable.

One political fact of life is that when a project does not work, corporate politicians look for a scapegoat. They want to blame someone else for their own mistakes and incompetence, to save their own skins. The poor programmer is a logical scapegoat because of limited knowledge of the business and often short job tenure. (I was once made the scapegoat on a project. Since then I have promised myself that if I ever write a computer dictionary,

I will include the word "scapegoat." I suspect that no computer dictionary includes it.)

How can programmer productivity be increased in a political environment, or in spite of politics? Here are some suggestions.

1. Be diplomatic in your dealings with management and with other programmers.
2. Study *The Psychology of Computer Programming* (Weinberg, 1971).
3. Try to maintain good relations with everyone. Be clear about what you want, and gently insist on it if you are right.
4. Set up your goals. If they are not in conflict with your job, let your boss know about them. If they conflict with your job, resolve them, or change jobs.
5. If your strength is in technical areas, get help from others, preferably your supervisor, in fighting political battles. Show him how your technical contribution can help to achieve *his* goals.
6. Try to do the best professional job under all conditions, and then forget about it.
7. Do not become intimidated. When you are right, let management know about it in clear and firm, but polite language.
8. Keep records, especially on your time spent, problems reported, and productivity records, for your protection.
9. Even though you are absorbed in technical work, keep your eyes and ears open.
10. Hiss, but do not bite. This suggestion is based on a parable from Sri Ramakrishna (see the *Gospel of Sri Ramakrishna* by Mahendranath Gupta). Let me relate the story briefly.

Once a holy man was passing through a village. Some children warned him not to continue down that street as a poisonous snake lived there. The holy man said that he knew a mantra, and the snake could not harm him. The snake dashed towards the holy man. The holy man recited the mantra, and the snake couldn't harm him.

Then the holy man gave a mantra to the snake, asked him to repeat it, and instructed him not to injure anyone. In due course, he would be liberated, the holy man promised.

After several years the holy man returned to the village and asked about the snake. The children said that it was dead. The holy man couldn't believe it. He went near the snake's hole and called him. The snake slowly crawled out.

"Why are you so thin?" asked the holy man.

"I didn't injure anyone. So children picked me up and threw me against the wall. They bothered me all the time. At night, when they were gone, I came out to find food."

"Shame on you! I asked you not to injure anyone, but I did not tell you not to hiss!"

The snake realized his mistake and followed the guru's advice.

The above are a few tips to help increase programmer productivity. You may add your own tips from your experience. Also start clipping from periodicals and making notes from books. Thus you will have a collection of ideas for increasing programmer productivity.

# *Logical Retrofit For Enhancing Maintenance Programming Productivity*

# 16

"Let's stop groping in the dark world of software maintenance as it is now. Warnier has shown the light. Let's follow him!"

Jean-Dominque Warnier begins his classic book *Logical Construction of Programs* (Warnier, 1974) with the following intriguing questions.

> Can programs be designed, coded, debugged and implemented 5 to 10 times faster than is usual? Can programs be written so as to run correctly at the first effective trial? Can program memory occupation and processing time be considerably reduced and, above all, can perfectly clear program documentation be obtained thus reducing maintenance time to a minimum?
>
> The answers to all these questions, from the experience in several hundred companies, in France as in other countries, is "yes."

The method that achieves the dramatic results in program development, as well as in maintenance, is Warnier's LCP (Logical Construction of Programs). In fact, Warnier wrote the world's first book on software maintenance titled *Program Modification* (Warnier, 1978). Thus Warnier is the pioneer in this neglected, but vital area of software technologies. He gives precise, step-by-step procedures to modify LCP programs. The modifications are reliable and work on the first or second effective test, and the testing is thorough. In the process the documentation is updated since the design of modification is done using the clear and complete documentation of existing LCP program. Even after several changes, the program remains like new.

Since the original LCP program is correct to start with, and it reflects the specifications, corrective maintenance—that is, correction of errors and abends—almost disappears. What remains is modification of LCP programs to meet the changing requirements of the users and changes in external requirements (e.g., government rules and regulations). This is systematic and specialized work in which a programmer can be trained. The work becomes exciting as the modifications are done using the precise techniques defined by Warnier.

---

## WHAT IS LCP?

LCP is a powerful structured programming technique based on data structured concepts developed by Warnier. The method is based on mathematical principles, especially set theory and Boolean algebra. The coverge of LCP is beyond the scope of this chapter; refer to *Logical Construction of Programs* (Warnier, 1974), *Program Modification* (Warnier, 1978), and *Practical LCP: A Direct Approach to Structured Programming* (Gardner, 1981) for details.

Thus LCP gives the best of all worlds, including the world of development, and the world of software maintenance.

## STRUCTURED RETROFIT

The term "structured retrofit" was coined by my good friend Cris Miller. Miller explains the term "retrofit" thusly:

> Retro means to go backward. Fit has many definitions, one of which is to alter or modify. Retrofit is generally applied to mechanical assemblies. In general, design improvements developed subsequent to production are "retrofitted" to the existing assembly, to gain the benefits of new design without assuming all the costs of new production. The term is used in exactly this sense for the improving of systems in production. Note that design improvements may relate to performance, reliability, or ease of maintenance—none of which affect the system inputs or outputs—as well as to new requirements, in which inputs and outputs may change.

See Chapter 1 in this book, and the chapter "Structured Retrofit" by Miller in (Parikh, (1982a), or (Parikh and Zvegintzov (1983a), for a brief introduction to Miller's pioneering concepts. The Bibliography in this book lists papers by Lyons and Miller on structured retrofit.

"Structured retrofit" (primarily based on "functional" structured programming concepts pioneered by Miller) was a step forward in solving some of the problems of maintaining existing unstructured programs. However, I believe "logical retrofit" (primarily based on "data" structured concepts pioneered by Warnier) offers a better solution.

## WHAT IS LOGICAL RETROFIT?

Logically restructuring existing programs using LCP concepts is called "logical retrofit." This process can be partially automated. Total automation, even if feasible, may not be advisable. Logical retrofit is data structured translation of an existing program into an LCP program. The program translation involves logical reconstruction of the program; however, the programming language of the new program may remain the same as that of the original program. The retrofit is *not* done according to "functional" structured programming techniques, but it is data structured retrofit according to Warnier's logical approach, so it is called logical retrofit.

### Concepts of Logical Retrofit

Logical retrofit provides semiautomated procedures of restructuring existing programs into LCP programs. It includes techniques based on the work of Warnier, and Gardner; appropriate graphic diagramming tools such as the Warnier diagram, the Warnier flowchart, truth tables, and (Gardner's) structure diagrams; and training for programmers and programming managers. Instead of Warnier's tools (Warnier diagram, Warnier flowchart, and truth tables), structured diagrams (which are hierarchical boxes with additional symbols and conventions) can be used.

### Guidelines for Restructuring an Existing Program into an LCP Program

Extract the logical output structures, logical input structures, and process structures from the existing program—proceeding from output, then input, then processes. How much time should you spend in understanding an existing program? In some cases, however hard you may try, you may not be able to decipher a program completely! Restructure the required processes (to get outputs from inputs), if they are obscure in the existing program.

The outputs and inputs of the program are available. Use them. The logical documentation developed for the existing program can also help current maintenance work. The program can be converted into an LCP program in two ways: incremental replacement, and total replacement. Total replacement may be preferable in order to preserve the logical integrity.

## Logical Retrofit of Systems

In the discussion above, logical retrofit of programs was described. The long-range plan may include retrofitting systems. In the short range, program retrofits can save substantial money, providing funds for systems retrofit. The process of logical retrofit for systems can be developed using LCS (Warnier's Logical Construction of Systems) concepts.

## How Much Money Can Logical Retrofit Save?

Using the worst-first maintenance concept (Weinberg's 80/20 rule, see Parikh, 1982a), that is, improving the worst parts of a program or a system by logical retrofit, will save money to pay for further retrofitting work. The increased processing speed of retrofitted programs may also save a substantial amount of money. Also, improved maintenance programming productivity may payoff handsomely.

According to one industry guru, $30 billion are spent annually worldwide on software maintenance. How much is maintenance cost in the United States? According to one estimate, there are 500,000 programmers in America. Taking the average salary of each programmer at $20,000 per year, this would cost $10 billion. If they spend on average 50 percent of their time on maintenance, as several studies reveal, the maintenance costs would be $5 billion annually. (This is a very conservative figure.) If logical retrofit can save 10 percent, the savings would be a whopping $500 million annually in programming costs alone, not to mention the savings in processing time.

## Increases in Programmer Productivity with LCP Programs

Parikh productivity metrics (see Chapter 7) can help determine the productivity gains obtained by converting existing programs into LCP programs. Also bebugging technique (see Tom Gilb's chapter in Parikh, 1982a) can help in assessing the benefits of logical retrofitting. The bebugging technique involves inserting an artifical bug in a program, and then giving it to a programmer who does not know about it, for debugging. The programmer's performance can reveal the maintainability of the program. Insert the same bugs in the old program and the new LCP program, and give to two programmers with same experience and competence. (The programmer selected to work on the LCP program should be trained in LCP program modification.) The improved performance of the LCP programmer would indicate the benefits of retrofitting. The bebugging concept can be extended to test the ease of enhancing LCP programs. Maintenance can become exciting work with logically retrofitted programs.

### Logical Documentation

The logical documentation generated during the logical retrofit is generally independent of hardware and programming language. This documentation can be saved and possibly automatically updated for reference. This can provide valuable documentation for future redevelopments.

## WHY LCP/LCS FOR SOFTWARE REDEVELOPMENT?

Why use LCP/LCS for redevelopment, not a functional method? (See Chapter 13 for a discussion of functional and data structured methods.) With LCS, you design relational data files, and programs are done with LCP, the method which is also based on the concepts of sets and subsets. In fact, the input and output data and programs are considered data in logical methodologies. This means that design of data and programs are based on the same principles of set theory. Also, the precise guidelines for maintenance work are available for LCP. The methods of program development as well as modification can be taught. To my knowledge, no other methods (except Jackson's, to some extent) have provided precise guidelines for maintenance.

### Logical Redevelopment

When the creation of a new LCP program from an existing one is not an exact translation, but there are new features or improvements in the new program compared to the old one, we may call the process "logical redevelopment." Logical redevelopment is also based on Warnier's methodologies.

The entire software systems can also be redeveloped. The modern hardware and software technologies, such as data base management systems (DBMS), and fourth-generation languages, may be used when appropriate with Warnier's methodologies for redeveloping software. (Incidently, the fourth-generation languages themselves can be designed using LCP/LCS.) The logical redevelopment of software systems is based on Warnier's "logical structured methodologies," the primary methodologies being LCS and LCP. (For a brief overview of Warnier's methodologies, see Warnier's paper in Parikh, Zvegintzov, 1983a.)

## CONCLUSION

Thus, logical retrofit may save a substantial amount of money and costly maintenance effort, and improve programmer morale. Management and technicians should consider logical retrofitting of programs and systems.

# Maintaining/Enhancing Applications Software Packages Productively

# 17

There has been a phenomenal growth in the applications software package industry. The annual sales of all standard software packages is expected to skyrocket from $2 billion to $25 billion during the 1980s. The rising cost of programming is one of the reasons for the unprecedented growth of the software package industry.

Programming expenses include the maintenance programming costs. Many companies allocate 50% of their budgets for ongoing software maintenance. Most programmers devote 50 to 80% of their time doing maintenance. According to one authority, worldwide software maintenance costs are over $30 billion annually. One way to reduce the maintenance burden is to buy software packages with maintenance contracts from reliable vendors.

The right software package may eliminate development chores; however, it usually needs custom modification. Postinstallation, ongoing maintenance and enhancements are also necessary.

## WHAT IS SOFTWARE MAINTENANCE?

What is software maintenance? A clear definition is necessary to protect customers as well as vendors. Maintenance is generally defined as any work done on a software system after it becomes operational. The work may include corrective (correcting processing, performance, or implementation failures), adaptive (satisfying changes in the processing or data environment), and perfective (enhancing performance or maintainability) maintenance. Helping users with various aspects of software is also considered maintenance.

## APPLICATIONS SOFTWARE PACKAGE MAINTENANCE

There are two aspects of applications software package maintenance: maintenance by the vendor, and maintenance by the customer. The contract should clearly define the responsibilities of both parties. Even though the vendor is totally responsible for maintenance, the customer almost always gets involved in the process to some extent. In some cases both vendor and customer may do maintenance. This chapter describes applications software package maintenance from the customer's point of view. It includes tips and techniques, based on my experience, study, and interviews with professionals, for making such maintenance more productive.

## ASSESSING MAINTAINABILITY

Before acquiring a software package, assess its maintainability. There are several way to do this. Review the source code (most vendors provide source code) and documentation. If possible, select samples for reviewing at random. Let your programmers review the material. Is the package designed using modern development methodology, such as structured design? What types of documentation techniques are used? What programming language(s) are used? One way to assess maintainability is to use the bebugging technique. Insert artificial bugs in selected code and give to a programmer to debug it. The programmer's performance indicates maintainability. (See Parikh, 1982a, for Tom Gilb's article "Guaranteeing Program Maintainability.") The enhanceability of software can also be assessed by modifying this technique.

## MAINTENANCE CONTRACTS

Maintenance for the first year is generally included in the contract. After the first year it is optional; however, it is usually cost-effective and in some cases even necessary to continue vendor support. As a developer, the vendor knows the package inside out. Also, he has a large stake in the package and should keep it running and updated. The maintenance contract usually costs a percentage (generally 10 to 15%) of the then-current package price, per year.

Study the contract. What are the responsibilities of both parties? What kind of support is provided in emergencies? What are the implications if the customer modifies the software? If source code is not provided, is it made available if the vendor goes out of business? Ask your legal department to review the contract.

## MAINTAINING/ENHANCING APPLICATIONS PACKAGES PRODUCTIVELY

The following are some tips and techniques for maintaining applications software packages productively. Tips are also included for making the most of vendor support.

### Keep Records

Keep record of your changes and vendor-supplied updates. Also keep track of the problems. Document them and send them to the vendor. Also keep a record of applying the vendor-supplied changes. (Always save the original program before applying changes.) Design simple forms to keep records. Appropriate records not only help the customer in maintenance, but also protect him.

### Telemaintenance

Solving maintenance problems on the phone (or by other telecommunications means) may be called "telemaintenance." If the vendor has a "hot line" number, give it to the responsible persons. Here are some suggestions for effective telemaintenance.

Before calling, study the vendor-supplied instructions and documentation related to the problem area. Make sure that all updates sent by the vendor are correctly installed. Check the job control statements.

If the problem still cannot be resolved, collect pertinent data (such as inputs and outputs, program listing, and dump), prepare concise notes about the problem, and dial for help. A systematic approach to problem solving on the phone makes telemaintenance efficient.

Telemaintenance will become more important with the advent of microcomputer software packages. Such packages are usually inexpensive, and telemaintenance may be the only economical and timely way to help numerous customers having distant geographic locations. While writing this chapter on a microcomputer using a word-processing software, I experienced this. I struggled for about an hour to print the chapter, but the printer kept overprinting the lines! I had heard high praise about the software from other users, and didn't doubt that there was a bug. In desperation, I picked up the phone and called the vendor. The help came immediately. The printer switch was to be set. I was ecstatic to see the chapter printed flawlessly after setting the switch.

## Standards and Guidelines

Vendors normally send program temporary fixes (PTFs). Periodically, the vendor may consolidate previous PTFs and issue permanent fixes or a new program release. Understand the vendor procedures and develop guidelines for the in-house persons. Such guidelines may include a procedure for recording fixes (such as when the fix was received, reason for the fix, programs affected, installation date, who installed, and problems, if any).

Standards and guidelines can also be developed for implementing other maintenance techniques described in this chapter.

## External and Internal Documentation

Carefully document the in-house changes to the programs internally (within the program) as well as externally (external specifications). The internal documentation consists of flagging the lines added or changed and inserting comments for deleted lines (see Chapter 5). Incidentally, the technique described in that chapter was developed while I was a member of a maintenance team of a large applications software package.)

The external documentation, keyed with internal flags, includes change specifications.

## Organizing the Maintenance Function

If the maintenance volume justifies it, organize a separate group for this purpose. Those who helped install the package are the ideal candidates for such a group. The word "maintenance" may be changed to "software support" if that helps improve programmer morale.

A trained human librarian may be included in a maintenance group to provide clerical and light technical support.

## Productivity Tools

Programmer productivity tools include software packages that help programmers to do their jobs more productively. They are also called software tools. Examples of such tools are: source library management systems, preprocessors which include reformatting functions, and source code autitors (see Chapter 12).

A variety of tools are available. Most of the tools selected for maintenance environment can also be used in development. Study software product directories (e.g., International Computer Programs directories; see the Bibliography) to select appropriate tools.

## Education and Training

Provide training to maintenance programmers. Check whether the vendor has such a program. For a small package, a training program may not be available. Are the manuals and the documentation clear for self-education? If on-the- job training is the only way to learn, would the vendor help in this process?

A newsletter, if published by the vendor, may provide valuable information for ongoing education. Save the issues for future reference. The user conferences, if held by the vendor, may also provide excellent education. The users and operators of the software system also need education and training.

## User Involvement

Try to understand the package from the user's view as well as from technical angles. Coordinate and review changes with users. When appropriate, make users aware of technical problems.

Thus there are several ways for maintaining applications software packages productively. The managers and technicians responsible for maintaining software packages should consider the guidelines outlined in this chapter.

# *The Missing Link In DP Training: Software Maintenance*

# 18

A chain is as strong as its weakest link. But what if one of the strongest links in a chain is missing!

In data processing training the missing link is software maintenance (see Figure 18-1). Looking at the following statistics published in several sources, software maintenance is without question one of the strongest links in data processing.

1. In a software life cycle, 67% is software maintenance; only 33% is new development.
2. Most companies allocate about 50% of their DP budgets for software maintenance.
3. Most programmers spend 50%, and in some cases 80% of their time on maintenance.

We often hear about a "software crisis." Software maintenance is one of the most critical areas in software field.

This chapter gives ideas on software maintenance training [see also Parikh (1982a), Parikh and Zvegintzov (1983a) in the Bibliography]. It includes material on understanding software, as understanding of systems and programs is crucial to software maintenance. Unfortunately, most DP education and training in industry as well as in academic institutions concentrate on the front-end work of development, and ignore the lengthy, expensive, and in some cases critical stage of maintenance.

---

Most of the material in this chapter is excerpted from *Tutorial on Software Maintenance* by Girish Parikh and Nicholas Zvegintzov [see Bibliography]. 

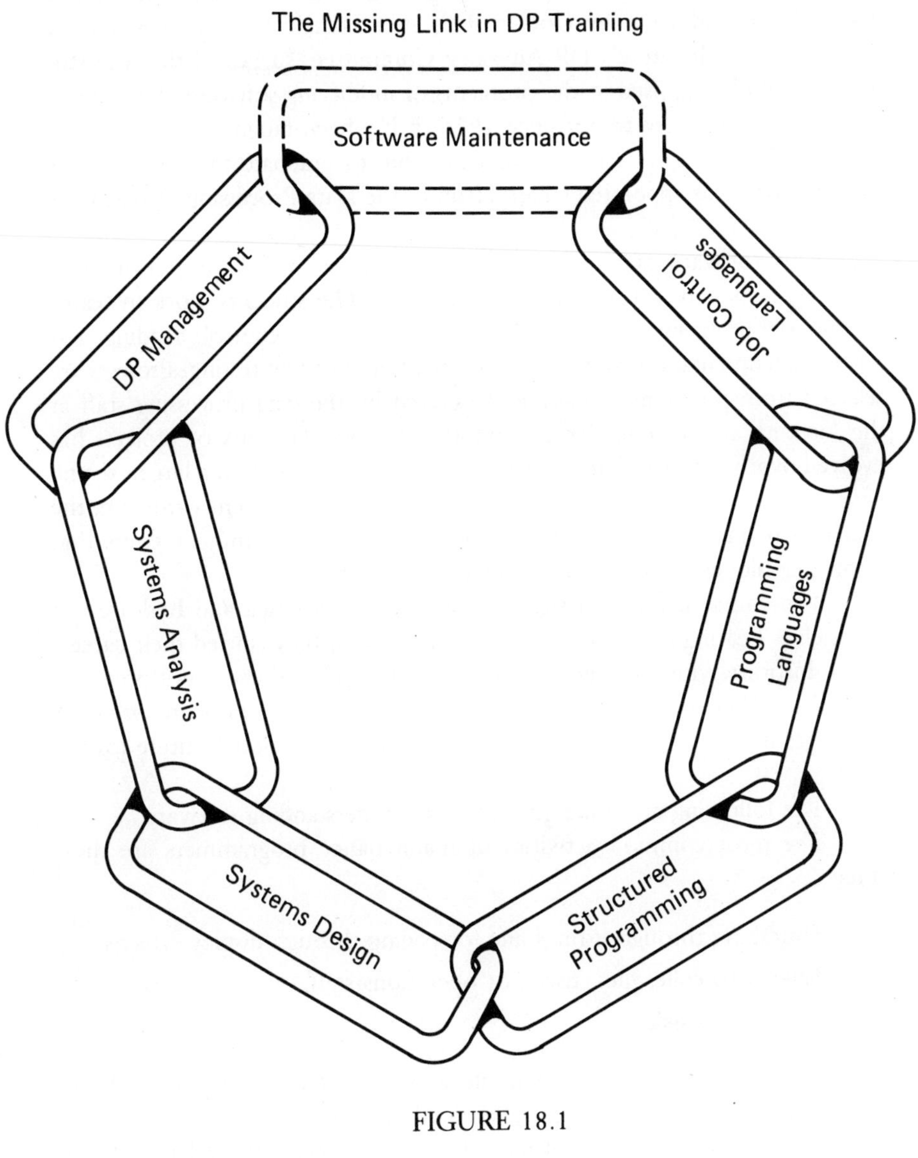
The Missing Link in DP Training
Software Maintenance
Job Control Languages
Programming Languages
Structured Programming
Systems Design
Systems Analysis
DP Management

FIGURE 18.1

One of the first college courses on maintenance offered in North America was at the National Technical Institute for the Deaf, which is a college within the Rochester Institute of Technology, and is a required course in the second year of a three-year associate degree in data processing. The course was originated in 1976 by Donald Beil, after Donald Stabley of Kodak, a member of the Institute's DP Advisory Committee, suggested that the students should be exposed to the problems of modifying software. The course has been taught every spring since 1976; it has been taught for the last few years by Robert Berl. The current class, due to graduate in 1983, has 23 students. Beil was appointed Chairperson of the Data Processing Department in 1979.

This software maintenance course has a real-world, project-oriented character rather than a theoretical orientation. The students work in teams of two on problems of conversion, program library control, reading and writing documentation, system enhancement, and system testing. Projects are selected from problems actually encountered by the data processing staff at the Institute and at other local computing centers. The mix of projects has evolved over the years. The current set of projects is based on a large existing payroll system; the students handle the conversion to different hardware, the updating of tax tables, and modifications based on government flyers that inform employers about legal and regulatory changes.

The course is given in sign language. Insructors Beil and Berl are not themselves hearing-impaired; like other instructors, they started their careers at the Institute with intensive courses in signing. The course is not presently offered to other students at the Rochester Institute of Technology, which is the larger institution which includes the National Technical Institute for the Deaf.

The following are some guidelines for understanding software.

The most common activities of maintenance programmers are these three:

Thumbing through listings and/or paging through display screens.

Talking to colleagues, users, or operations staff.

Staring into space.

Assuming that these are more than idle activities, what are they for and how do they help in maintaining an operational system?

Maintainers spend at least half of their time trying to understand—the request, the existing system, and its documentation. We infer that these activities are part of the effort of understanding the system, where understanding is defined as: *a relationship between the maintenance staff and the system that enables maintenance staff to make changes and explain the system correctly.*

If this definition is to be more than circular ("You handle the system correctly because you understand it; I know you understand it because you handle it correctly"), we need some analysis of the processes of understanding, some guide to appropriate tools and techniques, and some criteria for adequate performance. These needs are extraordinarily difficult to meet.

One way to develop a perspective on the understanding of software is to ask the classic WHO?–WHAT?–WHEN?–HOW?–WHY? questions.

## WHO SHOULD UNDERSTAND SOFTWARE?

Each element of a software system—the code, the data, the procedures—has a primary "understander." When the system operates, the code is "understood" by the processors, the data is "understood" by the storage devices or data base systems, and the procedures are "understood" by the users and operations staff. This is the minimum level of understanding necessary for the system to run at all. If the understanding goes no further, the system will continue to run only if nothing ever changes. When the system changes, the staff concerned with change—which includes maintenance programmers, development programmers, operations staff, quality assurance staff, and all their respective managers—must demonstrate understanding that goes beyond the existing documents.

## WHAT SHOULD BE UNDERSTOOD?

A large system is beyond the capacity of any one person to understand, even if that person dedicates an entire lifetime to it. The manager must assign parts of the understanding to individuals to achieve a collective understanding and a group coverage of the system. The manager must decide how the system should be partitioned for the best coverage.

The most common criteria for partitioning are the following:

Distinct units of the system as viewed by the users (the functional classification).

Units that are most often changed.

Units that give the most trouble.

There is much commonality in these classifications because the functions as the user sees them are the functions in which the most changes are demanded, and the functions in which the most changes are made are often those that give the most problems. The logic of concentrating on the outside of a system as a path to understanding its inside is not paradoxical:

The external environment of a system has a simplicity which is limited by the constraints, conventions, rules, and habits of the real world.

No system need be more complex than the operations it embodies.

The necessary simplicities of a system's function can be exploited to cut through the accidental complexities of that system's implementation.

## WHEN SHOULD SOFTWARE BE UNDERSTOOD?

When you need to put out a fire, you have no time to dig a well! You must understand the system before you attempt to change it. The manager must be committed to familiarizing the staff with the system. Several methods can be used to achieve this:

Long-term dedication of the staff to the system ("the elite team")

Scheduled walkthroughs, presentations, seminars, etc., in which staff members cover the system on a rotational basis

A one-time intensive initialization

The demand mode, in which an analyst "scopes" a section of the system from the narrow point of view of executing a particular change.

These methods form a continuum from the most broadly strategic approach to the most narrowly tactical. The manager or programmer can achieve the swiftest and smoothest performance at the top end of the continuum, but real-world circumstances, particularly staff reassignments, often put these strategies beyond reach. The wise manager uses the short-term methods when necessary, meanwhile developing long-term experience in the team by installing a policy of maintenance reviews, change logs, and system walkthroughs.

## HOW SHOULD SOFTWARE BE UNDERSTOOD?

A person understands a system by:

Knowing the different levels, point of view, and constituencies from which the behavior of the system can be described.

Knowing the objects and activities that characterize each level.

Being able to relate the objects and activities of one level to those of another.

## WHY SHOULD SOFTWARE BE UNDERSTOOD?

If a system is not understood, it is out of control. Its users have only the alternatives of accepting it entirely, which is slavery, or rejecting it entirely, which is revolution. The maintainers stand as a bridge between these costly alternatives, allowing the system and its users the freedom to evolve. In software, as in politics, the price of freedom is vigilance.

Jean-Dominique Warnier, the French systems scientist and the author of the world's first book on maintenance *Program Modification* (Warnier, 1978) emphasizes training. Warnier also emphasizes the need for training in the four phases of his (logical) approach to accomplish development of reliable software. He also recommends user training in DP techniques, especially where logic is involved.

Warnier's rigorous, logical approach also allows smooth integration of a new application into an existing system. With this approach modification of an existing system becomes a systematic process. Warnier also warns regarding the proliferation of microcomputers:

> I have grave misgivings when I see microcomputers invading schools and students being taught by teachers who are most interested in the technical aspects of the computer, but are not at all prepared to teach logical reasoning. As a result, we risk training a generation of brilliant handymen whose minds will be completely warped by bad habits learned since childhood. One will then see the lack of reliability of systems and her twin sister, maintenance, returning in force.

A variety of structured methodologies are advertised in manuals, books, and courses, and most claim to produce maintainable software. However, to our knowledge, none of the founders of these methodologies has probed as deeply as Warnier into the modification of systems and the integration of newly structured components into existing systems. In his books, Warnier demonstrates the modifiability and modification of systems by examples and/or case studies. He has done pioneering work in "logical maintenance" of systems developed according to his methods. He argues that with his approach tedious maintenance disappears, and a highly specialized job of "systems modification specialist," requiring extensive training and a strong experience in computer science, emerges in its place. His work may be used as a model for developing "maintenance technologies" for other methodologies.

According to Warnier, the problems encountered are essentially management problems. It is necessary to get decisions from top management concerning the objectives of the firm and, consequently, the objectives of the DP system.

The other problem is teaching the people involved. There are two solutions for teaching DP people as well as end users:

> Teaching the students in schools and universities as is done in France and in many other countries: Japan, Spain, Portugal, and other countries in Europe, Africa, Asia, and South America.
>
> Teaching employees on the job by public or private organizations.

The logical concepts are not very difficult to learn, but teachers must have a good practical experience concerning the logical construction of systems and programs.

By providing education and training in software maintenance to DP personnel we can increase the overall productivity in data processing. The management should look into the available training material, such as seminars and professional books. The industry and educational organizations should also develop software maintenance courses at all levels. The courses should address managerial as well as technical aspects. Thus the missing link in DP training can be completed and we get closed-loop DP training program addressing development as well as maintenance.

# *Are You an Illiterate Programmer?*

# 19

The title of this chapter may be an insult to a few programmers who are professionally literate; however, most programmers are illiterate! That may seem to be a strong statement; however, I think it is an understatement.

In several instances I found that most programmers do not read professional books and only leaf through professional journals. It seems that only students read books. Most working professionals ignore professional books. The problem is really serious. Let me cite two instances:

I talked with two supervisors who had more than a decade of experience each. One of them did not know what ACM was, and the other one had never heard about Warnier or the Warnier/Orr diagram. (The later instance is like working in physics and not knowing Newton! In the former case, probably the Association for Computing Machinery needs more institutional promotion, and pragmatic (or people) orientation.)

It seems that programmers want to keep pushing buttons on terminals. They do not want to take time to study and think about the problems. They usually rush to computers, hoping they will solve the problems for them. What is needed is to get away from machines occasionally and devote time to contemplation, self-analysis, and self- improvement. (See the section "Let's Get Away from Machines" in Chapter 15.)

---

It is a disgrace that most professionals do not read computer books. Most programmers are poorly educated. What are the remedies to correct this situation?

My good friend Lem Ejiogu suggests that "management should use subtle persuasion to encourage self-education by professionals." The performance of programming managers should be evaluated by their bosses by their success in encouraging programmers to read appropriate technical material. But programming managers themselves should be readers. (Remember the slogan "Readers Are Leaders." See Chapter 20 if you are a manager.)

I believe that managers should be more aggressive in making programmers read technical material. How can they do this? One sure way to make programmers read would be to consider when giving a raise or promotion, what the programmer has read. The programmer should furnish a list of books and articles he has read.

Programmers should read at least five to six books and several technical articles pertaining to their work, each year. How should they select the reading material?

The manager should allocate the task of screening books and periodicals to a senior programmer in the group. In a large company a full-time individual may be assigned to this task. This person should keep in touch with current literature and developments, and make reading recommendations. The department should purchase the necessary reading material. Programmers should be allowed to read some material in their working hours (it is an ongoing education), and other material may be read in their spare time.

After the group reads a particular book or set of articles they should get together and discuss the contents. [For example, in the text books of the video course "Measuring Programmer Productivity" developed by Parikh (1983) with DELTAK, Inc., an annotated reading list and discussion questions are included.]

In most EDP shops the process of learning is not congenial. The prevailing atmosphere is "do your own thing." Group discussions can help change the situation. Even while working individually, programmers should be encouraged to ask questions and to get new ideas. One-to-one discussions can also be productive. In some shops you are looked down on when you ask questions. Asking questions may be thought of as "you don't know." In such an environment, programmers shy away from asking questions. As a result, they may not learn better ways of doing things and even commit costly mistakes. The habit of reading may help develop a questioning attitude in programmers.

How to read technical material? Some material is worth digesting by reading it several times, whereas other material may be read just once. Cursory reading or skimming may suffice for some material. The craft of reading may be learned by practice. What are your professional goals? What are your current problems? Which are your favorite authors? (After you form the habit of reading, you will come to like the work of some authors. You will enjoy their style and contents.) What strengths do you want to enhance? What weaknesses do you want to correct? These questions would guide you in selecting reading material and developing a reading program. By the way, books are inexpensive training tools that you can use in your own time at your own pace. Select material at your own level—whatever you are capable of understanding.

The best known trade periodicals that programmers should leaf through are: *Computer Decisions, Computerworld, Datamation, Infosystems,* and *Mini-Micro Systems.* They should be clipped to provide for future reference.

The following are my 10 favorite books. I believe they should be required reading for every programmer. How many have you read? Most of them have a bibliography for further study.

1. *Practical LCP: A Direct Approach to Structured Programming* by Albert C. Gardner [McGraw-Hill Book Company (UK) Ltd., 1981]. Teaches LCP (Logical Construction of Programs—a data structured method developed by Jean-Dominique Warnier), a powerful structured programming methodology with COBOL, BASIC, and FORTRAN examples. The method helps produce correct, efficient programs quickly, uses machine time and resources more efficiently, and improves programmer productivity.
2. *The Soul of a New Machine* by Tracy Kidder (Little, Brown and Company, 1981). An exciting story about the development of a super-minicomputer (Data General Corp.'s MV/8000). It also details the lives of the engineers dedicated to developing the machine. What makes them tick under heavy pressure and exploitation? Once you start reading this book, you may not put it down until you are finished!
3. *Structured Systems Development* by Ken Orr (Yourdon Press, 1977). A highly readable and interesting introduction to data structured design concepts. It also includes an excellent introduction to a powerful structured tool, the Warnier/Orr diagram, with numerous examples.
4. *How to Measure Programmer Productivity* by Girish Parikh (Shetal Enterprises, 1981). How much are you worth? When your boss asks "Why has it taken so long?", can you give a satisfactory answer? This book, based on experience, research, and interviews with professionals, overviews available and emerging programmer productivity measurement techniques.
5. *Techniques of Program and System Maintenance* by Girish Parikh (Little, Brown and Company, 1982). The first American book on

software maintenance. A book of readings collected from the vast computer literature, and some original material. An entire section is devoted to "Practical Tips for Maintainers." The book originated while working in a depressing maintenance environment. As a result it has become a treasury of practical tips, techniques, and guidelines for improving programmer productivity in a maintenance environment.

6. *Tutorial on Software Maintenance* by Girish Parikh and Nicholas Zvegintzov (Silver Spring, Md.: IEEE Computer Society Press, 1983). This is a complementary volume to *Techniques of Program and System Maintenance.* The use of wit, humor, and personal anecdotes in the introductions make the book fun to read.
7. *Programmer Productivity: Achieving an Urgent Priority* by Girish Parikh (Reston, Va.: Reston Publishing Co., Inc., 1984). This book. I hope this chapter hooks you on books. Being the author, I have a vested interest, but don't you have an interest too? After all, it's your career.
8. *The Psychology of Computer Programming* by Gerald M. Weinberg (New York: Van Nostrand Reinhold Company, 1971). This classic introduces "a radically new point of view by depicting the human element in computer programming—man over machine." The lively style and real stories from the world of computer programming make the book fascinating reading.
9. *Understanding the Professional Programmer* by Gerald M. Weinberg (Boston: Little, Brown and Company, 1982). The lively essays in this book sparkle with "Weinberg wit." "Primarily, [the book] is intended as an exercise in self-examination for the professional programmer," says the author. While waiting at the terminal, or while sneaking a coffee break, why don't you keep this book handy?
10. *Techniques of Program Structure and Design* By Edward Yourdon (Englewood Cliffs, N.J.: Prentice-Hall, Inc., 1975). An excellent introduction to (functional) structured programming techniques.

That is enough to get you started. (See the Bibliography for further reading.) If you get a raise or promotion when you become a better professional by reading books, let me know, and also let me know which book(s) did it.

# *Are You an Illiterate Programming Manager?*

# 20

Programming managers rarely read books. When asked to read books, they may complain about lack of time. Usually, they are busy or at least keep themselves busy. However, a busy manager may not be a good manager! When he is too busy, he does not have time to think about better ways. And better ways may come from reading professional literature.

Good technical leaders are readers. A programming manager should be a good technical leader and keep himself updated with the current developments in the field. That means that he should leaf through the trade journals and some technical periodicals on a regular basis. He can clip important articles applicable to his environment. He may also subscribe to newsletters covering his area. The following two periodicals can be invaluable in keeping him updated: *Data Processing Digest* (P.O. box 1249, Los Angeles, CA 90028) and *EDP Analyzer* (925 Anza Avenue, Vista, CA 92083).

The most popular trade periodicals in data processing are: *Computer Decisions, Computerworld, Datamation, Infosystems,* and *Mini-Micro Systems*. Except for *Computerworld*, all are available free to qualified subscribers. Take advantage of this offer. It will keep you aware of new trends in the field.

---

What can a manager do to encourage programmers to read? One sure way to induce programmers to read is, at evaluation time, to consider the quality and quantity of professional books read by programmers during a certain period. The raise and promotion may even be made subject to reading professional books and literature. But generally you cannot force a programmer to

FIGURE 20.1 You can lead a programmer to a book but you can't force him to read

read books. As the saying goes, you can lead a horse to water, but you can't make him drink.

You may dump books on the shelves of programmers—they may do nothing other than decorate or clutter up (depending on how organized the programmer is) the programmer's working space. How can you make him *read*?

Selecting right books is crucial to developing the appetite of programmers for books. Select the books pertinent to the work of the programmer. For example, if he is working on designing programs to be developed with structured techniques, *Practical LCP* (Gardner, 1981) would be one of the essential books if data structured approach is to be used. If a functional approach is to be used, *Techniques of Program Structure and Design* (Yourdon, 1975) is a good source. If he is primarily involved in maintenance programming, *Techniques of Program and System Maintenance* (Parikh, 1982a) and *Tutorial on Software Maintenance* (Parikh and Zvegintzov, 1983a) are essential books. All programmers should be asked to read a few selected books, such as *The Psychology of Computer Programming* (Weinberg, 1971) and *Understanding the Professional Programmer* (Weinberg, 1982).

How do you select pertinent books? So many books are published that it is hard to make the right selection. You may use an outside consultant (who himself is a reader, like the author of this book!) to review your environment and to suggest appropriate books. After a particular book is studied, ask your programmers to get together and discuss the contents. The consultant may lead such a discussion. If you have many programmers, you may break them up into groups. In such an environment, you may also consider creating a position of in-house "technical literature consultant."

How do you justify the costs of a reading and discussion program? Again, measuring programmer productivity can help you. Measure programmer productivity before such a program, and after such a progam is in progress. I believe that the programmer productivity of the reading programmers will be enhanced.

Thus programmers should be allowed to read pertinent professional books during working time. Once they are hooked on books, I believe they will keep reading books on a regular basis in their own time.

An aggressive "reading campaign" is needed. A programmer literacy drive is extremely important in improving programmer productivity. Managers should themselves start reading, and then ask programmers to start reading, or else!

I recommend the following books. I believe these books should be must reading for every programming manager. (Most of them have bibliographies for further study.)

1. *The Mythical Man-month and other Essays on Software Engineering* by Frederick P. Brooks, Jr. (Reading, Mass.: Addison-Wesley Publishing Co., Inc., 1974). A classic by the father of IBM System/360. It includes many anecdotes from the author's experiences. He is candid in relating even a multimillion-dollar mistake in assigning a design project to a multitude of designers instead of assigning it to a small team of highly competent designers. The lively style makes the book exciting reading.
2. *The Soul of a New Machine* by Tracy Kidder (Boston: Little, Brown and Company, 1981). An exciting story about the development of a super-minicomputer (Data General Corp.'s MV/8000). It also

details the lives of the engineers dedicated to developing the machine. What makes them tick under heavy pressure and exploitation? Once you start reading this book, you may not put it down until finished!

3. *Structured Systems Development* by Ken Orr (New York: Yourdon Press, 1977). A highly readable and interesting introduction to data structured design concepts. It also includes an excellent introduction to a powerful structured tool, the Warnier/Orr diagram, with numerous examples.
4. *How to Measure Programmer Productivity* by Girish Parikh (Chicago: Shetal Enterprises, 1981). This book, based on experience, research, and interviews with professionals, overviews the available and emerging programmer productivity measurement techniques.
5. *Techniques of Program and System Maintenance* by Girish Parikh (Boston: Little, Brown and Company, 1982). The first American book on software maintenance. A book of readings collected from the vast computer literature, and some original material. This is primarily a manager's book. It is a treasury of practical tips, techniques, and guidelines for improving programmer productivity in a maintenance environment.
6. *Programmer Productivity: Achieving an Urgent Priority* by Girish Parikh (Reston, Va.: Reston Publishing Co., Inc., 1984). This book. I hope this chapter hooks you on books. Being the author, I have a vested interest, but don't you have an interest too? After all, it's your career.
7. *Tutorial on Software Maintenance* by Girish Parikh and Nicholas Zvegintzov (Silver Spring, Md.: IEEE Computer Society Press, 1983). This is a complementary volume to *Techniques of Program and System Maintenance.* The use of wit, humor, and personal anecdotes in the introductions make the book fun to read.
8. *The Psychology of Computer Programming* by Gerald M. Weinberg (New York: Van Nostrand Reinhold Company, 1971). This classic introduces "a radically new point of view by depicting the human element in computer programming—man over machine." The lively style and real stories from the world of computer programming make the book fascinating reading.
9. *Understanding the Professional Programmer* by Gerald M. Weinberg (Boston: Little, Brown and Company, 1982). The lively essays in

this book sparkle with "Weinberg wit." Understanding the programmer is essential to increasing his productivity. This book will provide you with insights into how programmers work.

10. *Managing the Structured Techniques*, 2nd ed., by Edward Yourdon (New York: Yourdon Press, 1979). An excellent introduction to the (functional) structured techniques. If you are considering introducing structured techniques, this book should give you many ideas.

Study the Bibliography for further readings.

It is also possible that the ideas you get from your readings may save a fortune. Or may even make you a fortune. I am not hinting that you go on your own. But if you do, you will have to be your own manager. Also, right reading will provide you with a gold mine of information. If you do save a fortune (or make a fortune), let me know. I want my share!

# *Annotated Bibliography*

Applied Data Research (1976a). *MetaCOBOL Concepts and Facilities.* Princeton, N.J.: Applied Data Research, Inc., Form SM1G-00-00. An excellent introduction to the facilities and benefits of the preprocessor approach, and a guide to more detailed MetaCOBOL literature.

———(1976b). "Toward COBOL Structured Programming" (MetaCOBOL Techniques Manual), Princeton, N.J.: Applied Data Research, Inc., Form SMIG-51-00. An excellent introduction to MetaCOBOL.

Ashcroft, E. and Manna, Z. (1971). "The Translation of 'GOTO' programs into 'WHILE' Programs," *Proceedings of the 1971 IFIP Congress.* [This paper is included in Yourdon (1979b).] This paper presents, by examples only, the concepts of two different algorithms for converting programs with GOTO's into WHILE programs.

*Baker, F. T. (1972). "Chief Programmer Team Management of Production* Programming," *IBM Systems Journal*, vol. 11, no. 1, pp. 56–73. [This paper is included in Yourdon (1979b).] Describes the New York Times Project, the use of structured techniques, and increased programmer productivity.

Boehm, B. W. (1976). "Software Engineering," *IEEE Transactions on Computers*, vol. C-25, no. 12, December, pp. 1226–1241. [This paper is included in Yourdon (1979b). Excerpts are included in Parikh (1982a).] This excellent paper provides a definition of "software engineering" and a survey of the state of the art and likely future trends. It covers the technology available in the various phases of the software life cycle, including maintenance, and in the overall area of software management and integrated technology management approaches. 104 references are provided.

Bourrut, Drew (1976). "HIPO Charts, Pseudocode Called Good Design Pairing." *Computerworld*, September 6, pp. 13, 14. Emphasizes the adequate training necessry to work with the HIPO technique. Automating the HIPO is not recommended, since the purpose of HIPO is to aid in the design and documentation of a system, and minimizing the human element makes human–computer interaction more difficult. Recommends pseudocode instead of flowcharts for program logic development.

Brooks, Frederick P. Jr. (1974). *The Mythical Man-Month and Other Essays on Software Engineering*. Reading, Mass.: Addison-Wesley Publishing Co., Inc. A classic by the "father of the IBM System/360."

Brownstein, Irv, and Nancy Lerner (1983). "Nurturing Your Own Productivity," *Computerworld*, April 25, "In Depth" section. This excellent article raises many questions on productivity in corporate DP environments.

Canning, Richard G. ed. (1972). "COBOL Aid Packages," *EDP Analyzer*, May, 14 pp. This excellent report discusses the COBOL aids, and the benefits some users [Ford Motor Company, U.S. Navy Fleet Material Support Office (FMSO), Computer Machinery Corporation] have obtained from them.

——— (1974). "Improving the System Building Proccess," *EDP Analyzer*, December, 12 pp. This report includes the discussion of user experiences and a description of Warnier's LCP, a standardized procedure for designing programs.

——— (1978). "Progress in Software Engineering, Part 1 & Part 2," *EDP Analyzer*, February, 13 pp., and March, 13 pp. An excellent overview of the state of software engineering. Software engineering seeks to impose a methodology and a discipline on the development and modification of software, and the management of software development and modification. The reports point out that software maintenance needs more attention.

——— (1979). "The Production of Better Software," *EDP Analyzer*, February, 13 pp. This report includes a discussion of Warnier's LCS, which supports the analysis phase and system design.

Carnegie, Dale (1948). *How to Stop Worrying and Start Living*. New York: Simon and Schuster (paperback). An excellent antidote to one of the worst problems of the programmer or manager—worry!

Clark, D. M. (1980). "Maintenance Programming," *Computerworld*, July 28, "In Depth" section. This article is one of the gems in the sparse but urgently needed literature on how to do maintenance.

Couger, Daniel J. (1980). "Half-Asked Questions on Productivity." *Computerworld*, December 1, pp. 43,48. This article begins with the question: "What is the time comparison for writing vs. processing a programming instruction?" The ratio of processing to coding is more than 100 million to 1. To improve productivity the redesign of the motivational environment for programmers is as important as technical improvements. The article is an introduction to the book by Couger, and Zawacki (1980).

Couger, Daniel J., and Robert Zawacki (1980). *Motivating and Managing Computer Personnel*. New York: John Wiley & Sons, Inc. See also Couger (1980).

Crosby, Philip B. (1979). *Quality Is Free: The Art of Making Quality Certain*. New York: Mentor Books (paperback). This classic contains down-to-earth advice for ensuring quality. Some ideas can be adapted for ensuring program quality and for measuring programmer productivity.

*Data Processing Digest* (1971–1972). "COBOL Support Packages . . . Programming and Productivity Aids," July 1971, Introduction; August, COBOL Subset; September, COBOL Manual; October, COBOL Shorthands; November, Decision Table Translators; January 1972, Data Management Systems; February, Test Data Generators; March, Debugging Systems; April, Documentation Aids; May, Summary. An excellent and detailed overview of the whole area of COBOL aids, by the editors and staff of DPD.

———*(1977) THEME/PAK: Structured Programming*. Los Angeles Calif.: Data Processing Digest, Inc. (Revised and updated.) It includes all the *DPD (Data Processing Digest)* articles and book reviews on structured programming from December 1973 through March 1977. An extensive bibliography of other references to structured programming contained in professional journals and conference proceedings is also included. Names and address of publishers of these original items are detailed. Includes an index.

de Balbine, Guy (1975). "Better Manpower Utilization Using Automatic Restructuring," *Proceedings of the AFIPS 1975 National Computer Conference*, vol. 44. Montvale, N.J.: AFIPS Press, pp. 319–327. [This paper is included in Parikh (1982a)]. This excellent paper describes results achieved by restructuring existing FORTRAN programs into a "structured" FORTRAN superset called S-FORTRAN, using a proprietary package that operates as a "structuring engine."

DeMarco, Tom (1978). *Structured Analysis and System Specifications*. New York: Yourdon Press. This very readable book includes a brief reference to J. D. Warnier, *Logical Construction of Programs*, (1974), the Warnier diagram, and Ken Orr. A decision tree is like a Warnier diagram, it states.

Dijkstra, E. (1972). "The Humble Programmer," *Communications of the ACM*, vol. 15, no. 10, October, pp. 859–866. [This paper is included in Yourdon (1979b)]. Edward Yourdon, in the introduction to this paper in his *Classics in Software Engineering* (Yourdon, 1979b), states: "In my opinion, Dijkstra's 'Humble Programmer' ought to be required reading for everyone who claims that programming is his or her profession." The paper was presented as the 1972 ACM Turing Award Lecture.

——— (1976). "Structured Programming," in *Software Engineering: Concepts and Techniques*, Peter Naur, Brian Randall, and J. N. Buxton, ed. New York: Van Nostrand Reinhold Company, pp. 222–226. (Originally published in *Software Engineering Techniques*. Brussels, Belgium: NATO Scientific Affairs Division, pp. 84–88.) [This paper is included in Yourdon (1979b).] A landmark paper from the father of "structured programming."

Ejiogu, Lem, (1983). *Effective Structured Programming*. Princeton, N.J.: Petrocelli Books.

Elliot, R. W., and E. R. Story (1975). "Audio Techniques for Program Documentation," *Data Management*, November, pp. 32–35. This article describes the economics of audio documentation (about one-fourth of the cost of conventional techniques), together with a test of its effectiveness for maintenance purposes.

Freedman, Daniel P., and Gerald M. Weinberg (1982). *Guide to Walkthroughs, Inspections and Technical Reviews: Evaluating Programs, Projects, and Products*. Boston: Little, Brown and Company. Excerpted in Parikh (1982a). An excellent handbook for ensuring software quality through reviews. Also covers MECCA methods with examples.

Freeman, Peter, and Anthony I. Wasserman (1983). "Comparing Software Design Methods for Ada: A Study Plan," University of California, Irvine. This is part of a larger report, "Software Development Methodologies and Ada," that includes "Ada Methodologies: Concepts and Requirements," and "Ada Methodology Questionnaire Summary" (both published in ACM *Software Engineering Notes*, January 1983). Proposes a plan similar to the one described in Chapter 13 in this book. The purpose of the plan is to answer the question: "What is the effect of various software design methods on the maintainability of systems, specifically, ones that are constructed in Ada?" The following are some thought-provoking quotations from the report:

> The results of this study will not be definitive and will be open to interpretation in most instances. It is essential that an open forum be held to permit discussion of the results, questioning of the methods used, and investigation of the data collecting techniques....

> We *do not* anticipate a strong differentiation between the various design methods employed. Indeed, it would not surprise us if the final conclusion is that what has been shown is that the use of *any* explicit design method produces significant improvements in maintainability. While the "true believers" know that already, a convincing demonstration would go far toward facilitating the adoption of improved methods....
>
> If the software field is in its infancy (as is often said), then objective investigation, let alone experimentation in the true sense, has not even been conceived. It would be superfluous for us to outline other possibilities here (a recent issue of *Software Engineering Notes* [vol. 7, no. 1] contains several concrete proposals), but we would note the value of replicating this (or any) investigation several times in different circumstances....
>
> We do want to emphasize two things, however. First, we strongly believe that objective investigations of the ways in which software is developed must be carried out to permit us to make more rational decisions regarding the way we organize and carry out system development. Second, the investigative process must be refined greatly from its present state.

Gardner, Albert C. (1981). *Practical LCP: A Direct Approach to Structured Programming*. Maidenhead, Berkshire, England: McGraw-Hill Book Company (UK) Ltd. "Do you need to produce correct, efficient programs quickly? Or train novice programmers fast? Use your machine time and resources more efficiently? Or improve programmer productivity?" If your answers to these questions are yes, the practical LCP is the structured programming methodology for you. Based on Warnier's LCP methodology (see Warnier, 1974), it also increases maintenance programming productivity.

Gause, Donald C. and Gerald M. Weinberg (1982) *Are Your Lights On? An Introduction to Problem Definition*. Boston: Little, Brown and Company. A series of lively, casually written essays, built on anecdotes. They provide approaches to problem definition and solving. This is not a heavy textbook for solving problems. Only two problems in the book involve computers. However, the principles suggested from the examples can be applied to highly technical problems, including, I believe, maintenance. The illustrations are entertaining.

Gilb, Tom (1979). *Software Metrics*. Originally published by Winthrop Publishers (acquired by Little, Brown and Company, Boston). Available only from Studentlitteratur AB, Magistratvagen 12, S-221 01 Lund, Sweden. Gilb presents his own MECCA method, among other topics, and details the experience of leaders in the field, such as TRW Systems and Lockheed.

——— (forthcoming). *Design by Objectives.* Amsterdam: North-Holland Publishing Co. A clear exposition of DbO, a method developed by Gilb. Regarding the Parikh productivity metrics, Gilb writes in a letter to Parikh: "It seems to me that you are really basing your measure on what I would call multi-dimensional metrics, used in the context of a System Attribute Specification (SAS), which is a cornerstone method of my *Design by Objectives.*"

Goetz, Martin A. (1973). "Soup Up Your Programmers with COBOL Aids," *Computer Decisions*, March, pp. 8–12. Discusses several types of COBOL aids, such as preprocessors, debugging/testing packages, and documentation aids. Gives ideas and rules for successfully introducing and using COBOL aids. A survey of the available aids as of early 1973 is included.

——— (1977). "New Software Tools Increase Productivity", *Infosystems*, February, pp. 66–70. Discusses four major software tools (preprocessors, automated documentation systems, source program control systems, and on-line programming systems) and how they can increase productivity.

Grauer, Robert T., and Marshal A. Crawford (1977). "Cobol Precompilers Seen Lacking in User Popularity", *Computerworld*, April 25, pp. S/10 and S/12. This article refutes the objections against precompilers. It briefly describes the features of precompilers, such as abbreviations, relative addressing, and logic generation, and cites CL*IV (Informatics), MetaCOBOL (ADR), SPLICE (SMM), and work Ten (NCI), each claiming a bottom-line reduction in coding of at least 50%.

Higgins, David A. (1977). "Structured Program Design," *Byte*, October, pp. 146–148, 150–151. The Warnier-Orr technique holds much promise for program design applications. It stresses design over coding, and contends that once a problem is designed, it can be coded in any programming language. The resulting code is easy to read and understand, easy to change and maintain, already documented, and logically correct. Also, the program will run the first time. The technique is easy to learn and use; however, it is not trivial. This excellent article further teaches the technique with examples—Warnier/Orr diagrams and a listing of Higgins' first BASIC program that worked the first time.

——— (1977–1978). "Structured Programming with Warnier/Orr Diagrams." *Byte*, December 1977, pp. 104, 106, 108–110; and January 1978, pp. 122–126, 128–129. The Warnier/Orr diagram allows people to produce super programs without being superprogrammers. This two-part article ("Part 1: Design Methodology" and "Part 2: Coding the Program") shows how to develop and code a structured program using Warnier/Orr methodology from start to finish. Although the language used is BASIC, the concepts are applicable to almost any programming language.

——— (1979). *Program Design and Construction*. Englewood Cliffs, N.J.: Prentice-Hall, Inc. Every programmer must read and digest this book; especially if he or she wants to master the Warnier/Orr diagramming technique. The first part of the book emphasizes methods for analyzing problems and synthesizing their solutions. Chapters in this section include an introduction to Warnier/Orr diagramming and instruction on its effective use, and material on logical output and input structures, event analysis, physical design, and logical process design. The second part treats techniques for transforming logical solutions into useful programs, covering common mistakes and questions, advanced concepts (e.g., concurrency, assembly-line diagramming, and hierarchy inversion), and coding in BASIC, the language used for examples. However, coding can be done in any programming language.

IBM Corporation (1974a). "Improved Programming Technologies—An Overview." White Plains, N.Y. (GC20-1850). This excellent document briefly describes the six techniques designed to improve the program development process: structured programming, top-down program development, chief programmer teams, development support libraries, HIPO, and structured walkthroughs.

——— (1974b). "Structured Programming," Independent Study Program, Poughkeepsie, N.Y., Textbook (SR20-7149), Workbook (SR20-7150). Excerpted in Parikh (1982a). Assignment 3 of this course is "Structuring Unstructured Flowcharts." Assignment 7 of this course provides an excellent introduction to HIPO, team operations, walkthroughs, and development support libraries.

——— (1974c). "HIPO— A Design Aid and Documentation Technique." White Plains, N.Y. GC20-1851. A technical bible for HIPO users.

——— (1975a) " An Introduction to Structured Programming in COBOL." White Plains N.Y., GC20-1776. This excellent text describes and illustrates structured programming with two examples of structured COBOL programs.

——— (1975b). "Improved Programming Technologies—User Experience, Crown Zellerbach," *Advanced Systems Programs Productivity*, SM-75-012, June 25.

——— "HIPO: Design Aid and Documentation Tool," Audio education package, Form No. SR20-9413. It consists of Part I, Introduction to HIPO; Part II, Drawing HIPO diagrams; and Part III, Editing HIPO diagrams.

——— (1976a). *HIPODRAW, Program Description/Operations Manual.* Palo Alto, Calif. SH20-1728.

——— (1976b). *Business Systems Planning and HIPO at the University of Illinois* (Installation Management). White Plains, N.Y., GK20-0967. Excerpted in Parikh (1982a).

*Infosystems* (1977). "Non-Standard COBOL Programs Get Treatment (Users Report)," July, pp. 82–83. Excerpted in Parikh (1982a). Describes how a paper manufacturer solved the problem of redoing 1000 nonstandard COBOL programs with half of its original staff.

International Computer Programs, Inc. *The ICP Interface Series: Data Processing Management.* ICP, 9000 Keystone Crossing, Indianapolis, IN 46240. This periodical, containing articles, case studies, product descriptions, etc., is distributed free of charge to qualified readers by ICP. Its purpose is to provide an effective interface between the buyers and the sellers of the software.

Johnson, James R. (1980). *Managing for Productivity in Data Processing.* Wellesley, Mass.: QED Information Sciences. Discusses five kinds of productivity: individual, project development, maintenance, DP division, and DP corporate.

Jones, Martha Nyvall (1976). "HIPO for Developing Specifications," *Datamation*, March, pp. 112–114, 121–125. Describes how HIPO was used sucessfully to develop specifications at John Hancock Mutual Life Insurance Company in a series of meetings between the programmers and users. Preliminary steps to take before using HIPO to define requirements are given. The guidelines to follow after selecting project and personnel are also given. The major benefits using HIPO are detailed.

Jones, T. C. (1981). *Tutorial, Programming Productivity. Issue of the Eighties.* New York: IEEE Computer Society, Catalog No. EHO 186-7. A compendium of 35 papers with Jone's reflections.

Katzan, Harry, Jr. (1976). *Systems Design and Documentation: An Introduction to the HIPO Method.* New York: Van Nostrand Reinhold Company. Provides a readable, comprehensive introduction to the

HIPO method. To my knowledge, this is the only major work on the subject not from IBM. As such, it is essential that HIPO users study it. It explains HIPO and its graphic conventions with numerous excellent illustrations. (See also Yourdon, 1976a).

Kidder, Tracy (1981). *The Soul of a New Machine*. Boston: Little, Brown and Company. An exciting account of the development of a super minicomputer (Data General Corp. MV/8000). It reveals what makes the designers of the machine work under high pressure and corporate exploitation and produce a powerful machine. Once you start reading this book, it is hard to put it down. Although the book deals with hardware engineers and programmers, it is a gripping story for other programmers as well—I can vouch it from my own reading.

Lyons, Michael J. (1980). "Structured Retrofit—1980," *Proceedings of SHARE 55*, pp. 263–265. An introduction to the evolving structured retrofit concepts pioneered by Jon Cris Miller.

——— (1981). "Salvaging Your Software Assets (Tools Based Maintenance)," *AFIPS Conference Proceedings*, vol. 50, pp. 337–341. According to Lyons, "structured retrofit" is an effective alternative to rewrites and purchased software." The critical tool in structured retrofit is the COBOL structuring engine.

Martin, James (1982). *Application Development without Programmers*. Englewood Cliffs, N.J.: Prentice-Hall, Inc. Examines a major change in which "packaged" routines deliver applications software to order. Includes languages and application generators for end users, data base user languages, end-user-driven computing and APL. The ideas in this book could have a profound impact on programming and programmer productivity.

McCracken, D. (1973). "Revolution in Programming: An Overview," *Datamation*, December, pp. 50–51. [This paper is included in Yourdon (1979b).] This article introduces a four-article group on structured programming.

McNurlin, Barbara C. (1977). "Using Some New Programming Techniques," *EDP Analyzer*, November, 13 pp. This report describes some uses of improved programming technologies (categorized into three groups: (1) for designing software (includes HIPO), (2) for building software, and (3) for testing software (to improve the software development process. The experiences of three companies [TRW Defense and Space Systems Group (DSSG), Columbus Mutual Life Insurance Co., and Mellon Bank of Pittsburgh] are described; and a literature search is summarized.

——— (1979). "Program Design Techniques,"*EDP Analyzer*, March, 13 pp. This report discusses the three major program design methods [the Warnier/Orr technique (which uses the Warnier/Orr diagram), the Jackson method, and the Constantine-Yourdon method], with a case study of the user of each method. Guidelines for choosing and introducing a technique are included. It also speculates on the future program design process.

Miller, Jon Cris (1976). "Improved Programming Technologies Retrofit (A Study of the Application of Improved Programming Technologies to Systems Developed without Improved Programming Technologies.)" Chicago: an unpublished report for Montgomery Ward CSD. This pioneering study may open a new field in software maintenance. [Miller's chapter "Structured Retrofit" in Parikh (1982a) includes some of the ideas from this report.] Together with other techniques, it describes the application of the preprocessors in an improved programming technologies retrofit environment. He cites CBLSHORT and SWAPPER among the preprocessors.

——— (1981). "Structured Retrofit—1981," *Proceedings of SHARE* 57, Chicago, August. This progress report on structured retrofit, presented by the pioneer of the concepts, includes case histories, reasons for retrofit software, and the lessons learned externally and internally.

Miller, Larry K., and David Ostrom (1976). "Source Program Management," *Datamation*, December, pp. 67–70. A good automated source program management system can go a long way in helping the maintenance programmer. The article describes a system developed in-house.

Mills, Harlan D. (1983). *Software Productivity*. Boston: Little, Brown and Company. "Contains 20 chronologically arranged articles that focus on software productivity, especially the technical and managerial means necessary to achieve both high productivity and increased quality. Responsible for a new approach to software development and management, these articles have supplied a basis for many IBM software management directives and education programs. The book provides a unique synthesis of theoretical foundations and practical applications in complex computing systems." It includes the classic paper "Mathematical Foundations for Structured Programming."

Naftaly, Stanley M., Bruce G. Johnson, and Michael C. Cohen (1972). *COBOL Support Packages: Programming and Productivity Aids*, New York: John Wiley & Sons, Inc. A "definitive" book on COBOL aids. The excellent series of articles on COBOL aids published in the July 1971 through May 1972 issues of *Data Processing Digest*[see *Data Processing Digest* (1971–1972) in this Bibliography] was reedited and published as this book. At the time of this writing, the book was out of print.

Noll, Paul (1977). *Structured Programming for the COBOL Programmer.* Fresno, Calif.: Mike Murach & Associates, Inc. This book presents a practical method of structured programming. One chapter shows how to create structure charts (VTOC of HIPO), while another chapter teaches a simplified version of HIPO documentation. Other topics include top-down testing, structured walkthroughs, chief programmer teams, and development support libraries.

——— (1978). *The Structured Programming Cookbook.* Fresno, Calif.: Mike Murach & Associates, Inc. This book is an easy-to-use reference book covering standards and guidelines, and the complete solutions (with HIPOs, in simplified version) for four model programs.

Omlor, Dennis (1977). "Hierarchical Diagram Seen Better for Documentation," *Computerworld,* March 28, p. 26.

Orr, Ken (1977a). "Structured Systems Design: Blue Printing the Future," *Infosystems,* February, pp. 73, 74, 76. This excellent article describes how the Warnier/Orr diagram came about. After describing problems with traditional documentation, HIPO is considered "a clear step forward from no consistent method of design and documentation at all." However, to overcome the shortcomings of HIPO, HIPO/DB was developed. But it still produced too much paper. The compact Warnier/Orr diagrams, hierarchical and including all the basic structured forms (sequence, alternation, and repetition) provides the most powerful documentation and design technique. (See also Orr, 1977b.)

——— (1977b). *Structured Systems Development.* New York: Yourdon Press. This book must be read by everyone involved with systems analysis, design, and development. Programmers would also find it enlightening. Chapters 4 and 5 describe the Warnier/Orr diagram, with numerous examples. More examples of the Warnier/Orr diagram are given throughout the book. One chapter is devoted to other structured design tools, such as structured narratives, structured flowcharts, HIPO, and HIPO/DB (HIPO/DATA BASE); however, the basic Warnier diagram is considered "the fastest, easiest, and best communicating device." The book presents logical analysis, design, and development methods. Other topics include systems analysis and problem solving, process flow, systems building, and systems design.

——— (1979). "Warnier-Orr Technology and Systems Maintenance," *Future(s)* (a newsletter published by Ken Orr and Associates, Inc., 1725 Gage Boulevard, Topeka KS 66604), vol. 3, no. 2, Spring, pp.

1–3. The Warnier-Orr diagram has been used successfully to document existing systems. In this activity, the "in-out" or "assembly-line" versions of the diagram are often used. The article includes excellent ideas on redesigning existing systems, and on structured maintenance.

Parikh, Girish (1981a). *How to Measure Programmer Productivity*. Chicago: Shetal Enterprises. An overview of the state of the art and evolving programmer productivity measurement techniques. Includes an extensive annotated bibliography.

——— (1981b). "Measuring Programmer Productivity in a Maintenance Environment," *Proceedings of SHARE 57*, Chicago, August. This paper, based on experience and research, overviews the state of the art and evolving techniques of measuring programmer productivity in a maintenance environment. The quantitative and qualitative aspects of programmer productivity are covered. The factors affecting maintenance programming productivity (e.g., management attitude, training, organization of maintenance function, documentation, software tools, experience, application knowledge, programming language, structure of software) are considered, and suggestions are made for evaluating performance.

——— (1982a). *Techniques of Program and System Maintenance*. Boston: Little, Brown and Company. A programming and management overview of software maintenance, compiled from the vast body of computer literature and some original material.

——— (1982b). "Who's Tending the Programs? Maintenance Training Suffers from Neglect" *Data Training*, July.

——— (1983). "Measuring Programmer Productivity," a video series developed with DELTAK, Inc. This series provides an introduction to the state of the art and evolving techniques for measuring programmer productivity. The titles of the four courses are: Productivity Issues, Measuring Techniques, Productivity Techniques and Structured Technologies, and Productivity Techniques for Maintenance.

Parikh, Girish, and Nicholas Zvegintzov, ed. (1983a). *Tutorial on Software Maintenance*. Silver Spring, Md.: IEEE Computer Society Press. A compendium of 31 papers with editors' reflections and lively introductions to each paper and author. Includes an annotated bibliography and an index.

——— (1983b). "Software Maintenance Training," *Data Training*, May.

Peterson, Norman D. (1970). "Shorthand Converters," *The Journal of Data Education*, November, pp. 53–57. Describes the capabilities of shorthands, such as using abbreviations, enhancing documentation by formatting output coding, flagging illegal (for a particular installation), coding, etc. It lists 20 software packages, which include COBOL shorthand converters.

Reifer, Donald J., and Stephan Trattner (1977). "A Glossary of Software Tools and Techniques," *Computer*, July, pp. 52–60. This paper provides a comprehensive listing of the software tools and techniques currently available. It describes the three major stages of a typical software life cycle (conceptual and requirements, development, and operations and maintenance) and the six categories of software tools (simulation, development, test and evaluation, operations and maintenance, performance measurement, and programming support). A table relates the life-cycle areas to the various categories of software tools, and a matrix relates the specific tools/techniques listed in the glossary to categories of software tools of which they are a part. The glossary of aids briefly describes 70 tools/techniques.

Rigo, Joseph T. (1976). " 'Son of HIPO' Proposed As Easier Charting Vehicle," *Computerworld*, August 9, p. 21.

——— (1978). "New documentation Aids Should Show Data Flow," *Computerworld*, July 17, pp. 23, 24. Discusses the trend in documentation aids. The (program) flowchart and program narrative have almost disappeared. HIPO charts (called "a transition phenomenon") may also belong to the past. Despite strong backing from IBM, they never caught on. We need a wider variety of graphic techniques to document data flow. It commends the work of the Yourdon organization, and Chris Gane in this area.

Rudkin, Ralph I., and Kenneth D. Shere (1979). "Structured Decomposition Diagram: A New Technique for System Analysis," *Datamation*, October, pp. 130–133, 136, 140, 144, 146. This article describes the approach called the Structured Decomposition Diagram (SDD) technique, based on SADT (Structured Analysis and Design Technique, a registered trademark of SofTech, Inc.) for specifying system requirements. The first phase of this approach decomposes system functions in a hierarchical manner, specifying information/data flow requirements, and uses SADT, and when appropriate, the Warnier/Orr technique. (In phase two, the required data characteristics are specified, and the data/function matrix is systematically analyzed to determine the data requirements of each activity. The SDD technique thus seems to reconcile the two approaches of structured analysis/design, based on functional decomposition and data structure, respectively.) The article includes a brief but excellent introduction to the Warnier/Orr diagram.

Shelly, Gary B., and Thomas J. Cashman (1977). "Introduction to Structured Design and Structured Programming," *The Compiler* (published by Anaheim Publishing Company, 1120 Ash, Fullerton, CA 92631, for data processing educators), Fall, pp. 5–9. Advocates the use of an IPO (Input-Processing-Output) chart and pseudocode in writing structured programs.

Shneiderman, Ben (1980). *Software Psychology (Human Factors in Computer and Information Systems)*. Boston: Little, Brown and Company. This excellent book includes the topics of programmer productivity measures, peer reviews, Halstead's software science, and McCabe's complexity measure.

Stay, J. F. (1976). "HIPO and Integrated Program Design," *IBM Systems Journal*, November 2, pp. 143–154. Discusses a procedure of hierarchical functional design by which programming projects can be analyzed into system, program, and module levels. It shows that program design is made more efficient by applying the HIPO method at each level to form an integrated view of all levels.

Stevens, Bruce (1976). "Structured Techniques: Comparative Analysis." (Available from Ken Orr and Associates, 1725 Gage Boulevard, Topeka, KS 66604). This paper is an excerpt of a larger study of major structured techniques performed at the National Bank of Detroit. The objective was to find a method that would cause the least "upheaval" within the organization. It contains the most complete list of selection criteria in the literature. The techniques are viewed as design aids, programming aids, and as documentation aids with specific criteria being independency of hardware and software, user interface, control/consistency (as design aid), acceptance, teachability, aid to programming, drafting ease, reference value, maintenance, and ease of use. The techniques compared are: SADT (Structured Analysis and Design Technique, a registered trademark of SoftTech, Inc.); IBM; Langston Kitch (Warnier-Orr methodology using the Warnier/Orr diagram); Yourdon; and to some extent, Jackson. Langston Kitch techniques (using the Warnier/Orr diagram as a tool) are rated superior to the other techniques in many respects and in the (overall) comparative analysis results.

Taylor, Harold L. (1981). *Making Time Work for You: A Guide Book to Effective and Productive Time Management*. New York: Beaufort Books. This book can help you get control of your life. It can help you organize and make the most of your time. It teaches how to replace low-priority tasks with meaningful activity; develop a personal time policy; run effective meetings; efficiently delegate work; get rid of the backlog; and stay on top of paperwork.

Warnier, Jean-Dominique (1974). *Logical Construction of Programs*. New York: Van Nostrand Reinhold Company. This book, translated from an original book in French, presents Warnier's LCP methodology in a very careful manner. Numerous illustrations and exercises (with solutions) aid in learning the method. The Warnier diagram helps develop clear and precise structures for the output, input, and the program.

——— (1978). *Program Modification*. Leinden, The Netherlands Hingham, Mass. Martinus Nijhoff Social Sciences Division. This book on the modifications of programs constructed according to Warnier's method LCP described in Warnier (1974) is the translation of his book in French, entitled *La Transformation des programmes;* originally published in 1975 in France. Shows how to make modifications without losing the basic qualities of the original program constructed according to Warnier's method LCP (Logical Construction of Programs).

——— (1981). *Logical Construction of Systems*. New York: Van Nostrand Reinhold Company. This definitive book explores the data structured approach for designing data and systems. The logical approach of Warnier is based on the concepts of set theory. Relational data models are produced using the method.

Weinberg, Gerald M. (1971). *The Psychology of Computer Programming*. New York: Van Nostrand Reinhold Company. This classic book must be studied and digested by every programming manager and programmer. It studies computer programming as a human activity and includes many interesting case studies and annotated bibliographies.

——— (1972). "The Psychology of Improved Programming Performance" *Datamation*, November, pp. 82–83, 85. Includes a summary of an experiment in which five teams of programmers were used and each was given a different objective. Each team excelled in the assigned goal.

——— (1979). "You Say Your Design is Inexact? Try a WIGGLE," *Datamation*, August, pp. 146–147, 148. WIGGLE is an acronym for Weinberg's Ideogram for Generating Graphics that Lack Exactitude. It's a method of sketching with wiggly lines that can be used with most diagramatic techniques. "A WIGGLE is a box or block or line with one or more rough edges. The rough edges indicate what parts represented by the box or line are imprecisely known." During the formative stage, the judicious use of wiggly lines can help maintain perspective on the knowns and unknowns of a design.

——— (1982). *Understanding the Professional Programmer.* Boston: Little, Brown and Company. The lively essays in this book provide pragmatic (in some cases philosophic) approaches to professional development and improvement. They help develop insight and make a professional "think" more deeply to become a better professional.

——— Stephen E. Wright, Richard Kauffman, and Martin A. Goetz (1977). *High Level COBOL Programming.* Boston: Little, Brown and Company. Excerpted in Parikh (1982a). This book must be read and digested by every (COBOL) programmer and (COBOL) programming manager. The chapter headings are: The Programming Business, Managing High Level Programming; Critical Program Reading; High Level Control; Style and Workmanship; Modularity; Refinement; Verification; Sheltering; Maintenance; Putting Theory into Practice; Appendix 1: The Meta COBOL System; Appendix 2: The LIBRARIAN System.

Wilke, Gary (1981). "Alleviating Flowcharting, Pseudo-Code Problem....with Yet Another Documentation Tool," *Software News,* November, pp. 38–39. An excellent article demonstrating the power of the versatile Warnier/Orr diagram, with numerous illustrations.

Wooldridge, Susan (1973). *Software Selection.* New York: Petrocelli. Gives practical advice on finding, evaluating, and acquiring proprietary packages.

Yourdon, Edward (1975a). *Techniques of Program Structure and Design.* Englewood Cliffs, N.J. Prentice-Hall Inc. An excellent introduction to the (functional) structured programming techniques, including top-down design, program testing, and debugging.

——— (1975b). "Making the Move to Structured Programming," *Datamation,* June, pp. 52–56. Regarding the use of structured programming techniques in maintenance, this excellent article suggests that the librarian and structured walkthrough concepts can be useful. Also, new sections of code can be added in a top-down structured manner. Eventually, a "structuring engine" automatically converting unstructured logic into structured form may solve the problem.

——— (1976a). "Users Want Too Much from HIPO," *Computerworld,* May 31, p. 24. Gives an illustration of an alternative diagramming technique called "structure chart" (with higher information content), together with a typical "hierarchy chart" and a "detailed HIPO." HIPO is considered "better than nothing." It points out technical complaints against HIPO, and its misuse.

——— (1976b). "Book Review: *System Design and Documentation: An Introduction to the HIPO Method* [by] Harry Katzan, Jr.," *The Yourdon Report*, December, pp. 5–7. "All things considered, I think the human race is considerably better off *with* Katzan's book than without it" concludes Yourdon in this critical review.

——— (1979a). *Managing the Structured Techniques*, 2nd ed. (formerly, *How to Manage Structured Programming)*. New York: Yourdon Press. Excerpted in Parikh (1982a). A concise management summary of structured programming, structured design, chief programmer teams, and other *programmer productivity techniques* (PPT). Yourdon is not in favor of detailed HIPO diagrams as a design tool. He gives excellent guidelines and suggestions for introducing new techniques.

——— ed. (1979b). *Classics in Software Engineering*. New York: Yourdon Press.

Zvegintzov, N. (1981). "Four Common Complaints—Tips Boost Maintenance Programmer Morale" *Computerworld*, March 30, "Special Report" section. [Also in Parikh and Zvegintzov (1983a).] This article deals with the human rather than technical content of communication within the maintenance group.

——— (1982). "The Eureka Countdown," *Datmation,*April, pp. 172-178. [Also in Parikh and Zvegintzov 1983a.] The Eureka Countdown is a five step process for displacing ignorance and replacing it with your brainpower:

5–The Five Questions

4–The Four Actions

3–The Three Places to Work

2–The Two Products

1–The One Golden Rule

Zvegintzov's approach to understanding is action oriented. It is significant that immediately after "the five questions" are "the four actions," which in his paper are: REVIEW, REFLECT, RECORD, REACT. The writing of Zvegintzov's article—content, style, and presentation—is superb.

# NAME INDEX



Mr. Siva P. Raparla helped compile the "Name Index" on an IBM Personal Computer using the word processing software Spellbinder™.

## J



## K



## L



## M



## N



## O



## P



## R



## S



## T

## V



## W



## Y



## Z

# TOPIC INDEX



Mr. Siva P. Raparla helped compile the "Topic Index" on an IBM Personal Computer using the word processing software Spellbinder™.

## H



## I



## J



## L



## M

## T



## U



## V



## W



## Y